SOMEBODY

WITH A LITTLE

HAMMER

SOMEBODY

WITH A LITTLE

HAMMER

MARY GAITSKILL

Pantheon Books
New York

Owing to limitations of space, information on previously published material appears following the text.

Library of Congress Cataloging-in-Publication Data
Name: Gaitskill, Mary, [date] author.
Title: Somebody with a little hammer : essays / Mary Gaitskill.
Description: First Edition. New York : Pantheon Books [2017].
Identifiers: LCCN 2016031697 (print). LCCN 2016038033 (ebook).
ISBN 9780307378224 (hardcover). ISBN 9781101871775 (ebook).
Subjects: BISAC: LITERARY COLLECTIONS / Essays. SOCIAL SCIENCE / Popular Culture. PSYCHOLOGY / Human Sexuality.
Classification: LCC PS3557.A36 A6 2017 (print).
LCC PS3557.A36 (ebook). DDC 814/.54—dc23.
LC record available at lccn.loc.gov/2016031697.

www.pantheonbooks.com

Jacket image: (bottom) from the cover of *Church & State*, vol. II, by Dave Sim and Gerhard
Jacket design by Oliver Munday

Printed in the United States of America
First Edition

9 8 7 6 5 4 3 2 1

CONTENTS

SOMEBODY

WITH A LITTLE

HAMMER

A LOT OF EXPLODING HEADS

ON READING THE BOOK OF REVELATION

I did not have a religious upbringing, and for most of my life I've considered that a good thing; I've since come to know people who felt nurtured by their religious families, but for a long time, for me, "religious upbringing" meant the two little girls I once walked home with in the fourth grade who, on hearing that I didn't believe that Jesus was the Son of God, began screaming, "There's a sin on your soul! You're going to Hell!" "Religious upbringing" meant my friend who, as a kid, was repeatedly exorcised in her mother's fundamentalist church and who still had nightmares about it at forty-five; it meant a thirteen-year-old boy who once told me he believed that God would punish his sexually active classmates by giving them AIDS. When I watched *The Exorcist* in theaters when it first came out and saw adult moviegoers jump up and stumble toward the exits, retching and / or weeping with fear, it was to me yet another example of what a bad effect a religious upbringing could have.

My mother, to her credit, told me that "God is love" and that there is no hell. But I don't think I believed her. Even though I have very little conscious religious anxiety, since childhood, I have had dreams that suggest otherwise: dreams of hooded monks carrying huge, grim crosses in processions meant to end in someone's death by fire, drowning, or quartering; of endless liturgies by faceless choirs to faceless parishioners in cavernous dark churches; of trials, condemnations, sacrifices, and torture. When I wake from these dreams, it is with terror. Such things *have* actually occurred, but I still have no idea why they are so deeply present in me. Horror movies and creeping cultural fear are obvious sources, but my unconscious has taken these images in with such kinetic intensity and conviction that suggestion and vague historical knowledge don't seem to have been the cause.

When I was twenty-one, I became a born-again Christian. It was a random and desperate choice; I had dropped out of high school and left home at sixteen, and while I'd had some fun, by twenty-one, things were looking squalid and stupid. My boyfriend had dumped me and I was living in a rooming house and selling hideous rhodium jewelry on the street in Toronto, which is where the "Jesus freaks" approached me. I had been solicited by these people before and usually gave them short shrift, but on that particular evening I was at a low ebb. They told me that if I let Jesus into my heart right there, even if I just said the words, that everything would be okay. I said, "All right, I'll try it." They praised God and moved on.

Even though my conversion was pretty desultory, I decided to pray that night. I had never seriously prayed before, and all my pent-up desperation and fear made it an act of furious psychic propulsion that lasted almost an hour. It was a very private experience, one that I would find hard to describe; suffice to say that I felt I was being listened to. I started going to a bleak church that had night services and free meals, and was attended heavily by street people and kids with a feverish, dislocated look in their eyes. And, for the first time, I started reading the Bible. For me, it was like running into a brick wall.

I was used to reading, but most of what I read was pretty trashy. Even when it wasn't, the supple, sometimes convoluted play of modern language entered and exited my mind like radio music—then, of course, there was the actual radio music, the traffic noise, the continual onrush of strangers through the streets I worked, the slower, shifting movements of friends, lovers, alliances, the jabber of electricity and neon in the night. All of which kept my mind and nervous system in a whipsawed condition from which it was difficult to relate to the Bible. *The earth was without form, and void; and darkness was on the face of the deep. And the Spirit of God was hovering over the face of the waters. Then God said, "Let there be light"; and there was light.* I couldn't even appreciate the beauty of the words. The phrases seemed like big dumb swatches of form imposed on something swift-moving and endlessly changeable. The form was mute, huge, and absolutely immobile. It made me feel like I was being smothered. One clergyman after another would quote from it so intensely, as if its big, majestic opacity was meaningful in and of itself, and I would try to at least feel the meaning if I couldn't comprehend it. But all I felt was that persistent sense of truncation, the intimation of something enormous and inchoate trying to squeeze through the static form of written words.

This feeling became most intense when I read Revelation. Next to Job, Revelation is the most cinematic and surreal part of the Bible—it's a little like a horror movie, which is probably why it was relatively easy for a modern teenager to take in: There're a lot of explosions. It seemed terribly real to me; I would walk out into the streets, amid the big buildings in which commerce ground forward, and I would feel the violence, the lies, the grotesque pride, the *filth*, pitching and heaving under the semblance of order. The air would crackle with the unacknowledged brutality of life, and I would feel acutely all the small, stupid betrayals I committed daily, against both myself and others. The angels with their seven stars and their lamps, the beast with his seven heads and ten horns—the static imagery was sinister and senseless to me, and yet all the more convincing for it. I could imagine angels and beasts looming all about us, incomprehensible and invisible to our senses the way the images in a photograph would be incomprehensible and invisible to a cat. Their stars and lamps and horns seemed like peculiar metaphors on the page, but, I feared, when the divine horses came down, with their fire and teeth and snake tails, their reality would be all too clear. I lay in my bed and prayed, trying to convince myself of God's love, but my prayers seemed a rag in a typhoon.

Besides, I couldn't help but think it was awfully harsh. Malignant sores, scorpions, fire, men "gnawing their tongues" with pain—I knew people were horrible, but even in my youth I could also see that most people did the best they could. Even as angry and fearful and disappointed as I was, I knew I wouldn't torture people like that, and I didn't see how I could be kinder than God. I was moved when I read, in 1 Corinthians 13: *Love suffers long and is kind; love does not envy; love does not parade itself, is not puffed up; does not behave rudely, does not seek its own, is not provoked, thinks no evil; does not rejoice in iniquity, but rejoices in truth; bears all things, believes all things, hopes all things, endures all things. Love never fails.* But I also remember thinking, And Love is not pathologically cruel, either.

The rage of Revelation sometimes made my compassion feel weak and mealymouthed, but my reservations were not only humanitarian. I was more perturbed by what to me was the mechanical quality, not just of Revelation but of the whole Bible. You had to worship God in exactly a certain way, according to certain prescriptions—and Revelation hinted that the rules set out in, say, the Ten Commandments were only one tiny piece of a vast schema in which human ambivalence was simply not a factor.

During this time I had a dream that was not about the Bible, but which embodied my consternation about it. In the dream I lived in a house with several other people. We could not get out of the house, and our relationships with one another had been preordained, regardless of feeling. Our actions were controlled by a master whom we never saw. One day a man came to visit us, ostensibly for lunch. He was very polite and even friendly, and we were also friendly with him. But it was understood that he was one of the people who controlled us, and the atmosphere was one of pure dread. During lunch, when one of the men of the house seized and killed one of the household cats, we knew it was because our visitor had somehow made him do it. I couldn't hide my horror completely, and our visitor looked at me a moment and then said, referring to the mangled body of the cat, "That's what I'm going to do to you one day." I understood him to mean that he was going to rape me, and I said, "But I'm married," not because it mattered to me, but because I knew that the only thing that mattered to him were his laws, including the law of marriage. Then I became too angry to go along with this and I added, "Even though I don't respect my husband." Very threateningly— after all, it's part of the law that we love our spouses—the visitor asked, "Do you have sex with your husband?" I answered yes, and it was clear from my tone that I did so in order to obey the law. "That's good," said the visitor, "because your husband is a very intelligent man." Even for a dream, this was a strange moment: There was such a sense of approval for the fact of my husband's intelligence, but it had nothing to do with the man he was; rather, the approval was all for the idea of an intelligent man and a duti- ful wife paying him the homage of sex. The hellish thing was, within the dream, it was true. Even though I didn't love my hus- band, I considered him intelligent. And so I said, "Yes, he is very intelligent." I said it for complicated reasons. Partly to please the visitor, whom I was afraid of, but more to make some emotional contact with him by invoking a concept he had codified as law, and making him see that I respected intelligence, too. The way

he looked at me when I said this was also complicated. It was a
look of respect for my miserable loyalty to my husband, for my
detached admiration for his mind. It was a look that appreciated
my humanity but would give it only a tiny space in which to live,
a look a torturer might give a victim who had just expressed a
sentiment the torturer considered noble, but that would not prevent the torture from taking place.

The prison house of this dream seemed to me to be a metaphor for our human state, the circumstances of our birth into
families not of our choosing, and our inability to free ourselves
from a psychological makeup learned before we can decide for
ourselves what we want to be. The visitor seemed like the God in
the Bible, who is kind only as long as you adhere to the rules, and
who will sometimes decide to punish you anyway. God famously
doesn't afflict Job because of anything Job has done, but because
he wants to prove a point to Satan.

Twenty years later, I am sympathetic with my first assessment;
to me, in spite of the soft, radiant beauty of many of its passages,
the Bible still has a mechanical quality, a refusal to brook complexity that feels brutal and violent. There has been a change, however. When I look at Revelation now, it still seems frightening and
impenetrable, and it still suggests an inexorable, ridiculous order
that is unknowable by us, in which our earthly concerns matter
very little. However, it no longer reads to me like a chronicle of
arbitrarily inflicted cruelty. It reads like a terrible abstract of how
we violate ourselves and others and thus bring down endless suffering on earth. When I read *And they blasphemed the God of heaven
because of their pain and their sores, and did not repent of their deeds,*
I think of myself and others I've known or know who blaspheme
life itself by failing to have the courage to be honest and kind—
and how then we rage around and lash out because we hurt.

When I read the word *fornication,* I don't read it as a description of sex outside legal marriage: I read it as sex done in a state of psychic disintegration, with no awareness of one's self or one's partner, let alone any sense of honor or even real playfulness. I still don't know what to make of much of it, but I'm inclined to read it as a writer's primitive attempt to give form to his moral urgency, to create a structure that could contain and give ballast to the most desperate human confusion.

I'm not sure how to account for this change. I think it mainly has to do with gradually maturing and becoming more deeply aware of my own mechanicalness and my own stringent limitations when it comes to giving form to impossible complexity— something writers understand very well. It probably has to do with my admittedly dim understanding of how apparently absolute statements can contain enormous meaning and nuance without losing their essential truth. And it has to do with my expanded ability to accept my own fear, and to forgive myself for my own mechanical responses to things I don't understand. In the past, my compassion was small—perhaps *immature* is a better word—and conditional. I could not accept what I read in the biblical book because I could feel the truth of it in my own psyche. Now I recognize, with pain, a genuine description of how hellish life can be, and that it is not God who "sent" us to this hell.

To me, these realizations don't mean I have arrived at a point of any real knowledge, but they are interesting as markers of my development. I imagine that twenty years from now, when and if I read Revelation, I will once again see it the same, but differently. I will look forward to it.

*Communion: Contemporary Writers Reveal the Bible in
Their Lives,* EDITED BY DAVID ROSENBERG, 1994

THE TROUBLE WITH FOLLOWING
THE RULES

ON "DATE RAPE," "VICTIM CULTURE,"
AND PERSONAL RESPONSIBILITY

In the early 1970s, I had an experience that could be described as "date rape," even if it didn't happen when I was on a date. I was sixteen and staying in the apartment of a slightly older girl I'd just met in a seedy community center in Detroit, where I was just passing through. I'd been in her apartment for a few days when an older guy (he was probably in his mid-twenties) came over and asked us if we wanted to drop some acid. In those years, doing acid with strangers was consistent with my idea of a possible good time, so I shared a tab with them. When I started peaking, my hostess decided she had to go see her boyfriend, and there I was, alone with this guy, who, suddenly, was in my face.

He seemed to be coming on to me, but I wasn't sure. LSD is a potent drug, and on it, my perception was just short of hallucinatory. On top of that, he was black and urban-poor, which meant that I, being very inexperienced and suburban-white, did not know how to read him the way I might have read another white kid from my own milieu. I tried to distract him with conversation, but it was hard, considering that I was having trouble with logical sentences, let alone repartee. During one long silence, I asked him what he was thinking. Avoiding my eyes, he replied, "That if I wasn't such a nice guy, you could really be getting screwed." This sounded to me like a threat, albeit a low-key one. But instead of asking him to explain himself or leave, I changed the subject. Some moments later, when he put his hand on my leg, I let myself be drawn into sex because I could not face the idea that if I said no, things might get ugly. I don't think he had any idea of how unwilling I was—the cultural unfamiliarity cut both ways—and I suppose he may have thought that white girls just kind of lie there and don't do or say much. My bad time was made worse by his extreme gentleness; he was obviously trying very hard to turn me on, which, for reasons I didn't understand, broke my heart. Even as inexperienced as I was, I could see that he wanted a sweet time.

For some time after, I described this event as "the time I was raped." I knew when I said it that the description wasn't accurate, that I had not said no, and that I had not been physically forced. Yet it *felt* accurate to me. In spite of my ambiguous, even empathic feelings for my unchosen partner, unwanted sex on acid is a nightmare, and I did feel violated by the experience. At times I even *elaborately* lied about what had happened, grossly exaggerating the threatening words, adding violence—not out of shame or guilt, but because the pumped-up version was more congruent with my feelings of violation than the confusing facts. Every now and then, in the middle of telling an exaggerated version of the story, I would remember the actual man and internally pause, uncertain why I was saying these things or why they felt true— and then I would continue with the story. I am ashamed to admit this, because it is embarrassing and because it conforms to the worst stereotypes of white women. I am also afraid the admission could be taken as evidence that women lie "to get revenge." My lies were told far from the event (I'd left Detroit), and not for revenge, but in service of what I felt to be the metaphorical truth—although what that truth was is not at all clear to me, then or even now.

———

I remember my experience in Detroit, including the aftermath, every time I hear or read yet another discussion of what constitutes "date rape." I remember it when yet another critic castigates "victimism" and complains that everyone imagines himself or herself to be a victim and that no one accepts responsibility anymore. I could imagine telling my story as a verification that rape occurs by subtle threat as well as by overt force. I could also imagine casting myself as one of those crybabies who want to feel like victims. Both stories would be true and not true. The complete truth is more complicated than most of the intellectuals who have written scolding essays on victimism seem willing to accept. I didn't even begin to understand my own story fully until I described it to an older woman many years later, as proof of the unreliability of feelings. "Oh, I think your feelings were reliable," she replied. "It sounds like you were raped. It sounds like you raped yourself." I didn't like her tone, but I immediately understood what she meant, that in failing to even try to speak up for myself, I had, in a sense, done violence to myself.

I don't say this in a tone of self-recrimination. I was in a difficult situation: I was very young and unready to deal with such an intense culture clash of poverty and privilege, such contradictory levels of power and vulnerability, let alone ready to deal with it on drugs. But the difficult circumstances alone do not explain my inability to speak for myself. I was unable to effectively stand up for myself because I had never been taught how.

When I was growing up in the sixties, I was taught by the adult world that good girls did not have sex outside marriage and bad girls did. This rule had clarity going for it, but little else; as it was presented to me, it allowed no room for what I actually might feel, what I might want or not want. Within the confines of this rule, I didn't count for much, and so I rejected it. Then came the less clear "rules" of cultural trend and peer example, which said that if you were cool, you wanted to have sex as much as possible with as many people as possible. This message was never stated as a rule, but, considering how absolutely it was woven into the social etiquette of the day (at least in the circles I care about), it may as well have been. It suited me better than the adult's rule—it allowed me my sexuality at least—but again it didn't take into account what I might actually want or not want.

The encounter in Detroit, however, had nothing to do with being good or bad, cool or uncool. It was about someone wanting something I didn't want. Since I had only learned how to follow rules or social codes that were somehow more important than I was, I didn't know what to do in a situation where no rules obtained and that required me to speak up on my own behalf. I had never been taught that my behalf mattered. And so I felt helpless, even victimized, without really knowing why.

My parents and my teachers believed that social rules existed to protect me and that adhering to these rules constituted social responsibility. Ironically, my parents did exactly what many commentators recommend as a remedy for victimism. They told me that they loved me and that I mattered a lot, but this was not the message I got from the way they conducted themselves in relation to authority and social convention—which was not only that I didn't matter but that *they* didn't matter. In this, they were typical of other adults I knew, as well as of the culture around them. When I began to have trouble in school, both socially and academically, a counselor exhorted me to "just play the game"— meaning to go along with everything from social policy to the adolescent pecking order—regardless of what I thought of "the game." My aunt, with whom I lived for a short while, actually burned my jeans and T-shirts because they violated what she understood to be the standards of decorum. A close friend of mine lived in a state of war with her father because of her hippie clothes and hair—which were, of course, de rigueur among her peers. Upon discovering that she had been smoking pot, he had her institutionalized.

Many middle-class people—both men and women—have learned to equate responsibility with obeying external rules. And when the rules no longer quite apply, they don't know what to do—much like the enraged, gun-wielding protagonist of the movie *Falling Down,* played by Michael Douglas, who ends his ridiculous trajectory by helplessly declaring, "I did everything they told me to." If I had been brought up to reach my own conclusions about which rules were congruent with my particular experience of the world, those rules would've had more meaning for me. Instead, I was usually given a set of static pronouncements. For example, when I was thirteen, I was told by my mother that I couldn't wear a short skirt because "nice girls don't wear short skirts above the knee." I countered, of course, by saying that my friend Patty wore skirts above the knee. "Patty is not a nice girl," replied my mother. But Patty *was* nice. My mother is a very intelligent and sensitive person, but it didn't occur to her to define for me what she meant by "nice" and what "nice" had to do with skirt length, and how the two definitions might relate to what I had observed to be nice or not nice—and then let me decide for myself. It's true that most thirteen-year-olds aren't interested in, or much capable of, philosophical discourse, but that doesn't mean that adults can't explain themselves more completely to children. Part of becoming responsible is learning how to make a choice about where you stand in respect to the social code and then holding yourself accountable for your choice. In contrast, many children who grew up in my milieu were given abstract absolutes that were placed before us as if our thoughts, feelings, and observations were irrelevant.

———

Recently, I heard a panel of feminists on talk radio advocating that laws be passed prohibiting men from touching or making sexual comments to women on the street. Listeners called in to express reactions both pro and con, but the one I remember was a caller who said, "I'm an Italian woman. And if a man touches me and I don't want it, I don't need a law. I'm gonna beat the hell out of him." The panelists were silent. Then one of them responded in an uncertain voice, "I guess I just never learned how to do that." I understood that the feminist might not want to get into a fistfight with a man likely to be a lot bigger than her, but if her self-respect was so easily shaken by an obscene comment made by some random guy on the street, I wondered, how did she expect to get through life? She was exactly the kind of woman whom the cultural critics Camille Paglia and Katie Roiphe have derided as a "rape-crisis feminist"—puritans, sissies, closet-Victorian ladies who want to legislate the ambiguity out of sex. It was very easy for me to feel self-righteous, and I muttered sarcastically to my radio as the panel yammered about self-esteem.

I was conflicted, however. If there had been a time in my own life when I couldn't stand up for myself, how could I expect other people to do it? It could be argued that the grown women on the panel should be more capable than a sixteen-year-old girl on acid. But such a notion presupposes that people develop at a predictable rate or react to circumstances by coming to universally agreed-upon conclusions. This is the crucial unspoken presumption at the center of the date-rape debate as well as of the larger discourse on victimism. It is a presumption that in a broad but potent way reminds me of a rule.

Feminists who postulate that boys must obtain a spelled-out *yes* before having sex are trying to establish rules, cut in stone, that will apply to any and every encounter and that every responsible person must obey. The new rule resembles the old good girl/bad girl rule not only because of its implicit suggestion that girls have to be protected but also by its absolute nature, its iron-fisted denial of complexity and ambiguity. I bristle at such a rule, and so do a lot of other people. But should we really be so puzzled and indignant that another rule has been presented? If people have been brought up believing that to be responsible is to obey rules, what are they going to do with a can of worms like "date rape" except try to make new rules that they see as more fair or useful than the old ones?

The "rape-crisis feminists" are not the only absolutists here; their critics play the same game. Camille Paglia, author of *Sexual Personae*, has stated repeatedly that any girl who goes alone into a frat house and drinks is cruising for a gang bang, and if she doesn't know that, well, then she's an "idiot." The remark is striking not only for its crude unkindness but for its reductive solipsism. It assumes that all college girls have had the same life experiences as Paglia, and have come to the same conclusions about them. By the time I got to college, I'd been living away from home for years and had been around the block several times. I never went to a frat house, but I got involved with men who lived in rowdy boy caves reeking of sex and rock and roll. I would go over, drink, and spend the night with my lover; it never occurred to me that I was in danger of being gang-raped, and if I had been, I would have been shocked and hurt. My experience, though some of it had been bad, hadn't led me to conclude that boys plus alcohol equals gang bang, and I was not naïve or idiotic. Katie Roiphe, author of *The Morning After: Sex, Fear, and Feminism on Campus*, criticizes girls who, in her view, create a myth of false innocence: "But did these twentieth-century girls, raised on Madonna videos and the six o'clock news, really trust that people were good until they themselves were raped? Maybe. Were these girls, raised on horror movies and glossy Hollywood sex scenes, really as innocent as all that?" I am sympathetic to Roiphe's annoyance, but I'm surprised that a smart chick like her apparently doesn't know that people process information and imagery with a complex subjectivity that doesn't in any predictable way alter their ideas about what they can expect from life. I trusted that the particular guys in their particular houses wouldn't rape me, not because I was innocent, but because I was experienced enough to read them correctly.

Roiphe and Paglia are not exactly invoking rules, but their comments seem to derive from a belief that everyone except idiots interprets information and experience in the same way. In that sense, they are not so different from those ladies dedicated to establishing feminist-based rules and regulations for sex. Such rules, like the old rules, assume a certain psychological uniformity of experience, a right way.

The accusatory and sometimes painfully emotional rhetoric conceals an attempt not only to make new rules but also to codify experience. The "rape-crisis feminists" obviously speak for many women and girls who have been raped or *felt* raped in a wide variety of circumstances. They would not get so much play if they were not addressing a widespread and real experience of violation and hurt. By asking "Were they really so innocent?" Roiphe doubts the veracity of the experience she presumes to address because it doesn't square with hers or with that of her friends. Having not felt violated herself—even though she says she has had an experience that many would now call date rape—she cannot understand, or even quite believe, that anyone else would feel violated in similar circumstances. She therefore believes all the fuss to be a political ploy or, worse, a retrograde desire to return to crippling ideals of helpless femininity. In turn, Roiphe's detractors, who have not had her more sanguine "morning after" experience, believe her to be ignorant and callous, or a secret rape victim in deep denial. Both camps, believing their own experience to be the truth, seem unable to acknowledge the truth on the other side.

It is at this point that the "date-rape debate" resembles the bigger debate about how and why Americans seem so eager to identify themselves and be identified by others as victims. Book after article has appeared, written in baffled yet hectoring language, deriding the PC goody-goodies who want to play victim and the spoiled, self-centered fools who attend twelve-step programs, meditate on their inner child, and study pious self-help books. The revisionist critics have all had a lot of fun with the recovery movement, getting into high dudgeon over those materially well-off people who describe their childhoods as "holocausts" and winding up with fierce exhortations to return to rationality before it's too late. Rarely do these critics make any but the most superficial attempt to understand why the population might behave thus.

In a fussing, fuming essay in these pages ("Victims, All?" October 1991) that has become almost a prototype of the genre, David Rieff expressed his outrage and bewilderment that affluent people would feel hurt and disappointed by life. He angrily contrasted rich Americans obsessed with their inner children to Third World parents concerned with feeding their actual children. On the most obvious level, the contrast is one that needs to be made, but I question Rieff's idea that suffering is one definable thing, that he knows what it is, and that since certain kinds of emotional pain don't fit this definition, they can't really exist. This idea doesn't allow him to have respect for other people's experience—or even to see it. It may be ridiculous and perversely self-aggrandizing for most people to describe their childhood as a "holocaust," but I suspect that when people talk like that, they are saying that as children they were not given enough of what they would later need in order to know who they are or to live truly responsible lives. Thus they find themselves in a state of bewildering loss that they can't articulate, except by wild exaggeration—much like I defined my inexplicable feelings after my Detroit episode. "Holocaust" may be a grossly inappropriate exaggeration. But to speak in exaggerated metaphors about psychic injury is not so much the act of a crybaby as it is a distorted desire to make one's experience have consequence in the eyes of others, and such desperation comes from a crushing doubt that one's own experience counts at all *or is even real*.

In her book *I'm Dysfunctional, You're Dysfunctional,* Wendy Kaminer speaks harshly of women in some twelve-step programs who talk about being metaphorically raped. "It is an article of faith here that suffering is relative; no one says she'd rather be raped metaphorically than in fact," she writes, as if not even a crazy person would prefer a literal rape to a metaphorical one. But actually, I might. About a year after my "rape" in Detroit, I was raped for real. The experience was terrifying: My attacker repeatedly said he was going to kill me, and I thought he might. The terror was acute, but after it was over, it actually affected me less than many other mundane instances of emotional brutality I've suffered or seen other people suffer. Frankly, I've been scarred more by experiences I had on the playground in elementary school. I realize that may sound bizarre, but for me the rape was a clearly defined act, perpetrated on me by a crazy asshole whom I didn't know or trust; it had nothing to do with me or who I was, and so, when it was over, it was relatively easy to dismiss. Emotional cruelty is more complicated. Its motives are often impossible to understand, and it is sometimes committed by people who say they like or even love you. Nearly always it's hard to know whether you played a role in what happened and, if so, what the role was. The experience *sticks* to you. By the time I was raped, I had seen enough emotional cruelty to feel that the rape, although bad, was not so terrible that I couldn't heal quickly.

Again, my response may seem strange, but my point is that pain can be an experience that defies codification. If thousands of Americans say that they are in psychic pain, I would not be so quick to write them off as self-indulgent fools. A metaphor like "the inner child" may be silly and schematic, but it has a fluid subjectivity, especially when projected out into the world by such a populist notion as "recovery." Ubiquitous recovery-movement phrases like "We're all victims" and "We're all codependent" may not seem to leave room for interpretation, but they are actually so vague that they beg for interpretation and projection. Such phrases may be fair game for ridicule, but it is shallow to judge them at face value, as if they hold the same meaning for everyone. What is meant by an "inner child" depends on the person speaking, and not everyone will see it as a metaphor for helplessness. I suspect that most inner-child enthusiasts use the image of themselves as children not so that they can *avoid* being responsible, but to learn responsibility by going back to the point in time when they should have been taught responsibility—the ability to think, choose, and stand up for themselves—and were not. As I understand it, the point of identifying an "inner child" is to locate the part of yourself that didn't develop into adulthood and then to develop it yourself. Whether or not this works is pretty questionable, but it is an attempt to accept responsibility, not to flee it.

When I was in my late teens and early twenties, I could not bear to watch movies or read books that I considered demeaning to women in any way; I reflexively evaluated what I saw or read in terms of the attitude it expressed toward women—or the attitude I *thought* it expressed. I was a very PC feminist before the term existed, and by the measure of my current understanding, my critical rigidity followed from my inability to be responsible for my own feelings. In this context, being responsible would have meant that I let myself feel whatever discomfort, indignation, or disgust I experienced without allowing those feelings to determine my entire reaction to a given piece of work. In other words, it would have meant dealing with my feelings and what had caused them, rather than expecting the outside world to assuage them. I could have chosen not to see the world through the lens of my personal unhappiness and yet maintained a kind of respect for my unhappiness. For example, I could have decided to avoid certain films or books because of my feelings without blaming the film or book for making me feel the way I did.

My emotional irresponsibility did not spring from a need to feel victimized, although it may have looked that way to somebody else. I essentially was doing what I had seen most mainstream cultural critics do; it was from them that I learned to view works of art in terms of the message they imparted and, further, that the message could be judged on the basis of consensual ideas about what life is, and how it can and should be seen. My ideas, like most PC ideas, were only slightly different from mainstream thought—they just shifted the parameters of acceptability a bit.

Things haven't changed that much: At least half the book and film reviews that I read praise or condemn a work on the basis of the likability of the characters (as if there is a standard idea of what is likable) or because the author's point of view is or is not "life-affirming"—or whatever the critic believes the correct attitude toward life to be. The lengthy and rather hysterical debate about the film *Thelma & Louise,* in which two ordinary women become outlaws after one of them shoots the other's would-be rapist, was predicated on the idea that stories are supposed to function as instruction manuals, and that whether the film was good or bad depended on whether the instructions were right. Such criticism assumes that viewers or readers need to see a certain type of moral universe reflected back at them or, empty vessels that they are, they might get confused or depressed or something. A respected mainstream essayist writing for *Time* faulted my novel *Two Girls, Fat and Thin* for its nasty male characters, which he took to be a moral statement about males generally. He ended his piece with the fervent wish that fiction not "diminish" men or women but, rather, seek to "raise our vision of" both—in other words, that it should present the "right" way to the reader, who is apparently not responsible enough to figure it out alone.

I have changed a lot from the PC teenager who walked out of movies that portrayed women in a demeaning light. As I've grown older, I've become more confident of myself and my ability to determine what happens to me, and those images no longer have such a strong emotional charge; they don't *threaten* me in the same way. It's not that I think I'm safe, that I can't be hurt by misogyny in its many forms. I have been and can be. But I'm not so afraid of it that artistic representations of it viscerally disturb me, especially not if they are truthful depictions of how the artist sees his or her world, including the ugly elements. Stories or imagery like that help me to understand, to feel the ugly places in myself, to see the anguish and violence of it from somebody else's view, even if the view is a privileged one. The truth may hurt, but in art, anyway, it also helps, sometimes profoundly.

I consider my current view more balanced, but that doesn't mean my earlier feelings were wrong. The reason I couldn't watch "disrespect to women" at that time was that such depictions were too close to my own worst experience, and I found them painful. I was displaying a simplistic self-respect by not subjecting myself to something I was not ready to face. Being unable to separate my personal experience from what I saw on the screen, I was not dealing with my own personal experience—I think, paradoxically, because I hadn't yet learned to value it. It's hard to be responsible for something that isn't valuable. Someone criticizing me as dogmatic and narrow-minded would have had a point, but the point would've ignored the truth of my unacknowledged experience, and thus ignored me.

Many critics of the self-help culture argue against treating emotional or metaphoric reality as if it were equivalent to objective reality. I agree that they are not the same. But emotional truth is often bound up with truth of a more objective kind and must be taken into account. This is especially true of conundrums such as date rape and victimism, both of which are often discussed in terms of unspoken assumptions about emotional truth anyway. Sarah Crichton, in a cover story for *Newsweek* entitled "Sexual Correctness," described the "strange detour" taken by some feminists and suggested that "we're not creating a society of Angry Young Women. These are Scared Little Girls." The comment is both contemptuous and superficial; it shows no interest in *why* girls might be scared. By such logic, anger implicitly is deemed to be the more desirable emotional state because it appears more potent, and *scared* is used as a pejorative. It's possible to shame a person into hiding his or her fear, but if you don't address the cause of the fear, it won't go away. Crichton ends her piece by saying, "Those who are growing up in environments where they don't have to figure out what the rules should be, but need only follow what's been prescribed, are being robbed of the most important lesson there is to learn. And that's how to live." I couldn't agree more. But unless you've been taught how to think for yourself, you'll have a hard time figuring out your own rules, and you'll feel scared—especially when there is real danger of sexual assault.

After my experience in Detroit, I was a lot more careful about getting high or drunk with people I didn't know. I never had another experience I could call "date rape" again. But sometimes I did find myself having sex with people I barely knew when I didn't really want to all that much. Sometimes I did it for the same reason I did in Detroit: I was secretly afraid things might get ugly if I said no. But sometimes it was for a different reason, one that may be subtly related to the prior one: Part of me wanted the adventure, and that more questing side ran roughshod over the side of me that was far more sensitive and shy. I'll bet the same thing happened to many of the boys with whom I had these experiences. Regardless of gender, all people have their strong, questing aspects as well as their more delicate aspects. If you haven't developed these characteristics in ways that are respectful of yourself and others, you will find it hard to be responsible for *any* of them. I don't think it's possible to develop yourself in such ways if you are attuned to following rules and codes that don't give your subjective experience enough importance.

I am not idealistic enough to hope that we will ever live in a world without rape and other forms of sexual cruelty; I think men and women will always have to make an effort to behave responsibly. But I think we could make the effort less difficult by changing the way we teach responsibility and social conduct. To teach a boy that rape is "bad" is not as effective as making him see that rape is a violation of his own masculine dignity as well as a violation of the raped woman. It's true that children don't know big words and that teenage boys may not be much interested in dignity. But these are things that children learn more easily by example, and learning by example runs deep.

When I was in my mid-thirties, I invited to dinner at my home a man I'd known as a casual friend for two years. We'd had dinner and drinks a few times when I'd been on the East Coast; I was living on the West Coast, where he was visiting, so he'd looked me up. In the original version of this essay, I wrote that I "didn't have any intention of becoming sexual with him," but it's closer to the truth to say that I didn't have strong intentions one way or the other. He was ten years younger than I was and I wrongly assumed he wouldn't be interested in a woman my age—so I wasn't thinking about him that way, either. But after dinner we slowly got drunk and soon were making out on the couch. I was ambivalent not only because I was drunk but because I realized that although part of me was up for it, the rest of me was not. So I began to say no. He parried each no with charming banter and became more aggressive. I went along with it for a time because I was charmed and touched by the sweet junior-high spirit of the thing. But at some point I began to be alarmed, and then he did and said some things that scared me. I don't remember the exact sequence of words or actions, but I do remember taking one of his hands in both of mine, looking him in the eyes, and saying, "If this comes to a fight, you would win, but it would be very ugly for both of us. Is that really what you want?"

His expression changed and he dropped his eyes; shortly afterward he left.

In the original version of this essay I didn't mention that when I woke up the next day, I couldn't stop thinking about him, and that when he called me, I invited him over for dinner again. I didn't mention that we became lovers for the next two years. I just went on to say that I considered my decision to have been a responsible one "because it was made by taking both my vulnerable feelings and my carnal impulses into account," and that I "respected my friend as well by addressing both sides of his nature." I stand by what I originally wrote. But in omitting the aftermath of that "responsible" decision, I was making the messy situation far too clear-cut, actually undermining my own argument by making it about propriety rather than the kind of fluid emotional negotiation that I see as necessary for personal responsibility.

In the original version of this essay, the last lines I wrote were: "It is not hard for me to make such decisions now, but it took me a long time to get to this point. I only regret that it took so long, both for my young self and for the boys I was with, under circumstances that I now consider disrespectful to all concerned."

But I don't truly regret most of the experiences I've had, even the halfhearted ones. They are part of who I am. The only circumstance I truly regret is the one I remember most vividly: the one in Detroit. Because as I remember him, that young urban-poor black man was no rapist. He was high on acid and was misunderstanding, just as I was. If I had held his hands and looked in his eyes and said some version of "It could be ugly for both of us. Is that really what you want?" everything might've been different. I'm not sure. But I regret that I wasn't even able to try, and that I lied about it instead. Far more than any sex act, these lies were "disrespectful to all concerned."

Harper's, 1994

A LOVELY CHAOTIC SILLINESS

A REVIEW OF *THE FERMATA* BY NICHOLSON BAKER

Nicholson Baker's last novel, *Vox*, was supposed to be a sexy book, but I didn't think so. Witty, pleasant, and technically admirable, yes, but sexy, no. It depicted a phone-sex session in which the participants are too decorous to talk dirty, and the fantasies it describes seem little more than circuitous exercises in kookiness. In *Vox*, Baker seemed to tiptoe around the subject of sex as though it were a plump, daydreamy girl, giggling behind his hand, every now and then running up to pinch at her, and then running away, still giggling.

When I heard that Baker's new novel, *The Fermata,* was supposed to be even hotter than *Vox*, I thought, Yeah, right. Ten pages in, I was eating my words. *Hot* doesn't even begin to say it. *Sex-positive* is hopelessly inadequate. The book is bountifully Rabelaisian and intensely refined—but its refinement is so fully realized that it has its own kind of bounty as well.

The book's wonderful sexiness is manifest not only in the actual sex scenes (and there're a lot of 'em) but in its comic vibrancy. The rigor and tenderness with which Baker gives form to this vibrancy through his language is extraordinary; I have never seen anything quite like it.

The Fermata (the word means a pause during a piece of music) tells the story of Arno Strine, a lonely office temp who is able to stop time. Rather than steal vast sums or pursue world domination or even play practical jokes, Arno uses "the Fold," as he calls it, to Christmas shop in peace, to perform his temp assignments with alacrity, to help him remember people's names, and to strip women naked. Or partially naked, as when he ties a coworker's dress up around her hips so that he can revere her pubic hair: "To think that I could have died and not seen this . . . I wanted to feel it, the dense sisaly lush resilience of it, which makes that whole hippy part of her body look extraordinarily graceful. It is a kind of black cocktail dress under which her clit-heart beats—it has that much *dignity*."

He also likes to write his own private porn, stash it where a woman of choice will find it, watch her read it, and, if all goes well, watch her masturbate under its influence while he hides in, say, her laundry hamper. As can be imagined, his adventures become complicated. But he's ultracareful never to harm or frighten or even cause puzzlement; he gets upset if he "inflicts some rending injury to the network of cosmic worm-holes" he treads on.

Much of the book is pornographic and, as such, will not be to everyone's liking. After all, not everyone will want to read about the intrepid housewife who attaches her mail-order, freshly battered "Van Dilden" to the seat of her five-horsepower ride 'em lawn mower and "mows that fucking lawn like she had never mowed it before." Certainly not everyone will want to read about her seducing her sweet teenaged neighbors into water sports and scatology amid the tulips. Misogynists will definitely not like *The Fermata;* there is not one iota of violence toward or contempt for women in this book. Arno uses the Fold to please and adore women, but never to demean them or himself.

The book does have pornography's limits. There is almost no emotional range; no one is ever sexually conflicted, ambivalent, scared, or damaged. No one ever has trouble reaching a shattering orgasm. Everything's all pretty much okay, except for some lower-class black muggers and a lower-class white doorman who expresses coarse, violent desires that sweet, sensitive Arno finds mystifying and horrible. I don't like the emotional finickiness, or the crass race and class stereotyping that makes its (thankfully) brief appearance, but that didn't prevent my enjoyment of the book. Whether or not you like Baker's sensibility, the verve with which he plumbs it is a true pleasure.

If *Vox*'s cute, giggly silliness was its weakness, the silliness of *The Fermata* may be its greatest strength—it's a lovely, chaotic silliness with reverence at its core. When one of Baker's heroines notices a cat in heat, he writes, "There was a purity and seriousness to the cat's simple wish to be fucked immediately that Marian found refreshing." Respect for the "purity and seriousness" of unadorned sex pervades Baker's book; such respect is largely absent from our modern, hideously sophisticated sexual sensibility, and the lack of it has just about smothered the kind of full, silly pleasure that Baker revels in. For that reason alone, *The Fermata* should be feted endlessly.

San Francisco Focus, 1994

TOES 'N HOSE

A REVIEW OF *FROM THE TIP OF THE TOES TO THE TOP OF THE HOSE* BY ELMER BATTERS, AND *NOTHING BUT THE GIRL*, EDITED BY SUSIE BRIGHT AND JILL POSENER

To the disinterested, a foot fetishist is ridiculous; right away you imagine a pathetic cringer who works at Thom McAn for the privilege of getting his fingers stepped on by sneering thirteen-year-olds. And while a yen for long, elegant legs is to be expected, a fixation on those that are short and thick, with fatty knees and cellulite squeezing out of weedy garter-belt straps is . . . not. Elmer Batters either never knew about such fastidious judgments or didn't care. His book of photographs *From the Tip of the Toes to the Top of the Hose* is a loving and lewd celebration of female feet and big ol' legs that says it loud and proud. Batters's photographs, taken from the mid-forties to the mid-eighties for magazines like *Black Silk Stockings, Leg Show,* and *Sheer Delight,* are stylish, energetic, humorous, and dirty. Because Batters is a fetishist, his compositions are based largely on a predictable set of images, a fantasy schema that would be flat if not for the inchoate feeling that comes squishing through the ultraspecific conduit of the fetish with a satisfying *ka-thump* all the more intense for the compression. Batters and his models somehow acknowledge the vulnerability and silliness of sexuality as well as its power—and then they go straight for the dirt.

In two of my favorite shots, a forty-something model, raunchy mom with a shaved snatch, poses in nothing but an open silk shirt and black stockings in a Technicolor backyard dart-game setting, and then, on the next page, bends over by the clothesline, legs spread wide and black panties pulled down, offering up that shaven thing like she's serving a tray of peanut butter sandwiches cut into triangles. In a black-and-white photo from the fifties, a tough no-nonsense-looking girl in a checked business suit sits in her fancy car studying a bird-watcher's guide with one foot on the open door and her skirt up, revealing her pantiless majesty. There's stateliness in her beehive hair, a stern refinement in her vinyl handbag and bird book—but you can somehow feel as well as see her muscular inner organs working in her meaty, solid body.

Not all the pictures are so explicit. Many are arresting shots of women flirtily revealing their legs; others are photos of feet in various poses—for example, bared and rising up over a neutral prop, toes fiercely, almost menacingly, splayed. Grrr!

For those who share Batters's enthusiasms, this book must be especially terrific. But you don't need to be a foot freak; this book would please anyone with a sense of humor and eros.

Nothing But the Girl: The Blatant Lesbian Image is also a book with a target audience. The collection of erotic photos by thirty-three lesbian photographers (the most well known being Catherine Opie) seeks to address the woeful paucity of such works—by dykes *for* dykes—on a broad cultural scale, and this mission, as articulated in the text, has a polemical, occasionally hectoring quality that may make some readers roll their eyes.

However, the images themselves are stylish, lively, and playful. They also have a vital seriousness that, instead of being dreary, gives them immediacy and weight. The women photographed are not professional models. They are ordinary people who have allowed themselves to be depicted in some of the most intimate possible poses and acts. At this particular cultural moment, in some circles anyway, such willingness (eagerness even) to display oneself can be tediously de rigueur—yet there is something undeniably moving in the faces and bodily turgor of these women. Even when they are clothed, even at their most self-conscious, they have a bare quality, an intense, visceral will to be seen for who they are that goes beyond exhibitionism. The cliché about women's erotica is that it's more emotional than carnal. These pictures are emotional all right—the strongest of them fairly reek of raw, fierce feeling that has its own kind of carnal wallop. One of the most compelling images is a self-portrait by Honey Lee Cottrell titled *Bulldagger of the Season, 1981*. She's posing in an open shirt and briefs, staring at the camera with deep eyes. Her protruding belly and strong thighs are almost grossly masculine, but her soft, low breasts are pure female. She looks terribly vulnerable, but she also has a power that comes from being present down to her roots. You may find her attractive and sexy or you may not. But, if you allow it, seeing her deep presence can make you feel that way-down part of yourself, the part that hungers for such vulnerability and intensity—whether you are gay or straight, male or female.

Artforum, 1996

CRACKPOT MYSTIC SPIRIT

A REVIEW OF *INVISIBLE REPUBLIC:*
BOB DYLAN'S BASEMENT TAPES BY GREIL MARCUS

Popular music is the most banal and most mysterious thing imaginable, and it's almost impossible to write about. A good song carries in each phrase fragments of thought, feeling, and sensation, all going by in a flash. It refers to things everybody knows, but it's rooted in the specific muck of whoever wrote it/sings it. If it's live, it includes the quick, erotic language of the body, a language at once too subtle and fundamental to be understood by the mind. So, along comes the intellectual writer and—oops! He's squeezing down on the poor thing so hard, you think he'll kill it, except he can't even get his hands on it. Unless he's Greil Marcus.

Invisible Republic, Marcus's latest book, is a history, an analysis, and an adoration of Bob Dylan's basement tapes. He starts with Dylan's notorious performance at Newport (where Pete Seeger tried to cut the band's power cables) and the subsequent outrage at Dylan's apparent betrayal of folk music, positing that those so outraged had no idea what folk music really was—the crackpot mystic spirit of the "old, weird America," much more dark and complex than earnest ballads like "Which Side Are You On?" could countenance. As Marcus quotes Dylan: "It comes about from legends, Bibles, plagues, and it revolves around vegetables and death. There's nobody that's going to kill traditional music. All those songs about roses growing out of people's brains and

lovers who are really geese and swans that turn into angels—
they're not going to die . . . traditional music is too unreal to die."

For Marcus, the basement tapes are a particularly eccentric
continuation of this tradition. In his imagination, the songs on
the tapes become a town he calls Kill Devil Hills, a place populated by loonies, loungers, doomed girls, rapt sluts, preach-
ers, criminals, con men, and rounders. They are the relations
and descendants of Smithville—that is, the famous *Anthology
of American Folk Music* created in 1952 by visionary nut Harry
Smith, a place of ha'nts, crime, and revelation, where "every day
is Judgment Day." Marcus tells their story as a great subhistori-
cal pageant that looms and dissolves with the inky dynamism
of a Max Fleischer cartoon. His cast of characters and walk-ons
includes Jonathan Edwards, Martin Luther King, Jr., the Ranters
of seventeenth-century England, Randy Newman, novelist Steve
Erickson, and Lincoln's bust in *The Manchurian Candidate.* Costar-
ring with Dylan are itinerant singers Frank Hutchison and Dock
Boggs (the resident of Smithville most often found in Kill Devil
Hills), who, according to Marcus, asks the musical question,
"Given the chance to destroy . . . wouldn't you take it?"

Marcus doesn't grope and crush his subject in the way many
critics do, because his writing works much like music: It flies by
in a comet tail, pieces of thought, feeling, and image all scrambled together. These components are often not fully developed in
the way one would typically expect of an essay, but, rather, play
off one another with enigmatic grace of sound. When it works,
it's brilliant and sensually delightful, broad, almost corny, at one
turn, piercing and refined at the next. Here, he describes Dylan's
performance at Newport:

> Dylan puffs himself up with the declamatory intonations
> of Humphrey Bogart at the end of *The Maltese Falcon,*
> Mary Astor in his arms but spurning her pleas for deliver-

ance: "I won't because all of me wants to." The rhythm is lost. Then "Phantom Engineer," an early version of what on *Highway 61 Revisited* would be called "It Takes a Lot to Laugh, It Takes a Train to Cry," and again the music is running. With Dylan singing a barbed Plain States drawl and his rhythm guitar pressing for speed, Bloomfield jumps the train and drives it: "I remember," said Sim Webb, Casey Jones's fireman when the Illinois Central 638 smashed into a freight train near Vaughan, Mississippi, on April 30, 1900, "that as I jumped from the cab, Casey held down the whistle in a long, piercing scream." Bloomfield gets that sound.

This style is great when it works, but when it doesn't, it can be vague and rambling, pursuing a too-abstract goal with the bombastic tenacity of a star guitarist who, planting one foot forward, leans into a solo and just won't let up no matter what. There's a sense of cataclysm to it that seems to have more to do with Marcus's taste for cataclysm than anything else; every second is Judgment Day, and once that happens, well, you can pretty much sleep through it.

I read one such passage to a friend who is not educated, nor intellectual, but who is a huge Dylan fan. "It's like a necklace of turkey wishbones," she said. "You come across one, it's pretty cool. You put 'em on a string and wear 'em around your neck, it's a geek show."

It wasn't meant as a compliment, but it could be taken as such; you could applaud this book as a geek show, the kind that makes you blink, scratch your head, and look at the world with different eyes for a moment. Or more to the point, hear it with different ears.

Artforum, 1997

like a kid, she asserts herself by kicking and screaming, which finally leaves her prostrate and exhausted before the authority. She has no authority of her own.

In chapter 1, she examines the story of Samson and Delilah (which she sees as a story of true love), duly criticizing it as demonizing the sexually powerful woman and deploring men who blame women for their failings. She has no problem, however, blaming men "for bringing women down . . . refusing to fulfill our needs, failing to give us what we want, knowing in some sadistic way that we don't have forever to wait the way men seem to."

She starts her second chapter by stating that Amy Fisher, the teenager who shot and paralyzed her married lover's wife, is "blameless." Because "the minute [the married man, one lunkish J. Buttafuoco] began to toy with Amy Fisher's 16-year-old mind, such as it was, he became responsible for its thoughts." Personally, I have sympathy with Amy Fisher because I believe her to be an injured girl who was brutally taken advantage of by Buttafuoco. But anyone who shoots an innocent party in the face is not blameless. Wurtzel states that the fact that Amy Fisher is still in jail five years after the shooting "proves just how scared we are of the inchoate violence of a woman scorned." What it proves, if anything, is that attempted murder will likely get you jail time, and there is nothing "inchoate" about shooting someone in the face. I would think Wurtzel is smart enough to see something so obvious, but she is apparently so immersed in her emotional reactions that she does not. It's as if some visceral tangle of hurt and anger makes her see all the people, living or dead, that she discusses as giant projections of her own experience—how else could she say about Mary Jo Buttafuoco, whom she has never met, that "her consciousness is not much more than that of an alligator who has been flushed down the toilet bowl and must only fight its way out of the sewer. Only she is not fighting. And that is why I am sorry she isn't dead."

On the surface, this is a vicious (but snappy!) statement. A little further down, though, I hear something that I understand. Wurtzel is raging against the contemptuous, cruel treatment of sexual women, the hypocrisy that lets "good" family men dally with them and then smugly enjoy the support of their good wives when they disown the slut. I hear her loud and clear. But her anger, again, is that of a wounded child, and it ruins the book, even when she has good points to make and good sentences to make them with. It is the voice of a victim, and it is a voice that cannot have real insight or compassion, not even for other victims.

In a chapter on abusive relationships, she discusses the particularly horrible case of Hedda Nussbaum, who was beaten so badly by Joel Steinberg that she was disfigured: "Hedda was so hideous that by the time we see her in police photographs we want to beat her up too, we can't blame anyone for what they might have done to a woman who allowed this to be done to her." I imagine that's exactly what Hedda felt like. I imagine that's why she was with Joel. I imagine she also felt that "women age into insignificance," that men have all the power, that being single is not a choice, it's a sentence.

Wurtzel spends most of her last chapter going on about how awful it is to be single, how pitiable and despised and tortured single women are, and truly she does become pitiable.

But then something happens. As in the first chapter, she goes back and forth; it's okay to be single, no it's not, I'll be old and ugly, they have all the power. Then suddenly, it's as if she quiets down and finally hears a different voice. She is talking about a character in the movie *Blue*, a woman who has lost everything and is very alone: "[She] makes for herself a new understanding of what love is: it is not about romance or marriage; it is about living in a world without pity, with little sense of community, and choosing to reach out and show love to people who one might expect to hate." This moment in the text is so open, so fresh, that it's arresting. She continues: "It is so hard to be more and better than the terrible things that have happened to you, but it helps to start seeing bad people as more and better than the worst things they've done."

Including the Buttafuocos? Maybe.

"All I would like in my life, what I wish for so very much, is to someday have the strength to be free of the resentment and anger that I carry around with me like Linus' blanket for just long enough to become one of those people who is better than the worst thing that happens to her.

"How I would love to be that woman."

Finally, after all the silly shit, here is an adult—a graceful, strong adult, a woman I would like to hear more from. Too bad she didn't show up until the last two pages.

The Village Voice, 1998

DYE HARD

A REVIEW OF *BLONDE* BY JOYCE CAROL OATES

Blonde is Joyce Carol Oates's novel about Marilyn Monroe, and it is a very easy book to make fun of if that's what you want to do. Monroe's story is a tragic soap opera that has already been set to every sound track imaginable, and now here comes a cerebral lady professor to pound it out on her piano. And I do mean *pound*. Norma Jeane Baker's life was terrible and strange, and Oates hammers that home with a vengeance, emphasizing the actress's every moment of degradation and shame. Indeed, the book is a masochistic festival of feminine shame, filled with incidents such as the childlike Monroe being raped in the ass by a sadistic producer for the privilege of trying out for a bit part in his film (*Scudda Hoo! Scudda Hay!*), for which she auditions with "ugly brown menstrual blood" soaking through her Kotex and a "searing pain in [her] anus." Such things happen, and maybe they happened to Monroe *a lot*. But Oates renders this and countless other moments in a tone of ululating hysteria that is often emotionally pornographic. The ass-raping chapter is called "Hummingbird," and it juxtaposes Monroe's helpless delicacy with the grossness of the action to needlessly heighten the pathos.

"*Love me, don't hit me.*" "Don't make me into a joke . . . I beg you." "Could you p-promise not to . . . Otto, please!" The Monroe of *Blonde* is an ideal Sadean victim, and Oates places her in a gothic landscape built of feverish language: "The secret place between her legs had been rent and bloodied and claimed by the Dark Prince." "Never had Warren been so big." "Never would we know." "But no, never will we hear."

I repeat, you can make fun of *Blonde*. You would even be right, except that, even with all the qualities just described, the book has real power, energy, and locomotive force reminiscent of Dickens or Hugo—who, if judged by today's standards, would also be deemed hysterical and melodramatic.

Oates's narrative voice here includes three modes: One runs up and down on the surface of the story, nearly incoherent with the horror of what it relates, yet relating it with the silly, affected phrases beginning "Never would . . ." Another is the voice employed by Oates the essayist—rigorous, observant, nearly cutting in its precision. The third is muscular and sensual—a stereotypically male voice. The three voices operate independently of one another, creating a rich, clashing jumble. The first one is the strongest, though, perhaps because it has been charged with insistently reminding the other, more sanguine ones that something terrible is happening. That first voice may be high-pitched and theatrical, but it is finally dignified by its genuine grief at the suffering of the fictional Norma Jeane Baker.

Blonde begins when Baker is six, in the clutches of a demented mother whose baroque cruelty toward her daughter is a casual by-product of her own self-destructiveness. The child is sent to an orphanage when her mother tries to kill her and is eventually farmed out to a rough, ignorant farm family, where she is betrayed by the mother, who is jealous of her beauty. From a forced marriage to a vigorous young oaf, to a tawdry start in films, to a treacherous ménage with two narcissistic bisexual boys, to stardom, addiction, more hollow marriages, a ghastly tryst with the president—along the way, there are too many disasters to catalog.

Oates has stayed faithful to Monroe's life to a great extent, but she has also invented and imagined, infusing the story with her exaggerated sense of degradation, which both relies on Monroe's icon status and distorts it. Monroe's sometime degradation at the hands of studios is well known, but Oates, perhaps out of outraged empathy, is so focused on the star's suffering that she underplays any positive aspect of her brilliance, delightfulness, and power. Most peculiarly, Oates does not even give the power of Monroe's beauty its due: She repeatedly describes men and boys reacting to the star's nakedness with derisive laughter rather than desire. In one such scene, the teen Monroe is at a swimming pool with some teenage boys; when her cheap suit gets wet, it becomes see-through. Instead of being struck with eye-popping lust, the boys burst into laughter—hard to imagine! There is little sense of the adored icon, about whom Clark Gable said, "Marilyn is a kind of ultimate. She is uniquely feminine. Everything she does is different, strange and exciting, from the way she talks to the way she uses that magnificent torso. She makes a man proud to be a man."

But *Blonde* is a novel, and even if it is based on an actual person, it is not bound to represent her literally. Oates's empathy and indignation may be somewhat misplaced, but it nonetheless has the force of larger truth. As a character, Oates's Monroe is viscerally alive, and, with vivid, compelling imagery, Oates makes the reader feel the strength and intelligence that coexists and conflicts with the slutty, manipulative allure, the in-turned rage of her ultrafemme victim. Through this characterization, Oates depicts the American fixation on glamour and ugliness as locked together in a grotesque polarity, feeding off and heightening each other:

> She'd freeze . . . she'd walk off the set staggering like a
> drunk woman sometimes she'd shake her hands at the

wrists so hard, it was like a hurt bird trying to fly . . . in this shimmering mostly transparent gown they'd concocted for Monroe showing these mammoth boobs & the twin cheeks of her fantastic jelly-ass & the dress dipped low in the back showing the entire back to practically her tail bone . . . there was this tragic terrified woman emerging out of Sugar Kane . . . like a confectioner's sugar mask melting & its Medea beneath . . .

In such passages, Oates's writing is beautiful and clear, and the seriousness of her passion honors her subject. With beauty and clarity, she evokes a world where private and public violently intersect, creating an arena of no safety and no sense; in this unmoored universe, the banal and the infinite crisscross and then run together garishly—as they do in life. Monroe goes to have an abortion, in a car driven by a studio chauffeur:

The woman with the gloved hands made a face that might be described as a smile-frown. There was a jolting stop. Norma Jeane was made to realize that they had traveled through Time. *Any role for the actor is a journey in Time. It is your former self from which you must depart forever.* A sudden curb! A flight of concrete steps! A corridor and a pungent medical-chemical smell . . .

One is given the impression of a soul that has been, by some impossible error, snatched from its deep place in the psyche and thrust into a maze of personality and persona, through which it must grope and blunder, trying to make sense of the earthly barrage of words, images, and ideas like "movie star." The Monroe of *Blonde* is like every other lost soul, except that her lost state is so brutally public; in this essential way, the character may be true to the real woman, who continues to touch our imaginations more deeply than can be explained by great beauty and brilliance alone.

When Oates has one of Norma Jeane's lovers describe her sexual style, he could, in a way, be describing the book:

> . . . she'd get so excited, so crazed, there wasn't any rhythm to it . . . her body was this gorgeous thing she'd stare at in the mirror but it wasn't her exactly, and she didn't know how to operate it worth shit. Funny! Norma Jeane having an orgasm was like stampeding for an exit. Everybody screaming and trying to push out the door at the same time.

Oates's writing in this book can be overexcited, and if you stay detached from it, it's easy to snicker. But if you get caught up in that feeling of everybody stampeding for the door, you forget what you were snickering about—and when she makes it out the door, you're blown away.

Bookforum, 2000

MECHANICAL RABBIT

A REVIEW OF *LICKS OF LOVE* BY JOHN UPDIKE

Three years ago, David Foster Wallace wrote a review of John Updike's novel *Toward the End of Time,* in which he expressed the opinion that the aging author, along with other "G.M.N.'s" (great male narcissists), is a solipsist concerned only with himself and his personal problems. According to Wallace, every character Updike creates is really himself, even when they are not; they are never redeemed by belonging to any "larger unit or community or cause"—yes, they have families, but they don't love them, at least not enough, so that doesn't count. (Nor apparently do jobs and churches count, even though they are the only type of "larger unit" most people belong to.) Having attributed the failings of Updike's characters to their author, Wallace then censoriously extended those failings to an entire generation, deploring the "joyless and anomic self-indulgence of the Me Generation," supposedly epitomized by said author.

This is a perennially popular line of thought, and, on the face of it, a legitimate one: Narcissism is bad; communities are good; the novel should have a "broad social sweep." Except that it ignores the following: Even though art is expressed through an individual personality, if it is any good at all, it is not about that personality in a literal sense. John Updike does typically feature male protagonists who are selfish, horny, socially conservative, and *irresistible* to young pussy. I'm sure that this reflects

Updike's personality in some way, but I would not be so quick to say exactly how, even if Piet, Rabbit, et al. seem to function as mouthpieces for their author's opinions. Because, at his best, Updike places these predictable characters in landscapes as mundane as, yet infinitely more mysterious than, the personalities of those characters seem to be. This is from *Rabbit Redux,* a description of Rabbit and his dad having a talk in the local bar:

> The bar television is running, with the sound turned off. For the twentieth time that day the rocket blasts off, the numbers pouring backwards in tenths of seconds faster than the eye until zero is reached; then the white boiling beneath the tall kettle, the lifting so slow it seems certain to tip, the swift diminishment into a retreating speck, a jiggling star. The men dark along the bar murmur among themselves. They have not been lifted, they are left here. Harry's father mutters at him, prying. "Has she seemed any different to you lately, Harry?"

It's as if Updike has entered a tiny window marked "Rabbit" and, by some inverse law, passed into a universe of energies both light and dark, expanded and contracted, infinite and workaday. In this place, Rabbit's flaws and opinions are just another bit of mutable energy, familiar and yet unknowable as the "jiggling star." If "Rabbit" is how Updike gets to this numinous place, it seems small to stand there fuming that the entry point is not the right one, or worrying that Updike's use of this entry means that he, personally, is narcissistic.

It was with this readiness to defend and adulate that I approached *Licks of Love,* Updike's new, ridiculously titled collection of stories plus a novella. Imagine my distress at finding myself unable to do either. The book isn't bad—it has some lovely moments—but it is nowhere near as good as Updike can be. In some ways, it reads as if he's been listening to his critics and trying to please them. The novella, *Rabbit Remembered*, features Rabbit Angstrom's son, Nelson, a mild-mannered, liberal social worker who describes his father as "a narcissist." There are no sex scenes, no distasteful thoughts about "cunts," and the only sexist, racist characters seem meant to be disliked. (There is one exception, when Nelson thinks, "Women lie the way blacks lie. If you're a slave race telling the truth gets you very little." Which strikes me as more weird than offensive; this nerd is walking around imagining himself as a master among slaves?) Generally, the son is kinder, gentler, and far less convincing or compelling than the father.

The same can be said of most of the twelve stories. They revisit the Updikean concerns of family life, adultery, and social drift, and while they are sometimes touching, too often they feel rote and careless. Updike's language can still be sensitive, even beautiful. But too frequently it becomes bloated and grossly imprecise:

> Divorce, which had been flickering at our edges for a decade while our vast pool of children slowly bubbled up through the school grades toward, we hoped, psychological sturdiness, was still rare, and sat raw on Frank, like the red cheek he had been pressing against my wife's.

There are exceptions, notably "My Father on the Verge of Disgrace" (a kid discovers his father's petty theft) and "Metamorphosis" (an aging playboy in love with this Korean-American eye doctor persuades her to give him Asian eyelids). All of these are elegant and engaging—but even they lack the surprising changes of depth, the multilevel richness that characterizes Updike's best stories. ("My Father" comes the closest, with its tender, intelli-

gent observations, especially of a high school play in which the
dad, to his son's horror, kisses another man for laughs.)

The novella is the most compelling piece in the book, dramatic in the unabashed, sweaty style of a good soap opera. It
begins as Rabbit's thirty-nine-year-old illegitimate daughter
(Annabelle) comes to visit his widow (Janice), whose current
husband (Ronnie) also had sex with Annabelle's mom (Ruth), a
sometime prostitute. (Rabbit once had an affair with Ronnie's
former wife, Thelma, but never mind.) Annabelle's mother had
revealed her father's identity just before dying, and Annabelle's
appearance is an unwelcome surprise to everyone but Rabbit's
son, Nelson. Nelson's marriage has fallen apart, and he lives a discontented half-life with his mother and stepfather: He's drawn to
Annabelle out of a muddled longing for his father. It's as ridiculous as life, and features dialogue like: "I forbid anybody getting
in touch with this twat." "Ronnie . . . this twat may be my sister."

Even when the dialogue is salty, the effect is often stiff, talking head–like. Updike's characters have always veered toward the
topical, but in the previous Rabbit books, the banal (and realistic)
talk was intercut with what Anthony Burgess characterized as
"the poetry of digression"—that is, apparently unrelated descriptions of, say, a television broadcast in a crummy bar. These
digressions are like hidden pockets of thought and feeling, and
they subtly elucidate the characters in ways that dialogue alone
can rarely achieve. Such poetry is sorely missed here; Updike still
uses description and physical detail, but his intuition is off, and so
the technique does not serve to deepen or illuminate his scenes.

The book has another problem, one that negatively echoes
one of Updike's strengths—his compassion. In the past, the
blunt, helpless ugliness of his characters was presented in such
a way that you could not overlook it—nor could you overlook
how it made them human. The detailed precision with which he

drew their lives was never merely aesthetic; it served to locate the reader in the characters' skin in a way that went beyond ideology, beyond personal affinity, even beyond words. Whether you liked Rabbit or not, you felt him. You felt his blundering animal questing in the sensate prose. For Updike to weave such vulnerable animality together with the opinionated stridency of Rabbit or one of his antagonists required a profound, tough-minded compassion that did not morally let Rabbit, the reader, or the author off the hook. In *Licks of Love*, that compassion has devolved into a lax acceptance that is merely sentimental. Here is Rabbit's widow thinking about their emotionally distant, adultery-ridden marriage: "Looking back from this distance, she can't think any more that Harry was all to blame for their early troubles, he had been just trying life on too: life and sex and making babies and finding out who you are."

It is true that time can make even crabby old women forgive that which once seemed unforgivable. But tonally, this passage reminds me of a crowd-pleasing lounge singer who ends his heartbreak ballad with cheesy, uplifting chords, his arms open wide, and a brave, desolate twinkle in his eye. Another example from the novella: During Thanksgiving, the oafish Ronnie viciously insults Annabelle's dead mother, calling her a whore who would "fuck anybody"; Annabelle weeps, and Nelson, though he does nothing in the moment, moves out. But the conflict is easily resolved when Janice makes Ronnie call Nelson at work to deliver a grudging apology, during which he refers to Annabelle as a "slick little twat." Then, Nelson feels "right with Ron," and, by New Year's Eve, they're all together again, with Ron smooching the little twat's kisser. (Insert happy music here!)

The same refrain sounds in the stories: In the title piece, a banjo player chosen to take part in a cultural exchange program meets a "little black-haired coffee-fetcher," who says to him, "Sir, you are my God." You know what that means—pretty soon, they're drunkenly rolling around in her bed. It's not a satisfying experience, but the coffee-fetcher nonetheless becomes obsessed, badgering the banjo player from one end of the Soviet Union to the other with demented love letters. That such extreme emotions have become roused by such a brief encounter is a psychologically rich trope—or at least it ought to be. I imagine it is a strange experience to sleep once with someone who thinks you are a god, to discover that she is profoundly disturbed, and then to be hounded by her across a continent and finally into your own home. I was very interested to see what Updike's character would think and feel about it, as well as what he might imagine the girl to be thinking and feeling. But all he feels is superficial irritation, combined with worry that it will be embarrassing if someone finds out about the affair, and he imagines the girl to be nothing more than a psycho. When he returns to America, his wife does find out, but she doesn't seem to mind all that much. Neither, it's revealed, does the musician, who, though he tells his wife that "it wasn't anything," concludes that you can't really be too pissed at someone who thinks you are a god, and that there is, after all, "nothing more wonderful and strange than the way men and women manage to get together." (Insert happy music here!)

The three-page "Oliver's Evolution" is even less satisfying. It is the compressed history of a neglected child, who, as a toddler, nearly drowns because his parents, "striving for romantic harmony in the wake of a late party and an alcoholic quarrel," swim off and leave him alone on the beach. It's one of the many occasions when the parents fail to be there for Oliver, and by page two, he's looking like he actually has problems worth telling a story about, but (insert happy music!) by the end of page three, he's married with children and it's all good. In this case, there isn't even a real song—just that inserted happiness. If Updike had shown how this painful situation was so beautifully resolved, if he had developed the subtle psychological twists innate in his story, it could have been a wonderful piece. In skipping straight to the happy end, he creates the impression of needing to reassure himself as much as the reader.

I understand this impulse, or at least I think I do—many authors must secretly itch to stop torturing their characters, to spread their arms and give it up, making everything right in the end. In *Rabbit Remembered*, Nelson thinks, "But order and organization must be kept in the world. Ties of affection must be expressed, or nothing holds," and the thought casually reflects one of Updike's great themes: the tension between emotion and order, indulgence and rigor, cruelty and love. In past books, you felt the characters' awkward, sometimes belligerent attempts to negotiate between the two poles, and you felt their disappointment when they failed; you also recognized their pained efforts to accommodate that failure. In glossing over the failures here, I think Updike means to show affection, not only for his characters but for the reader, even for life. It's an admirable and, I believe, sincere intention. But "affection" that makes light of ugliness and pain is not very deep. Weighted too heavily on the side of indulgence, this new book lacks dramatic tension; if everything's so easily all right in the end, it doesn't matter much what the characters do.

Nonetheless, *Licks of Love* bears the mark of a brilliant and still-engaged mind. As I read it, I kept imagining Updike as a prospector who, having already found enough gold to last a lifetime, is still sifting for the sake of sifting, making the motions in order to fulfill some private need and paying little attention to what's actually in his pan. If this is what he wants to do, he has more than earned it. But as a reader who thinks there is still more gold there, I wish he'd start paying attention again.

Bookforum, 2000

I'VE SEEN IT ALL

THOUGHTS ON A SONG BY BJÖRK

Most sound track albums exist completely separate from the movies they're attached to because the songs selected already have a vital popular character that the movie has borrowed to enhance itself; I don't know if this ever works the other way around. The exception is the old-fashioned musical—and that is what Lars von Trier's *Dancer in the Dark* is, sort of. This "sort of" applies in different ways to both the film and Björk's album of the same name, the movie because, instead of simply being a musical, it is self-consciously *about* musicals, and the album because it appropriates the genre in a somewhat tedious postmodern way. However, both the movie and the album have power that is wholly unique, almost secret, and it comes from the way they play off each other. Specifically, it shows up in one astonishingly beautiful song called "I've Seen It All," which makes the CD worthwhile. The song amplifies the meaning of the film, even surpasses it in elucidating what seems to me *Dancer's* most powerful theme. Yet the song couldn't really exist without the movie.

Dancer in the Dark is ostensibly about an oppressed factory worker named Selma (played by Björk) who is going blind and who is saving every hard-earned penny to buy an operation for her son in order to save him from this congenital condition. Her money is stolen by a loathsome cop who has pretended to be her friend, who then weirdly (unbelievably, you might say) insists that she shoot him. She complies, then gives the money to the eye surgeon, is betrayed, caught, and executed. Meanwhile, in her fantasies, everyone sings and dances.

Like von Trier's *Breaking the Waves,* this is a story of transfiguring agony experienced by a childlike innocent. In the earlier film, the heroine's masochistic sexual sacrifice, supposedly made to save her husband, makes emotional sense because of the intense mystical relationship von Trier built between the two characters. But in *Dancer,* he has Selma sacrificing herself for her child, and yet the child barely exists. She appears more involved with her imaginary musicals and seems absolutely indifferent to her son's emotional well-being. Neither the devotion of her best friend (played by Catherine Deneuve) nor the malevolent cop quite makes sense, at least as they are portrayed. However, in a deeper, stranger sense, *Dancer* is the more powerful film, its real force being an undercurrent that has only a refracted relationship to the supposed story. That force is derived not from the story of sacrifice, but from an ecstatic spiritual underpinning that includes the transcendence of character and plot.

This is where von Trier's genius shows itself: In making music so important in the film, and in choosing a pop singer with a forceful, otherworldly persona to be his star, he seems to understand that his irrational, ecstatic theme is better served by voice and sound than by story. In this light, the musical sequences are not just charming, weird delusions; they are there to show that under the "story" of these lives there is a broader reality in which people who are deadly enemies or dear friends are merely playing roles almost for the sake of the soul's exercise. Further, these roles are in fact flimsy and can be stepped out of for transcendent moments that expose human personality as a mask and human action, whether compassionate or cruel, as a kind of ridiculous theater. (For example, after Selma shoots the cop, he gets up off the floor and they sing together; he understands that she merely, as the lyrics say, "did what [she] had to do." In this context, Selma is not an innocent; she is a blind "seer" who understands all this through music in a way that the people around her do not. As a story, the movie fails this material, because if it is about the illusion of "character" and "plot" in human life, then paradoxically its own plot and characters need to be highly developed and believable illusions, not hastily constructed cutouts. But "I've Seen It All" very nearly redeems this failure, almost making the film and the sound track into a hybrid art form, and hinting at a way of creating stories through combinations of different media.

In the movie, the song is sung by Selma and a man with a hopeless crush on her who has realized she is going blind and confronted her with it. He pleads with her to get an operation to restore her sight, and she says she has no need to see anymore. They are on a train track when a train roars by; suddenly they are on the train itself, singing as they speed past domestic tableaux, while rail workers do balletic routines. It's essentially a love song of renunciation and it is very tender. The man lists all the things she will miss seeing, and she answers with what she *has* seen. "You've never been to Niagara Falls? / I've seen water, it's water, that's all." It's about outer abundance—all the great stuff like Niagara—versus the inner abundance that comes from being able to see what is right before you. The song opens and contracts; smallness becomes bigness, the man's idea of big becomes small, and then you can't tell which is which.

On the album, the actor is replaced by Thom Yorke of Radiohead, and he and Björk share the roles, so that sometimes it is she who interrogates him. (That makes sense in the song because it doesn't matter which character is answering or asking; it is the exultant feel of expansion and contraction, of acknowledgment and release.) Without the visual aspect, the song is stripped down and childishly simple, with Seuss-like lyrics and a monotonous industrial backbeat. It is also lush, expansive, emotionally complex. Björk's voice goes from crumpled, nearly retarded, to wide and powerful as a highway to heaven. Yorke's voice, sometimes rhetorically sentimental yet giving full honor to sentiment, has never been more beautiful or nuanced. He can also sound like a righteous therapist: When she asks, in the voice of a pinched imp, "What about China? Have you seen the Great Wall?" he replies, "All walls are great, if the roof doesn't fall," and he seems nearly too pleased with this bit of wisdom. But the stuck-up part is tonally cut with a gentleness that gets fully expressed on that last word, *fall*. When he asks, "Your grandson's hand as he plays with your hair?" his voice describes sorrowful tenderness in so many shades, you can't parse it. And so she answers with sing-song insouciance that is almost bratty: "To be honest, I really don't care." And then the music opens out like sky and Björk's voice opens even more, in an electric combination of pain and joy—because almost any woman would care. Her joy is that of a person with so little joy in her life that she's been forced to find it where she can, and both singers seem to understand this. "I've seen it all, I've seen the dark / I've seen the brightness in one little spark." Both voices sing this line in a duet, *West Side Story*–style, and together they give reality to lyrics that, taken strictly at face value, could be New Age treacle.

In fact, I've quoted lyrics here mainly to locate particular shifts in the song; it's the voices and music, not the lyrics, that mark these shifts most effectively. It's the voices and music that convey the mystery, the transient changeability of human feeling, better than the movie. The song creates a sense of beauty and abundance that the struggling movie characters, with their small lives, would not seem entitled to, yet which they not only can possess through the strength of their inner abundance but can also refuse. Because the song itself is finally a refusal, one that acknowledges the beauty of all it refuses—holding it, then letting it go.

It's also, more simply, a powerful example of what's populist in pop—its lovely ordinariness. "I've Seen It All" is a passionate evocation of what is great in ordinary people, with their crummy jobs and fantasies, people who are not even supposed to "have a life." When I interviewed Radiohead some time ago, bassist Ed O'Brien said pop songs are like snapshots meant to be thrown away the next day. That is very true. But in the sense suggested by "I've Seen It All," that is also true of everything human. And I mean that in a good way.

The Village Voice, 2001

AND IT WOULD NOT BE WONDERFUL
TO MEET A MEGALOSAURUS

ON *BLEAK HOUSE* BY CHARLES DICKENS

I first became acquainted with Charles Dickens in the way I suspect most people of my generation have—by watching various versions of *A Christmas Carol* on TV. It's not a bad introduction. Dickens is fantastically visual and dramatic, full of broadly drawn characters ideally designed to bloom out of the cinematic darkness, their faces glowing with goodness or vice. Many of the film versions do an excellent job of rendering the thematic layer of Dickens's famous novelette—the struggle of good and evil, the purity of children, the redemptive power of charity—and the best ones suggest the deeper layers with their dark cinematography, their earthy depictions of minor characters with their gap-toothed grins and sparse hair standing on end. The 1951 version (starring Alastair Sim) is the most gorgeous film and probably the most faithful to the spirit of Dickens. But it is by pure serendipity that it most wonderfully serves the author: Because the film is very old and fragile, weird moving squiggles appear in the primitive dark borders and sometimes even in the shimmering, flickering skin of the stock; the foregrounded figures play out the story against a backdrop that seems to quiver with invisible life, dissolving and re-forming on the margins. This incidentally suggested backdrop, this dark world of teeming movement, subtly represents the locus of Dickens's genius—which would be virtually impossible to put into film as we know it.

G. K. Chesterton described the teeming world of *Bleak House* as a kind of literary accident, great because of "the unconscious or *accidental* energy of his genius which broke through at every gap" of the social satire. I don't know if it was an accident— Dickens's prose strikes me as quite purposeful. But *Bleak House* has a fecund ball of life at its core that seems to live independently of its author's purpose, and without it, the story would be a soap opera played by hand puppets. This in itself is not unique; a story is the outer weave, or conscious personality of a novel, but its numinous unconscious—which the reader can feel if not so easily see—is in the secret life that glimmers in the margins or bleeds out from the core. What is particularly striking in Dickens is the contrast between his melodramatic narrative tropes and the protean force that infuses them with kinetic, dreamlike power more fully dimensional than psychological realism.

The plot and characters of *Bleak House* are a great busy rattletrap that would lumber and creak if not driven by this protean force. The overarching social theme is the grotesque nature of the British court system Chancery, introduced in the fantastical first pages, with the lord chancellor, droningly addressed as "M'lud," proudly presiding in a filthy city covered in mud, where filthy pedestrians, human, horse, and dog, slip and slide in the streets and ". . . it would not be wonderful to meet a Megalosaurus, forty feet long or so, waddling like an elephantine lizard up Holborn Hill." Waddling out of this muddy mass comes the generations-long suit, Jarndyce and Jarndyce, through which "whole families have inherited legendary hatreds" and "[t]he little plaintiff or defendant, who was promised a new rocking-horse when Jarndyce and Jarndyce should be settled, has grown up, possessed himself of a real horse, and trotted away into the other world." Out of it come characters, strange little heads that poke up to yell at "M'lud" and then fall back down, among them a crazy suitor named Miss Flite, bearing her reticule of "paper matches and dry lavender," and two young people, yet unnamed, who will become major characters, Ada Clare and Richard Carstone.

It has been remarked that the glaring legal absurdities satirized in *Bleak House* had ceased to exist twenty years before the book was written; it has also been remarked that it scarcely matters. It doesn't matter because of that Megalosaurus and that rocking horse and that real horse, on which a breathing shadow figure leaves this world for the next. These cartoon homunculi— and there are many others throughout the book—extend the life in the novel beyond the frame of the story, in this case back into a cartoon prehistory, then forward into a cartoon death. Like them, like everything in the churning world of these first pages, Chancery is both temporal and forever—a castle made of mud convinced of its eternal nature, its fancy-dressed lawyers and judges acting as hosts for primitive forces of madness and destruction.

Chesterton called the beginning of *Bleak House* "an alpha and omega," and he is right in that it suggests a primeval world seen through the palimpsest of evolved, codified society. It suggests also the contrast between eternal forces and the mortals who live within them—twittering Miss Flite flying by, Tom Jarndyce blowing out his brains in a coffee shop, and "the little counsel with a terrific bass voice" who rises from the fog and then drops back down. ("Everybody looks for him. Nobody can find him.") These contrasts are huge, frightening, and comic; Dickens puts the emphasis on comedy, not because he is coarse, but because he is mature in the truest sense of the word; he may have written in part to protest social evil, but he accepted reality on reality's terms. Here is his ghastly slum, Tom-all-Alone's, where crime and pestilence rule:

> Much mighty speech-making there has been, both in and
> out of Parliament, concerning Tom, and much wrathful

disputation how Tom shall be got right. . . . In midst of which dust and noise, there is but one thing perfectly clear, to wit, that Tom only may and can, or shall and will, be reclaimed according to somebody's theory but nobody's practice. And in the hopeful meantime, Tom goes to perdition head foremost in his old determined spirit.

But he has his revenge. Even the winds are his messengers, and they serve him in these hours of darkness. There is not a drop of Tom's corrupted blood but propagates infection and contagion somewhere. It shall pollute, this very night the choice stream (in which chemists on analysis would find the genuine nobility) of a Norman house, and his Grace shall not be able to say Nay to the infamous alliance. There is not an atom of Tom's slime, not a cubic inch of any pestilential gas in which he lives, not one obscenity or degradation about him, not an ignorance, not a wickedness, not a brutality of his committing, but shall work its retribution, through every order of society, up to the proudest of the proud, and to the highest of the high. Verily, what with tainting, plundering, and spoiling, Tom has his revenge.

On the top layer, this passage is a grim moral anthem of social revenge; deeper down, it shows an amoral, gut-level affinity for sheer, rich ugliness, which Dickens the artist could revel in with childishly amoral freedom.

The book is baldly theatrical, almost primitively so, and the main characters are nearly like playing cards with their static defining traits: Esther, a pious, good, wise young orphan who narrates about a third of the book. Ada Clare, a beautiful and angelic inheritor of the suit's legacy, who becomes Esther's best friend.

Richard Carstone, Ada's cousin and lover. John Jarndyce, a benef-
icent elderly bachelor who nobly turns his back on the loathsome
suit. He becomes the guardian of Richard, Ada, and Esther. Sir
Leicester Dedlock, a foolish, pompous baronet who "has a general opinion that the world might get on without hills, but would
be done up without Dedlocks." He is married to the beautiful,
inhumanly cold Lady Dedlock, who "if she could be translated
to Heaven tomorrow . . . might be expected to ascend without
any rapture." Unknown to her husband, she harbors a secret that
could destroy her, and Mr. Tulkinghorn, a lawyer who works
for Sir Leicester, is onto her and is determined to expose her.
Running around these, banging into one another and bellowing,
are: the Smallweed family, a malevolent, half-crazed clan of loan
sharks. Mr. George, a good-hearted vagrant soldier who owns a
ramshackle shooting gallery. Mrs. Jellyby, a phony philanthropist
with a filthy house, enraged children, and a husband who sits
with his head against the wall. Harold Skimpole, a dainty little
monster, a self-described "child" who would send a real child to
his death. Jo, a miserable street urchin who unwittingly gives
Tulkinghorn his weapon against Lady Dedlock. This is a bare list
of characters and the mere suggestion of a story that crescendos
and crashes like a Puccini opera, all the while careening like the
Little Rascals meet the Three Stooges.

Dickens used a method of characterization that would be
unthinkable to the hypersophisticated modern writer: He tells
you exactly what characters are like, not just on meeting them,
but throughout the acquaintance. Then he shows you what they
are like through description and dialogue. Then he tells you
again—and again and again. Most writers could never get away
with this; they would simply repeat themselves. On the face of
it, Dickens certainly repeats himself; he can use the same ironi-
cal, jesting phrase to describe a character several times in a span
of pages. But on a more subtle level, Dickens is not repeating.

He is *deepening,* rapidly taking you through layers of images and movement that develop your sense of the character and his world almost nonverbally—an extraordinary thing in a verbal medium. Dickens accomplishes this by using words to make concepts into visceral pictures, as eloquent and fluid as dream images. The inhuman longevity of Chancery leaps into the physical form of a rocking horse that mutates into a real horse that trots into eternity while mothers become grandmothers and a man blows his brains out, all in the space of two sentences. Emotions, ideas, and events become physical and alive; they roar about and won't be confined to the words that have brought them into being. The images made of words transcend words to become something more primal in their effect, and the apparently simple characters become conduits for essential forces that we can just glimpse in these rushing images. In a pedestrian sense, some of the characters are too exaggerated to be realistic. In a larger sense, they are faithful to the comic reality that we spend our lives as conduits for forces we don't understand, and which form our characters in a sometimes extreme fashion over which we have limited control.

In the chapter "Sharpshooters," two members of the Smallweed family visit Mr. George in his shooting gallery. These characters are morally static; the former will be eternally wicked and grasping, the latter stalwart and plain-spoken. Granddaughter Judy Smallweed so resembles a monkey that, "attired in a spangled robe and cap, she might walk about the table-land on the top of a barrel-organ without exciting much remark as an unusual specimen." Grandmother screeches grim nonsense, "like a horrible old parrot without any plumage," and grandfather screeches back, "You brimstone pig!" Whereupon he is, by Judy, "shaken up like a great bottle, and poked and punched like a great bolster" until he and his wife resume staring "like a couple of sentinels long forgotten on their post by the Black Serjeant, Death."

They are scarecrow opposites of the tall, broad, jovial

George, with his "sounding voice" and "his large manner, filling any amount of room." When the lunatic Smallweeds come to visit George in his shooting gallery, these character traits, while repeated and amplified, become a mad ballet of stasis and movement. Mr. George's man, Phil, has just been declaring his willingness to be hit in the head, shot at, wrestled, and thrown as a lightweight on George's behalf, while bodily illustrating these activities, culminating with a devoted head butt. Into this tornado of personality come old Smallweed and Judy, the spiteful geezer borne aloft in a chair, panting and throttling a bearer.

The ensuing dialogue serves to forward the plot, but the continued imagery and manic action drop us into a surreal energy current running beneath it. Mr. Smallweed is constantly poked by Judy, pounced on, shaken up, poked again, and prodded while he slides down in his chair and claws the air, squeezes his cap, and snarls. His goblin face with its "skittle-ball of a head" looms out of the narrative with exaggerated size, his "nails . . . long and leaden, and his hands lean and veinous, and his eyes green and watery . . ." These outsize images and antics do not increase our understanding of Smallweed—rather, they saturate the scene with him, like heavy paint crosshatching a canvas. His character becomes one dark dimension in the multidimensional scene, which culminates with everyone riding off together like the Keystone Kops:

> Mr. George is quite confounded by the spectacle he beholds from time to time as he peeps into the cab, through the window behind him; where the grim Judy is always motionless, and the old gentleman with his cap over one eye is always sliding off the seat into the straw, and looking upward at him, out of his other eye, with a helpless expression of being jolted in the back.

But Dickens's lesser characters are (too blandly) accepted for their comic eccentricity. Modern readers have a lot more trouble with his major characters, especially the good ones. Esther of *Bleak House*, as the sainted housewife, caretaker, and healer of all who would be healed, is so good that, psychologically, she is scarcely believable as a person of either gender. Even Victorian critics, who presumably had a higher tolerance for feminine treacle than we do, complained about her, one gentleman confessing to a wish that she either do something "really spicy" or shut up and tend the jam pots. Vladimir Nabokov, in his lecture on *Bleak House*, pointed out that Dickens had to use a banal churchy voice when speaking through Esther—or to force his own voice into the character's insipid mouth. "I must say that despite the superb planning of the novel, the main mistake was to let Esther tell part of the story," he fussed. "I would not have let the girl near!"

It is true that Esther's unrelenting goodness is crude and simple next to the wild imagery and "accidental energy" that electrify the Smallweeds. But I think that's precisely why her voice is not a mistake—why, on the contrary, it increases the novel's power. Esther works in a sense that's abstract and nearly musical: Her voice is like that of an operatic singer—a pure, high ribbon of sound that simultaneously pierces and unites the complex "music" of the other voices, images, and kinetic movement. It works through the dramatic contrast of light and boiling darkness, and it creates a feeling of ardent expansion in what could otherwise have been an involuted and too-dense mosaic. A character like Smallweed has the density of one who has made his own personality into a baroque lockbox, and there are many such characters in *Bleak House*. An example is the stupid old poser, Mr. Turveydrop, a living gewgaw deformed by his own will, "pinched in and swelled out, and got up and strapped down, as much as he could possibly bear," made into a rhinestone-encrusted whirligig of twisted energy. Or the lawyer Kenge, a mechanical windup demon, who moves his hand "as if it were a silver trowel, with which to spread the cement of his words on the structure of the system, and consolidate it for a thousand ages." Characters like these pull the narrative into such tight, weird knots that you welcome the smooth expanse of Esther's conventionally idealized nature, even if the writing that comes with it is often cloying.

Esther's conventional point of view also has another function. When Dickens looks at certain wicked or complex characters through Esther's ingenuous eyes, he can perceive their gross faults with naïve clarity while pretending (as Esther) not to know what's wrong with them. It's a transparent device, but it nonetheless creates a feeling of openness and receptivity that is almost maternally tender, and which is complementary to Dickens's fierce comic knowingness. This function is most effective in relation to Lady Dedlock, the novel's dark queen. "My Lady" is introduced in a gorgeous onrush of wet, heavy, murky images that echo the primeval world of the first pages:

The waters are out in Lincolnshire. An arch of the bridge in the park has been sapped and sopped away. The adjacent low-lying ground, for half a mile in breadth, is a stagnant river, with melancholy trees for islands in it, and a surface punctured all over, all day long, with falling rain. My Lady Dedlock's "place" has been extremely dreary. The weather, for many a day and night, has been so wet that the trees seem wet through, and the soft loppings and prunings of the woodsman's ax can make no crash or crackle as they fall. The deer, looking soaked, leave quagmires, where they pass. The shot of a rifle loses its sharpness in the moist air, and its smoke moves in a tardy little cloud towards the green rise, coppice-topped, that makes a background for the falling rain. . . . On Sundays the little church in the park is mouldy; the oaken pulpit breaks out into a cold sweat; and there is a general smell and taste of the ancient Dedlocks in their graves.

Emerging out of this backdrop, the artifice of her figure is highly charged. Every time she appears, it is reiterated that she is perfectly fashionable, gracious, empty, and cold. She is an embodiment of social masking, its power and its idiocy. She is also an embodiment of female power and female pain, and she is like clashing cymbals of raw feeling and iron control. Tulkinghorn's pursuit of her has an unmistakable whiff of sadistic desire; he is awed by the perverse strength and courage of her facade, and lusts to strip it from her. The pivotal confrontation between them is rendered with an emotional eroticism more intense for its restraint:

> She falters, trembles, and puts her hand confusedly to her head. Slight tokens these in any one else; but when so practised an eye as Mr. Tulkinghorn's sees indecision for a moment in such a subject, he thoroughly knows its value. . . . He would know it all the better if he saw the woman pacing her own room with her hair wildly thrown from her flung-back face, her hands clasped behind her head, her figure twisted as if by pain.

When Lady Dedlock falls on her knees before Esther, revealing herself in a fury of abjection, Esther's deep, uncomplicated response creates a field of placid receptivity against which the frantic woman becomes more poignant than she might be if Esther were complicated herself:

Covering her face with her hands, she shrunk down in my embrace as if she were unwilling that I should touch her; nor could I, by my utmost persuasion, or by any endearments I could use, prevail upon her to rise. She said No, no, no, she could only speak to me so; she must be proud and disdainful everywhere else; she would be humbled and ashamed there, in the only natural moments of her life.

The tension is most obviously in the melodramatic emotional juxtaposition of an innocent, loving girl with a perverse, dark woman. But we feel it more deeply as a charged juxtaposition of female elements that have flashed into these painted figures like electricity and animated them. Like the little mortal beings that appear in the huge, grinding morass that is Chancery's introduction, Esther's very banality is affecting and stabilizing against the fierce, surging background that introduces Lady Dedlock and infuses her static character.

But Esther is not always banal. Through her comes some of the book's strangest, nearly mystical perceptions, such as her hallucinatory descriptions of a dangerous fever:

I am almost afraid to hint at that time . . . when I laboured up colossal staircases, ever striving to reach the top, and ever turned, as I have seen a worm turn in a garden path, by some obstruction, and labouring again. . . . Dare I hint at that worse time when, strung together somewhere in great black space, there was a flaming necklace, or ring, or starry circle of some kind, of which I was one of the beads! And when my only prayer was to be taken off from the rest, and when it was such inexplicable agony and misery to be a part of the dreadful thing?

It is also through Esther that Dickens shows us the harbor at Deal, where she has gone to meet Richard, where the sun makes "silvery pools in the dark sea," and the ships "brightened and shadowed and changed." In those fever visions and in those sunny, silvery pools there is a hint of a world unknown not only to the characters, but to the reader and even to the writer. This world, and the tingling peculiarity of its inhabitants, can be briefly revealed in moments and images that may be amusing or beautiful or terrible but which are finally mysterious. In the context of such a world, we are reminded of our own banality, and our need for the unalloyed goodness that Esther represents.

With all the roaring energy he summons, accidental or no, and all the ranting little heads popping out of his fantastic landscape, Dickens is excessive by modern standards. But modern standards have become denatured, and Dickens is excessive like Nature; like living things, his creatures must twist and turn, expand out or tunnel in until they have utterly fulfilled what they are. They must bang their tankards on the bar and sing the song, whether it's corny or not. Dickens can have one of them dying a supernaturally horrible death of drug overdose, and then, a few pages later, have an entire neighborhood of them crowding the street to hear of it, singing a popular song of the day about a boy boiled alive in the orphanage soup. It's very entertaining, but it's also faithful to human experience, which indiscriminately mixes trivia with genius, artificiality with raw power, sentimentality, and seriousness.

One of the most touching scenes in the novel is the transformation of Sir Leicester near the end. He has been severely humbled by the discovery of his wife's secret and her flight, jeered at by a servant, and crippled by a stroke. Society expects him to renounce his wife, but instead, before his household, he declares his loyalty to her with the pomp and bravado that have, until now, made him the novel's chief stooge:

> His formal array of words might have at any other time, as it has often had, something ludicrous in it; but at this time, it is serious and affecting. His noble earnestness, his fidelity, his gallant shielding of her, his generous conquest of his own wrong and his own pride for her sake, are simply honorable, manly, and true. Nothing less worthy can be seen through the lustre of such qualities in the commonest mechanic, nothing less worthy can be seen in the best-born gentleman. In such a light both aspire alike, both rise alike, both children of the dust shine equally.

A more tasteful writer would cut everything after the first sentence. I would cut it after the second, which seems to me simply accurate even if the volume is high. But it doesn't matter; even the melodramatic sanctimony of the last part is essential to Dickens's *Bleak House*—to cut it out would be like trying to stop a freight train on a dime.

Nabokov, in his *Bleak House* lecture, wished to hold Dickens "above the sentimental trash" and "theatrical nonsense" of the author's own making. It is a passionate compliment, maybe too passionate—for in wishing to idealize Dickens, Nabokov does not respect him quite enough. Dickens loved sentimental trash and nonsense as much as he loved beauty and rigor, and he had that rare form of intelligent innocence that perceives these qualities on their own terms, outside of conventional hierarchies. He gave each its due, and in doing so created art that was and will remain uniquely his.

INTRODUCTION TO *Bleak House,*
MODERN LIBRARY SECOND EDITION, 2002

REMAIN IN LIGHT

ON THE TALKING HEADS

Lost my shape—Trying to act casual!
Can't stop—I might end up in the hospital

—"Crosseyed and Painless"
Talking Heads, *Remain in Light*

In 1979, I was an almost total dork. I didn't know what was going on—in any way, really, but especially as regards culture and fashion.

My first encounter with culture and fashion was when I was seven and my mother took us to a roller-skating rink, where teenagers wearing dos and poodle skirts with flannel appliqués roared ferociously around in a circle while music played. One girl's skirt had on it slogans like "Do the Twist!" and "The Mashed Potato!" and I watched her ferocious movement around the rink with amazement and terror.

I was afraid because I was looking at a world of signifiers and abstraction, broad basic swatches of feeling and experience expressed in symbols that were both general and refined, a whole language of symbols that I didn't speak and which instantly struck me as too complex to learn. I was looking at the future.

Five years later, I would be required, along with everyone else in my junior high school, to fit my personality into a similar system of symbols that I couldn't get right. The only thing that kept me from social autism was music. Anything from Nancy Sinatra to the Four Tops to Mitch Ryder to the Association—it was refined and shapely, like the social styles that so defeated me, but it was also fluid and fundamental as preverbal sound. The songs did not have prescribed meaning for me, so they could mean anything. I would go to sleep at night with my transistor radio pressed against my head, letting the "anything" take forms that were too mysterious and personal to turn into a symbol that I could put on my skirt or my hair. It made me feel connected, even to the people who had mastered the art of style—because I understood in some way that they must hear this more mysterious thing, too.

Three years later, I dropped out of school and ran away from home. For a while it was like disappearing into the songs on the radio. But in five years I was struggling to get by, and by then I wasn't paying attention to any style system. I liked music a lot, but it was background to me, not any kind of main event. I liked Patti Smith, the Cars, 10cc, the Electric Light Orchestra, Robin Trower, Roxy Music, and it was all equal to me. It did not have prescribed meaning, and it did not define me in any way. When I decided to go back to school, I went to community college and hung out with people who got high in deserted housing developments and screwed to *Frampton's Camel*, then drove home meditating on Gary Wright's "Dream Weaver." I liked that, too.

Then I went to a real university and met people who knew what was going on. I briefly went out with a guy I'll call Jenkins, who introduced me to the Ramones, Elvis Costello, and the Talking Heads. He had excellent taste. He read *Rolling Stone* and *The Village Voice* and he knew exactly what these bands meant and why they were important. He and his friends had a softball team called the Psycho Killers (with individual shirts labeled "Ted Bundy" "Richard Speck," etc.) and *Texas Chainsaw Massacre* posters up in their house. It was like being at the roller rink. It was also like pressing the transistor radio to my ear. I didn't know how to separate the music from the pretense around it—college-kid pretense, both wonderful and idiotic, a mixture that felt so false and so true that I didn't know how to react to it. Like a dork, I would fume about snotty art students singing songs about murder—*I had experienced real violence, I said, and it wasn't funny*. But I said that because I didn't know how to say what I really felt— which was that the cleverness, humor, and sometimes perverse torque of the music was a nearly flawless form that I felt stunned by and locked out of.

I still don't know what was going on in 1979. What I remember is a mass dream of joy and pain, both slightly delirious, neither fully felt. The nonfeeling created a certain morbid innocence that in my mind looks like that of the victims in the disaster/murder movies that were popular then—an awful blank optimism, best expressed on the "face" of Mr. Bill, the cartoon victim on *Saturday Night Live*. Jenkins was right: "Psycho Killer" was the perfect song for this moment. And because it was he who was right, the music got mixed up with sex that was like twisting and crushing myself into weird forms until my "self" broke and something powerful and formless came out, then withdrew again.

I heard that in the music, too—the weird, twisting form, the bouncing, jerking, deliberate, and sophisticated childishness of it. I loved it and hated it. Maybe I felt mocked by it. The week Jenkins and I broke up, I published a story in a local paper about a hydrocephalic guy in a wheelchair who'd been wrongfully locked up in a state home for crazy retarded people because his poor, battered inner-city family had been unable to care for him or get him diagnosed correctly. My story about him got bounced out of the lead position by a million-word analysis of how important the Ramones were. There was a huge picture of the Ramones joyfully pretending to be retards, while the deformed beatific face of the hydrocephalic guy smiled from the corner. It was me and the hydrocephalic guy versus Jenkins and the Ramones, and they'd won! I felt like the fool David Byrne sings "No Compassion" at, and it was more humiliating than it should have been.

Or maybe it was exactly like it should've been. It was around then that I started waking up in the morning and having no idea who I was or where I was. I had to remind myself, and it took several minutes. I would call up images, pictures of myself doing things: walking to class, in a restaurant drinking tea, talking to someone. At first the pictures were bizarre and alien, then neutral, then I'd say, Oh, right, and get out of bed. My self, it seemed, really had broken, and something unfamiliar was trying to emerge. It was scary, but it was powerful, too. I wanted to know who it was that was looking at the pictures before I said, Oh, right. I started writing stories that were more real than anything I had written before. I started listening to music, really listening. Sometimes I wrote with headphones on.

It was during this time that I heard *Remain in Light*. It was like meeting an enemy and realizing he's an ally. It was like the hard, clever form of their old songs had burst, and something was pouring out of it—something that had always been there. Listening was like going through a tiny door and coming out somewhere vast, with thousands of doors and windows to a thousand other places. Sometimes the music flew past the places, and sometimes through them. One world might be the gauze through which you looked at another, and then it would be the world. I could be the person walking down the street or having tea and then I could be the person looking and not knowing who I was; each moved through the other, seen and not seen. I was changing shape, and it was an accident, and this music not only understood that; it celebrated it. It described something that was happening in me, and something that was happening in everybody, all the time, to the hydrocephalic guy and to psycho killer.

I wasn't saying this to myself while I listened to the music. It was something I understood deeper than words, in a way my mind could only glimpse. The understanding was like a seed, and it would be a long time before it began to germinate. It would be even longer before I had the means to communicate what was being grown. But that was okay. I knew it was there. I heard it.

LINER NOTES COMMISSIONED FOR THE COMPILATION CD SET *Once in a Lifetime*, 2003

VICTIMS AND LOSERS: A LOVE STORY

THOUGHTS ON THE MOVIE *SECRETARY*

In 1992 an inexperienced young director named Steven Shainberg first approached me about making a movie of "Secretary," my story about a naïve young masochist who yearns for emotional contact in an autistic and ridiculous universe, and who winds up getting her butt spanked instead. Mr. Shainberg was very young and very earnest, and while he got the yearning, he didn't get the ridiculousness. He seemed bent on assuring me that he would not belittle Debby's suffering, though I sought no such assurance. During one elaborate assurance, he brought up the movie *Pretty Woman,* which, he said, had been ruined by Hollywood philistines. The original script was very dark and ended with the angrily screaming prostitute being dragged out of a car by her three-day john and thrown on the sidewalk before he flies off to get married. He expressed outrage at the light and charming spin the movie had put on the innately painful and degrading subject; his indignation was so excessive that I actually felt roused to defend a film I didn't think much of. Yes, it was phony and insipid, but Hollywood is phony and insipid about housewives and mothers, and I wasn't especially indignant regarding this treatment of prostitutes, whom I didn't see as innately degraded. He seemed baffled and even offended. Ten years later, he made the *Pretty Woman* version of my story.

The bare plot of "Secretary" the story could be the plot of a classic wank book: Hopeful Innocent takes a job as a secretary where she is abused, spanked, and jerked off on by Mean Bossman. She is weeping and shamed, her face is as scarlet as her red-hot bottom—*and her pussy is dripping wet!* But life is dirtier than porn, and I didn't get the idea from a wank book. I got it out of the newspaper. It was a small story reprinted in the "No Comment" section of *Ms.* magazine, circa 1980, and it reported that, somewhere in the Midwest, a lawyer running for public office had been revealed to have abused his former secretary by spanking her and videotaping her standing in a corner repeating "I am stupid." On being revealed, he sought to make things right by apologizing and giving the woman two hundred dollars. I'm sure *Ms.* didn't intend it this way, but the blandly reported story, in addition to being ludicrous, had a great erotic charge, primarily because both players were faceless ciphers whom the imagination easily translated as archetypes. On reading it, I laughed, then shook my head in dismay, then thought, What a great story—funny, horrible, poignant, and gross, the misery of it as deep as the eroticism; the misery, in fact, giving the eroticism its most pungent force. The wank-book aspect was clearly indispensable, but what interested me most was, Who is this girl? The Hopeful Innocent in the porn story, the cipher in the news story—what would she be like in real life?

In any genuine piece of fiction, the plot is like the surface personality or external body of a human being; it serves to contain the subconscious and viscera of the story. The plot is something you "see" with your rational mind, but the unconscious and the viscera—what you can smell and feel without being able to define—is the deeper subject of the story. This is particularly true of "Secretary," the heroine of which is a knot of smothered passion expressed only obliquely and negatively in her outer self. I conceived her as someone of unformed strength and intelligence, which have never been reflected back to her by her world and so have become thwarted, angry, and peculiar. The deeper subject of "Secretary," then, is the tension between the force and complexity inside the heroine, and how it gets squeezed through the tiny conduit of a personality that she has learned to make small so that she may live in the small and mute world around her. Debby's parents are not abusive; they are defeated—to some extent by the severely limited world around them, but primarily by their own emotional ineptitude. Their daughter's desire to humiliate herself may be accurately described as self-hatred; however, looked at less judgmentally, it's an ardent and truthful desire to represent, with her own being, the distorted world around her and inside her, where force and passion are humiliated and punished by being ignored or twisted. Debby's passivity is so willed and extreme that it is an act of mutually annihilating aggression; there can be no "relationship" with the boss, even if he were to desire one (which he does not), and questions about whether or not she is victimized by him are irrelevant. His only superiority is in his ability to recognize her—as one of his own kind. For her passion is every bit as cruel as his, and this is what is horrible in the story.

However, coexisting with all this is the yearning that Mr. Shainberg perceived from the beginning. Whatever else she may be, Debby is a sensitive girl acutely attuned to the emotional world. Hunger for contact underlies her perversity and to some extent drives it. Early in the story, she recalls an instant of loving touch from her sister, wistfully noting that such an instant has never occurred again. At the height of her experience with her boss, she has romantic dreams in which they walk together in a field of flowers, holding hands and smiling with "a tremendous sense of release and goodwill." One room away from her family, she longs for real connection with them, and the fear that she will never have it plunges her into despair. Her unformed aggression and cruelty are surpassed only by her unformed tenderness. What a shocking relief when, at work, both impulses are poetically expressed through emotionally violent and intense sex that occurs without touching. Simultaneously, Debby and the lawyer achieve total intimacy and total isolation, and this paradox is the heart of the story's anguished comedy. The character's ability to hold this paradox is the source of her dignity, even if she holds it unknowingly. Without understanding how, she is aware that she bears equal responsibility for what is happening. Given this awareness, when the reporter calls, urging her to expose her boss, what can she do but hang up?

This is an almost impossible story to make a movie of. Its drama is internal, rendered in language very nearly like code and meant to be sensed rather than explicitly seen. I admire Steven Shainberg for attempting it, and for succeeding to the extent that he did. It bears almost no relationship to the original story because it couldn't—not in America anyway, where *Belle de Jour* or *Repulsion* would now be met with either fear or blank incomprehension. For it to be commercially successful, a relationship between boss and girl needed to occur, and so it does. To be successful, the relationship must end in marriage, and so it does. (Perhaps the most socially threatening thing about the story is that Bossman is actually not very important.) Unlike Debby in the story, the movie heroine (played by Maggie Gyllenhaal and renamed Lee) has just been released from a mental hospital and is an anorexic self-mutilator. She is puppy-eyed and slump-shouldered, but this melancholy affect is oddly superficial; it is quickly neutralized by Lee's big, glowing smiles, which unmistakably signal the assurance and ease of a happy and lovably ditzy person. When the boss says to her "You're closed up, tight," it doesn't make sense, because we're looking at a soft, receptive, essentially sunny face. When first spanked, she does show bewilderment and consternation, but her ambivalence is temporary and never reaches the level of conflict that might be uncomfortable to watch. Lee never seems humiliated; this truly painful feeling is present only symbolically, as if the screenwriter used anorexia and cutting to represent emotions she did not understand and was incapable of rendering. Right after spanking her, the boss hands Lee the letter she has retyped, with the comment "good job"; a look of sweet, simple joy possesses her face. These emotions are not incongruent with S/M. But considering that Lee is supposed to be an inexperienced and emotionally frail person, it is remarkable that she understands this so quickly—remarkably facile. Debby's arousal is so intense, it nearly breaks her. Lee's arousal is pleasant and improving, as is Lee herself.

This is not to say that the film shirks ambivalence entirely. It's the boss (played by James Spader) who is confused and anguished here, and it was an interesting choice to make him so. The jerk-off scene is done with a close-up on him, and Spader's face subtly reveals sexual feeling that is deep enough to include sadness and vulnerability as well as furtive, guilty meanness, which he does not himself understand. (Not cruelty; meanness. *Cruelty* is too strong a word for this film.) These qualities, as they are revealed, give him complexity and make you feel for him.

However, his ambiguity comes too dear, at the expense of hers. Gyllenhaal is a delightful and unaffected presence, so genuinely pleasing that she almost redeems a character verging on total insipidity. In one scene, in which she awkwardly spanks herself at home, her face and body are alive, radiating animal determination and geekiness that is funny and touching. It makes one doubly sorry that delightful and pleasing were all that the character was finally allowed to be. Shainberg was right to make Lee's cutting accoutrement beautiful and artistic; for some who practice it, cutting *is* beautiful. But he so emphasizes this perceived beauty that it becomes one-dimensional. As the film progresses, Lee begins to seem like a fantasy madonna in her unconditional approval and affirmation of her conflicted lover. When the boss has a crisis about what they're doing and fires Lee, any unpleasant feelings of hurt and anger on her part are quickly transcended. She's all the more accepting and approving, declaring that she wants to "get to know him" before she glues herself to his desk and starves herself for three days. If only the film had ended there, at the desk, its relentlessly positive fantasy could've been leavened with ambiguity, an open place that allowed the viewer his or her own response. But no; the boss lifts Lee out of the chair and carries her upstairs, where a curative bath awaits her. In the next sequence they are wed. The "takeaway" here is that S/M is not only painless; it's therapeutic: It has made both characters more confident, better-looking, happier, freer, and self-actualized. Best of all, it has led them straight to marriage!

The original screenplay, a sort of theoretical S/M romper room, was more real than this; in it, for example, Lee cries the first time she is spanked. But there is none of that in the film, which is like the flag for the S/M section of a gay pride parade reading WE USED TO BE SICK, NOW WE'RE SAFE. One critic praised the film for "opening up avenues of feeling and experience," for illuminating "the dark corners of the psyche." And it does illuminate these dark corners, just as dozens of American movies illuminate them every year—by shining a perfectly happy ending on them, so bright in this case that nothing dark remains. This insistence on the positive may seem compassionate, but it rarely is, for it cannot tolerate anything that is not happy and winning. I first saw *Secretary* at the director's house with several of his friends. During the opening scenes, while Lee elegantly maneuvered in an elaborate bondage costume, a woman loudly burst out, "She's not some helpless little victim! She's IN CONTROL and she's doing JUST FINE!" She spoke as if through clenched teeth, and considering that no one had suggested that Lee *was* a victim, her vehemence was startling. This vehemence, which may be the real driving motor of the film, revolves around what has become a contentious cultural belief: that Americans want to be victims, and that such "victimhood" must be denounced or denied.

But I think that this apparent desire to be a victim cloaks an opposing dread: that Americans are in truth profoundly, neurotically terrified of being victims, ever, in any way. This fear is conceivably one reason we initiated the particularly vicious and gratuitous Iraq war—because Americans can't tolerate feeling like victims, even briefly. I think it is the reason every boob with a hangnail has been clogging the courts and haunting talk shows across the land for the last twenty years, telling his/her "story" and trying to get redress. Whatever the suffering is, it's not to be endured, for God's sake, not felt and never, ever accepted. It's to be triumphed over. And because some things cannot be triumphed over unless they are first accepted and endured, because, indeed, some things cannot be triumphed over at all, the "story" must be told again and again in endless pursuit of a happy ending. To be human is finally to be a loser, for we are all fated to lose our carefully constructed sense of self, our physical strength, our health, our precious dignity, and finally our lives. A refusal to tolerate this reality is a refusal to tolerate life, and art based on the empowering message and positive image is just such a refusal.

What *Secretary* the movie and "Secretary" the story have in common is the theme of awakening. In the movie, the heroine awakens to her masochistic sexuality and lives happily ever after. In the story, the heroine awakens to her masochistic sexuality and learns a hard truth: that she is a small, fallible container for a primary force beyond her understanding. In the end, her self, that fetish object of anorexics and cutters, has become unknown to her. And it's not "such a bad feeling at all." She is alone on an ocean, with no idea where she's headed, without any nice boss to hold her hand. Whether or not this is a terrible ending is unclear even to me. She may discover uncharted territory or she may be eaten by sharks. But whether or not she learns to negotiate the sea she finds herself cast upon, it will remain unknown to her—as it will remain to all of us.

In spite of all this, I understand why people liked the film. In a perfect world, sweet, understanding masochists would meet and marry sweet, understanding sadists and go on to have hot, conflict-free fun in perpetuity. How can I be sarcastic about the earnestness of *Secretary* when, fifteen years ago, I gave an interview to *The Wall Street Journal* in which I earnestly told the world that "masochism is normal"? If falsely positive movies can be made about everybody else, why not make them about sadomasochists, who are surely an underserved population in this regard? Am I too high-and-mighty to scorn the need for empowerment, always, in every case? Who hasn't, at least once, come out of a movie glad to be uplifted, even if the uplift is specious? Apparently, young girls felt empowered by *Pretty Woman,* and I say bless their impressionable hearts. Indeed, somewhere, in a parallel universe, I can imagine my character Debby watching *Secretary* and feeling empowered!

Incidentally, Steven Shainberg was right about *Pretty Woman*. Some years after our initial conversation, I came across the original script, titled "Three Thousand." It's a beautiful piece of work, a dark and powerful story about a loser and a victim. And it was ruined by philistines.

Zoetrope, 2003

THE BRIDGE

A MEMOIR OF SAINT PETERSBURG

In Saint Petersburg, Russia, I got hit in the head with a bridge. It was a stone bridge, with a high arch and a low foot and a girdle of steel spotted with moss and green mold. There was a man walking across it with anger closing his face like a fist and a proud girl in a flashing skirt and a prancing dog looking up at them with eyes of love. We had just passed another boat full of screaming people, one of them a drunken man standing on the prow and acting like he was masturbating. I didn't see what he was doing at first, so I smiled at him: My husband laughed and said, "A guy goes by jerking off and you smile!"

We were in Russia teaching at a two-week writing conference. It didn't pay anything, but still we'd wanted to go. My husband's father had been born in Russia; he had escaped just before the Revolution, hidden under the straw of a vegetable cart, with a bag of jewelry down his shirt and an earwig in his ear. He came to New York and ran a catering service. When he and his wife (a Finn) fought, they did it in Russian, and in this way Peter had learned a bit of the language. I had grown up seeing the Russian premier pounding a shoe on a table as he threatened to storm our houses and lawns. I found him terrible and wonderful, and when I was ten, my parents gave me a subscription to a magazine called *Soviet Life* so that I could find out more about his country. Other girls played with Barbies and Beatle dolls with giant heads;

they walked around with transistor radios held to their ears. I held *Soviet Life,* taking it out in school and covertly smoothing it open inside my desk to look at pictures of ballerinas with huge Soviet faces in pink feathered headdresses. I said I was going to be a writer, and that I would go to Russia and spy on it. Forty years later, I was a writer in a boat on the Neva with my writer husband. The day before, Paul McCartney had played at the Hermitage; we could hear him and his band from our hotel blocks away, a dark roar of sound rolling through the streets, rolling past and present together.

If someone had told me when I was ten that I would grow up to be a writer, that I would be invited to read in Russia, and that a Beatle would be playing just a few blocks away, it would have made my life worth living. Now that it had all happened, I was simply put out by the lack of toilet seats and paper, the giardia in the water supply, and the animals starving in the streets because people put their pets out when they couldn't afford to feed them anymore.

During our six-hour layover at Charles de Gaulle Airport I had spent an hour running from toilette to toilette, looking for a sink that had hot water so that I could wash my face. I burst from the last one with wild eyes, complaining, "I never thought I'd say it, but maybe America really is better than everyplace else. Maybe our maniac government is right about maintaining our 'way of life,' and it really is our duty to take over everywhere and install hot water and toilets with seats. It's horrible about Iraq. But maybe it's finally worth it. My God, listen to me. I hate myself. But maybe it's the truth. Maybe it is!"

"I hate you, too," said Peter, but in a tolerant tone; we had been up all night and missed our connection. "A civilization is about more than plumbing."

"Yeah, it's also about buildings that stay up."

Soldiers with machines guns strolled past like animals with

heavy paws. They gazed about as if longing to kill someone—anyone. Just weeks earlier, a section of the airport had collapsed, and people *had* been killed.

"When I was on the pot in one of the stalls, the attendant banged on the door and yelled at me. She poked her broom under the door to roust me out, and I had just sat down!"

We laughed and went to a fancy bar and drank glasses of wine. Over the rim of my glass, a group of aged, ragged people appeared, as if a bag had been opened and they had come out of it. The two women had dust smeared on the backs of their skirts; one of them wore a brooch with its stone missing. The short man looked like a squashed head on a sack of clothes. The tall one had magnanimous eyes, a sclerotic nose, and a liver-spotted white head. Even from a distance, they exuded alcohol and urine; still, you could easily imagine the tall one twirling a walking stick. The maître d' hesitated, then showed them to a table.

"Where do you suppose they're traveling to?" I asked.

"Maybe they're poor people who live in the airport. Though it's hard to believe they're French."

"It's hard to believe that attendant poked her broom under the door while I was having a moment of animal relief. I just hope the airport doesn't collapse on us. I hope terrorism doesn't get us."

The first bridge was so low, even those of us sitting down had to put our heads in our laps; we shouted as we ducked, looked up to touch the molding steel roof of the stone mouth, then looked back down at its lapping black liquid tongue. I shouted with these people like I talked with them—excitedly, eagerly. All day and night we talked, in cafeterias, conference rooms, and bars, about Islamic extremism in Indonesia, American atrocities in Iraq, AIDS in Russia, our families, phobias, and times we had lost our bags. Earlier that day I had talked to a writer from Kenya named Binyavanga, a big man with deep, reasonable eyes and a richly glistening head. He had just led a panel discussion on African literature and was taking a cigarette break in a damp hallway painted a dull salmon. He rolled a cigarette as we talked about what was shocking to African readers, which was mostly homosexuality and black women having sex with white men. Recently, he said, an African woman had written from a white man's perspective about his lust for a fat black woman, and it had been accepted quite warmly. We talked about the ways in which the unacceptable could be not merely accepted but adored; he gave as an example his Kenyan neighbor who went around in jeweled robes and a turban and blasted the neighborhood with every recording Maria Callas ever made; in spite of the boys seen leaving his back porch early in the morning, people did not revile him as a queer, but instead revered him as a lovable eccentric. When a neighbor's son called him "homo," the gentleman demanded a public apology and got it when the father frog-marched the kid over in full view of everyone. In response, I told him about Sweet Evenin' Breeze, a black hermaphrodite hospital orderly much beloved in my parents' southern town, even by racists— Binyavanya paused in rolling his cigarette, a hot expression coming up through his layers of eye. He held it back and continued rolling his cigarette, and I continued talking about my grandfather, who, when my eight-year-old mother asked, "Why is that man wearing a dress?" replied, "Honey, that's not a man; that's an accident of nature. That's Sweet Evenin' Breeze."

"So strange," mused Binyavanga. "In some place inside them, people accept it all, as long as you keep to the conventions." In the courtyard outside, two dogs tore up an old hunk of bread. In my head my mother kept talking. "And he walked on down the street in this funny way," she said. "Like a woman, you know."

———

The screaming became a shapeless roar. *Like a woman, you know.* The previous night there had been fighting in the hotel; we heard shouting and somebody's fist beating a door. They were fighting over a woman.

My parents had argued once about Sweet Evenin' Breeze. People were over visiting, and my mother was describing to them how the whole racist town had loved the hermaphrodite orderly.

"Our town was not all racist," said my father; "don't slander us."

"Sam Blackburn was a real racist and you know it," she said.

"Sam Blackburn was not a racist!" He almost shouted it. "When Sam was in for a hernia, Sweets was the only one he would let hold him. He said, 'Only Sweets knows how to hold me without it hurting.'"

We came out the open mouth; everybody sat up and cheered. On the stone bank, two boys walked on their hands, one after the other. There were more cheers. One of the boys held his legs erect; the other let them dangle at the knee. Overhead, clouds parted and freed bursts of lavender rimmed with orange.

"Are you still sorry we came?" asked my husband.

"I don't know," I said, dazed. Another boat of drunken people plowed past, roaring lustily. "It's strange to be floating through, seeing all these things and not being able to understand or to fully experience them. But it's beautiful here and powerful in a way America isn't."

We ducked under another bridge. Its shadow woke at our

passing and tossed like an ogre with the boat lights prickling its skin.

Days before, I had given a reading with an American writer named Jeffery, who'd read about an escaping slave hiding his son in the ass of a white cow, then finding him later shit out and his skin mysteriously covered in a layer of white. We'd gone to dinner with him and his fiancée, Danielle, and our Russian host, Mischa; Danielle was a sexy, thick-bodied beauty with fake mauve nails and a skeptical attitude toward all writing, including her fiancé's. She ordered absinthe and tiger shrimp and then out of nowhere snapped at Jeffery: "What's wrong, too ghetto for you?" He looked hurt but forbearing.

From a bright, heat-steaming kitchen window, blue eyes stared out, suspicious and crouched in their expression. Mischa was saying, "Young people feel that when we were Soviet, at least we were number one. Everyone hated us, but it was okay because also they were afraid of us. We were number one." American rock music played on the sound system, but I was thinking of ballerinas in pink Soviet headdresses. In the real world, we were at war with Iraq, but when I dreamed of it, it was Russian soldiers who fought us. In the dream, Arabic women in veils saved me when the Russian soldiers came.

Another tunnel roared over us; we sailed out past a huge pale green building with beautiful beetling brows. It glanced at us, sighed, and folded its hands across its midsection as it returned its attention to the past. In the recent past, we had visited the Museum of the Defense and Siege of Leningrad. It was a small apartment up a short flight of stairs lined with great crude paintings in gilt frames of Stalin and the generals he had murdered. Deeper in were more paintings, these depicting dead, half-eaten horses lying in the streets, gutted buildings, and the city exploding under a flaming sky of clotted oil. Hanging just beneath them were enlarged newspaper cartoons of Hitler driving a pack of goggle-eyed Nazi dogs, military maps, and Soviet uniforms stiff and small enough for chloroformed children. On the floor were hoary broken-legged cannons, some shocked household items, tables of personal effects (buttons, ribbons, a diary with two pages filled in), and a broken loaf of sawdust bread ringing with starvation like a shell rings with the sea. A small, dim diorama protected a table, a rug, a chair, a child's cornhusk toy, and a wooden radio with a metronome sounding from the torn gold fabric of its speaker. "They played the sound of the metronome twenty-four hours a day," said Peter. "It meant that the heart of Leningrad still beat."

Clouds rolled in, white and profoundly blue, massed like great intense thoughts in a clear and joyfully humming mental field. A little blimp toiled distantly, finite, curved and occluded in the great mind of the sky. Binyavanga stood up to take a picture.

Two days before, Peter and I had gone to the Hermitage, the giant palace full of gold furniture, carriages, priceless art, and knickknacks; we read in a pamphlet that after the Revolution a delegation of peasants staying in there got drunk and shat in the gold tureens, vases, and marble baths. The next day, in the Siege of Leningrad Museum, we saw photographs of the peasants' emaciated sons with their limbs blown off—both legs and an arm in the case of one son, a large-eyed young man who stared raptly at the left-hand corner of the frame, his upturned face stunned as if by the glimpse of another world. "So moving," said Peter. The gray museum attendant coughed in the next room.

When I told Danielle about the peasants shitting in the tureens, she made a disgusted face. She suddenly turned to a table full of students, picked up a stray manuscript, and began reading it ferociously. She asked if she could sit in on my class. "I want to see if it's a game," she said.

"It is," I said, "to some extent."

The water flexed its cold, rolling muscle; the boat was turning slow and hard. After the war, the peasants' sons were starved again, shot, and worked to death in prisons. Today their daughters sat in the streets and begged. Every day we passed them, old women holding out cups or caps or selling bunches of flowers. The previous night, a group of us had passed one of these old women on our way to dinner at an expensive restaurant that was cheap for us. One of the writers looked at her and spoke in English. "Did you shelter any Jews?" he asked. Hopefully, she extended her cup. "I don't think so," he said, walking past.

Later, the organizers amused us over dinner, describing the time a writer had gotten lost in the subway system and been held prisoner by some toughs who slapped him, robbed him, and wouldn't let him go until he'd said "I am not the writer—you are the writers" fifty times, in Russian. "And they were probably right," said Peter, laughing.

Outside the window, another old lady stood and shouted in at us. "What is she saying?" I asked Mischa. He listened for a moment and then said, "I think she's asking how we make our money. She's asking, do we even work."

We sailed along on the Neva's lilting silver skin, listening to someone tell a story about the time one of Stalin's men put on a show for his boss by mimicking a purged apparatchik pleading shrilly for his life. Stalin roared with laughter, he gasped, "Stop, stop!" and pounded his knee.

"Did he kill the guy who told the story?" asked a student.

"Of course!"

Binyavanga sat down and put away his camera.

I wish I had not thrust racists on him while he was rolling his cigarette. I could've told a different story. I could've told him that many years ago I had been a dancer, a stripper, in clubs and sometimes bars for guys who hated queers, who might beat and even kill them, and that on one evening I had watched a room of these guys become enchanted by a troop of queers lip-synching and dancing as women. But then he might not have accepted me.

We were coming to a fork in the river, one direction of which was marked by a portal made of stone walls. There was a window of broken brick in one of the walls, and the midnight sun came through it, giving the river a restless patina of mauve and peach. In the distance was another bridge, a low embankment of ocher stone that curved around a wooded bend; beyond that was a meadow, a glimpse of forest, an enchanted lake of red and fiery purple streaming through the sky. Someone yelled, "I want to go there!"

And music came from below. In the hold, a Russian boy was playing a tape so a Russian girl would dance with him. *This is a man's world—* It was a James Brown song nearly forty years old, and it joined past and present with its saturating voice. *But it wouldn't be nothing—* Brown's voice was so dramatic that it made even the spaces between sounds glow with density and mass. *Without a woman or a girl*— The Russian boy pulled the smiling girl stiffly toward him. In my memory, a strip-club dancer leaned against a velvet pillar, his eyes down, one leg bent, one small knee tensely flexed, lithe white belly pressed moodily out as he arched his back, ecstatic and abject in the pale grainy light, and shining in the slow glandular fire of someone else's voice. *Man thinks about a little baby girls*— Jeffery and Danielle gently touched their faces together. We came near the enchanted place. *And a baby boys*— Down below, the boy and girl bantered, she tanned and blond, with sad, tired eyes and a long, sinewy neck; he white-skinned, with little burning blue eyes and a lewd red mouth. He was slight and effeminate, but there was something wild in him, leaping like a goblin in a dark and ancient forest. You would feel that with him inside you; his blue eyes promised you would feel it. But the girl just laughed; she'd already felt it in herself. *Even though the man makes money*— Eyes down, the naked dancer twirled his raiment of grainy light. The audience of men sat at their tables, getting teary as they lifted their beers. *To buy from other men*—

"I want to go there!" But we couldn't; the song was over, and the portal was closed off with a rusted chain. There was a sigh of disappointment. I closed my eyes, tired. "My name is really Traci," said Danielle. "I changed it when I got old enough." She'd said this at the bar, over golden-mouthed drinks. The ballerinas in their feathered headdresses fluttered up through the murk. *He said, "Only Sweets could hold me and not hurt me."* But Sweet Evenin' Breeze, with a lithe movement of his little hips, parted the darkness as if it were a curtain, slipped inside it, and disappeared.

"Walk the dog! Walk the dog!" Another bridge was coming, and boaters were shouting up at the people walking across it. Peter looked back at me and smiled; we put our heads down. A wing of foam took us forward. When I was ten, I slept in a redbrick house in a row of redbrick houses on lawns of bright sod, and dreamed of spying on Russia and writing books. Girls pressed their transistor radios to their ears and played with Beatle dolls that had tiny bodies and huge flawless heads. I had finally come, but Russia was broken; the lavender was pouring through and Paul McCartney was playing at the Hermitage, unintelligible but horribly audible blocks away. He had broken free of his tiny doll body, but now he had no shape. "Walk the dog, walk the dog!" I raised my head. There was a girl with a flashing skirt and a prancing dog. "Walk the dog!" I raised my head again; there was a man leaning over the rail, his face a fist of longing and rage. I thought, Everything is too mixed now; too many things are mixed. I am too small to hold it all, and if I try, I will break.

And then I was hit, as if by a blunt knife wielded like a punch. "What is it?" cried Peter, and we went under the bridge. Down under, I thought, where giant flowers lift and fall with the deepest waves. "Mary," he said, "are you all right?"

"I don't know. I feel sick." One of the flowers was a girl's face; she was rising to meet me, one eye alive, the other not. Her name was Valeria and the memory of her came with terrible feeling.

"God, look at the blood!"

We had come out the other side of the bridge; there was blood on my head. I had not thought of that girl in years. "Peter," I said. "I'm afraid."

Mischa came toward us; he looked like he was thinking, Oh no. My vision began to blur. "I just remembered this girl," I said to Peter. "Somebody hit her and she fell asleep and when she woke up, she wasn't right." One part of his eye came toward me; everything else in him moved away. I saw it all before me: a dark city street with its torn paper and discarded cans, a bag of spilled cashews, a wheel of flashing neon color. Then my vision blurred, so I could barely see at all.

"We're right here, sweetheart," said Peter.

"Don't let me fall asleep," I said, then fell.

It was dark where I fell; there were no giant flowers. But there were voices, hundreds of voices, unintelligible but still glimmering and filling the dark with movement. The dark had several strands of movement, each one a narrow door, all spinning so fast, I did not see how I could choose the right one. But I did not have to choose; it chose me. It drew me in as if I were smoke, and I was gone.

Imagine a bird flying in the dark of night. Suddenly, it flies into the rafters of a house; down below it there is a party, with people eating and drinking. Adults are talking and dancing lustily; kids are laughing and running between them. All of life is there with its lights, sounds, smells. Life rises up and pierces the bird's supple breast; the bird flies out the other end of the rafters and into the night again. It sees and knows and instantly forgets everything but the rhythmic beating of its own wings.

At first I was a bird. I saw, knew, and forgot everything. Then I was a person who knew nothing. I was at the party. People were drinking and eating; the room roared with their talking and laughing. Who were they? Music was playing. But something was wrong. I was curled in a corner, naked. Something bad had happened. What was it? Should I cover my nakedness or show it? A bird flew overhead and disappeared. A sharp smell flew up my nose; there was the blue-eyed Russian boy with smelling salts. As he drew away, he looked at me intensely and I saw the sexy goblin in his eyes. His eyes flashed pleasure at my seeing. I fell back again, though not so deep this time.

This time I was not naked at a party. I was curled safe in my bed. On one side of me was a wheel of color and spilled cashews. On the other was Peter's hand. "I'm right here," he said. I could feel his warmth and fear, but I could not see him. "They're stopping the boat," he said. "We're going to the hospital." I couldn't see. I was blind. This was the bad thing. This was my nakedness.

"How you doin'?" said Danielle. She was in front of me; I could feel her warmth and curiosity.

"I can't see," I said.

"You'll be fine," said Danielle. "Trust me."

"But I can't see."

"Oh God," said Peter.

"Yes, you *can* see." I felt her hands on mine. Warm, with plastic nails and rings. "You're looking right at me."

"But that's what I mean. I can't see you."

Instead, I saw the girl who got hit and went to sleep. I could see Valeria, obese and swollen, with dulled eyes and a slack mouth, moving absently on a dirty stage, half-aware of the men sitting rows before her. Maybe half-aware, too, of my pity and terror coming toward her from someplace far away.

"You *can* see; you *can* see."

"Traci," I said, "I'm afraid. I'm really afraid."

"You're going to be fine. I've seen worse, believe me."

"But I—"

And then I saw Traci/Danielle. I saw her lips and teeth first, flashing slightly, as if in a darkened room. I saw Valeria, too. From a distance the dull eyes and mouth, even the obese white flesh seemed to know something not sayable in words. Something I was about to know for the rest of my life and be unable to say. It would be terrible, but I must accept it because Valeria had.

Danielle came fully before me, glossy-haired, radiant, and snappy, the gold of her jewelry cast on her skin. I saw from her expression that she had not been trying to help me as much as boss me. But she had helped anyway, and I was grateful for it.

"We're here," said Peter, and he took my arm.

I broke away to kiss Danielle's forehead. "You're a wonderful person," I said. "Thank you." And for the first time I felt fear come from her, mixed with confusion and surprise.

We crossed over to land on a little wooden plank. A car had stopped and the blond Russian girl was leaning into it, persuading the drunk kid at the wheel to drive us to the hospital for some rubles. He agreed. Two rumpled girls climbed out of the front seat, smoothing their hair. "He says please excuse the mess," said the blond girl, and we climbed over a mound of refuse into the panting car. The kid looked curiously at me and hit the gas, with one arm out the window.

Because I was with the writers' conference, I went to the American Clinic, where they spoke English, gave you a private room and a toilet with a seat. The doctor had a high, reserved chest, a gentle, slightly bitter mouth, and precise eyes that held their object like gleaming tweezers. He was not interested in my brain, but it was his duty to take care of it and so he would.

My husband sat on the bed with me while we waited for the X-rays, and I told him about the girl who had come up to meet me on my way down.

"Several strippers I worked with were beautiful, but she was the most beautiful. Black hair, full lips, long legs, big breasts— she looked like Vampirella, except onstage, there was nothing fierce about her. She didn't dance; she posed in an almost trance-like way. Though she did have a powerful look in her eyes sometimes, and her eyes were deep. She did this complicated 'stocking act,' where she would hook the stocking on the end of her toe and change position, stretching it this way and that, so that she was looking at it over her shoulder, et cetera. She'd make it this precise, balletic thing, like a narcissistic ritual, her alone in her room—and then she'd look up and give the men these hot, deep eyes, and let them in the room with her. Let them inside *her*, but for just a second; then she was back with the stockings. That was the striptease really, this placid beauty who suddenly showed herself. Or seemed to. It's the cheapest trick, but she didn't realize that, which is why it worked.

"The place was an old-fashioned strip joint—the men didn't have any contact with the girls; there was no sticking money in underwear, no tipping allowed, though of course girls would accept it if it was a big-enough bill. Men would sometimes scream obscene abuse, but they also wrote love letters, with cash or little presents, hoping the girl would meet them. One of them, a journalist, fell in love with Valeria, and did a big story on her in the city magazine.

"The magazine did her hair and makeup like she was a for-ties movie star, and they put her on the cover with a tiara on her head. The journalist described going to see her night after night, fantasizing that she was *une belle dame sans merci*. Then, when he got to meet her for the article, he found out she was just an ordinary twenty-two-year-old from a small town in northern Quebec, the kind of kid who ordered a Blue Zombie just to see what it was."

The journalist had described that moment so vividly, I could recall it clearly almost thirty years later; at the private island of their table, the young man looks with abashed disappointment at the impossible girl reaching for a frosted blue drink loaded with umbrellas and striped straws. There is the waiter's retreat-ing arm, the jaundiced light from the bar glowing about the dark heads of strangers.

Valeria started coming to work in low-cut white dresses with cinched waists and frothy skirts, and fancy broad-brimmed hats with flowers. When she came in, men would turn around and say, "There she is!" Women sometimes would come back to the dressing room and ask for her autograph.

"What a great story," said Peter. "It would never happen today, and it's wonderful."

It was wonderful. Then one night, a bunch of us left work

at midnight and went out for drinks. It was summer, the street was crowded with sweating, half-dressed people, and the air was heavy, like something had burst inside it and swelled it with juice. Again and again hot, rhythmic neon burst and dissolved against the night sky. Valeria wanted to get a bag of cashews, so we stopped at a stand. She was wearing a fancy dress and a big lacy hat, and a red-faced man scratching his scabby chest through his open shirt stopped dead and gawked. "Great God!" he screamed. "You are beautiful!" We all ignored him as he followed us down the street screaming, "You're beautiful!" until finally he screamed, "You're beautiful, but you stink, you stinking whore!" She flew at him so fast, her cashews sprayed the street; he shrank back, blinking and weaving his head confusedly. She screamed as loud as he did, "I don't stink. You stink, man, too bad for me to talk to!" For a second, a bolt of feeling connected them. Then he swung on her, hitting just hard enough to knock her off balance. She wobbled on her high heels, then fell and banged her head on the curb. The record store light flashed like an explosion. Somebody cursed him. He jerked his head fiercely, wiped his mouth, and walked away on bowed, toiling legs. The cashew man ran to get a cup of water to revive Valeria, but by the time he got back, she'd come to and was sitting on the curb, brushing off her hat.

Later she sat in the bar, drinking Blue Zombies and bragging. "Some people would just take it," she said. "But not me. I'm proud, and I don't let nobody get away with saying that shit. I fight back."

The next day she didn't show up for work. Two days later one of the soundmen broke into her apartment and found her asleep. She didn't wake up for a week; when she did, her mouth was slack and her eyes unmoored.

We were quiet a long moment. Peter kissed my temple and said, "When you were out, I had your forehead cupped in my hand the whole time." We were quiet some more.

The X-ray was okay. We each lay down in a crooked, creaking bed. Half-asleep, Peter said, "I'm sorry about your friend." Light came under the door crack.

"She wasn't really my friend," I said. "That's why I forgot until now."

"Still," said Peter.

"I know."

The room stretched out and became enormous between our beds. Peter began to snore. I turned and scratched myself and felt my head with my fingers.

Fifteen years ago, I had returned to the town where I had been a stripper with Valeria. I had come to participate in a literary festival. The little club where we used to dance still existed but had become seedy and charmless. There was no pretense of a show; women stomped across the stage, then stripped and squatted to let men finger-fuck them for tips. I asked the bouncer if anyone from the old days was still there; Valeria was the only name he knew. She had gotten fat, he said, and puffy from alcohol and drugs. He glanced at the stage to be sure the finger fucking hadn't turned ugly, then looked back at me and tapped his forehead. "Other problems, too," he said.

I turned and turned and tried to calm my breath. The wordless knowledge I had seen when I could not see was near me but not on me; for now I would be spared it. I tried to give it a form, a garment, a hem I could cling to, and lay my head against. But it had no form, no garment. Light grew and elongated under the vinyl blind, revealing a layer of dreaming dust. How gentle it was, the light and dust, the cheaply painted sill, the blind.

Peter stirred. "Are you okay?" he said in a furred voice.

"Yes. I think so."

Outside, a woman shouted a string of words, a grudging and slatternly command; she was answered by a torrent of hammers, a storm of industry and hopelessness. Peter got up and looked out the window. Construction was under way; violence echoed between the buildings in rising red rings of sound. "That's the most primitive scaffolding I've ever seen," he said. "There's nothing to keep them from falling off."

A technician, a middle-aged woman in a low-cut blouse and high heels, put my head in a long silver tube and took its picture with an ecstatic, spinning camera. She and Peter looked at the pictures, spoke Russian, and laughed. "She says everything is working fine," he said. "But is not so cute! She said that!"

When we got back to our hotel, we stopped by the conference office. People were lunching on canned meat, bread, and cold blintzes, eating off a low coffee table and from plates on their knees. The blond girl from the boat was there; her knees, small and bruised-looking without any bruise, were nearly as expressive as her eyes. She got up to give me tea in a plastic cup; she touched my shoulder and told me that everyone was distracted and upset about the disappearance of a student, a flaky, blowsy girl who had last been seen getting very drunk with Russian guys.

"Things like this happen every year," said one of the organizers, a small, scrappy American named Jeff. "People come to Saint Petersburg and enter a chaos vector. But it always works out. Anyway, I'm glad you're okay."

Peter came up and we sat down for some canned meat and bread. Mischa came in and embraced me. "I know what you went through," he said. "Me and my friends all had concussions. To get out of the Afghan war, we bashed our heads on the wall of the military building"—he jerked his head to show me—"we vomit and black out and don't have to go."

Peter went down to the café to check his e-mail, and I went down the hall to our room. The windows in our room were enormous and screenless, and took up most of the wall. I stood up on the wide sill and looked out, into the smaller windows across the street. On their sills were clay pots, the bent stems and leaves of plants, small jars and bottles lined up neatly, and the wily ears of a cat not yet put out. A mirror gleamed; a swollen hand methodically used a brush. The wind filled the air with white down. The curtains were a rough synthetic, a blend of pink and orange that put a glow on the room—lurid, artificial, but with a hint of the ideal. I shut them, and got into bed. The bent leaves, the ears, the little jars, the swollen hand, the drifting down—each came through the synthetic pores and was transformed into a garment whose wearer I could not see but trusted nonetheless. I lay my head on its hem and went dreamlessly to sleep.

In my class the next day, a stray red kitten came in the door and walked the length of the conference table with its tail up. The missing student came back, laughed, and said, "Couldn't you tell, those guys were gay!" We feasted on blintzes, herring, and borscht. We went to the opera to see *Carmen* and sat next to Jeffery and Danielle. The players were thin and seemed tired; Carmen's voice was tremulous and yearning; her shoulders were small and hunched, which she tried to hide by putting her hands on her unconfident hips. Danielle said Beyoncé was better in the MTV hip-hop-era version; Peter said, "But this one has such a soft, expressive throat." Jeffery said we should've gone to see *The Nose* instead. We had cake and caviar during intermission, then came back to the penetrating scent of fresh piss wafting through our box from the lavatory's open door. The painted cherub on the wall next to us had a crumbling foot, and I thought the whole box might crumble and pitch us into the human sea below.

But the orchestra played jauntily; the dancers gamely twirled their skirts. Aged matadors with turtle eyes stumped across the stage with their old backs staunchly humped. When we came out, the streets were full of girls wearing tight shirts with plunging necklines and light-colored pants with dark thongs showing underneath, and deep-eyed boys fiercely escorting them. Rattling cars came at us in waves; a clock tower, too, defaced by too much gold, bore down, and a giant rearing horse.

I took Peter's hand. He raised his arm. A car stopped for us, not a taxi, just a young guy wanting to make extra money. Peter told him where we were going and negotiated a price. The driver's face, sideways in the side mirror, was beautiful and full of wasted strength. He turned the wheel and took us into a speeding gray curve of traffic, nearly colliding with an oppositional curve. Above us clouds continued to move, slow and round, and massively white at the top.

Zoetrope, 2004

SOMEBODY WITH A LITTLE HAMMER

ON TEACHING "GOOSEBERRIES" BY ANTON CHEKHOV

Last September I was reading in my Syracuse apartment when something very large thundered down the street and stopped with a loud grinding of gears. I looked up; long pulses of light were coming through the blinds. Parting the slats with my fingers, I peeped out; there seemed to be a car parked in the air across the street. I opened the blind and saw that the car was actually mounted on a metal apparatus hauled by a mightily blinking truck cab. As I watched, the driver got out, carrying what appeared to be a very large wrench, and, stopping at various points on the contraption he had hauled, expertly unfolded it so that it formed a ramp from car to street. It was a fascinating sight, the car like a toy held by a giant robot hand, and I went out onto the sun porch to better see it. There is a park across from me, and from its leafy darkness I noticed several people emerge so that they, too, could see better.

I am an associate professor teaching full-time in the English Department at Syracuse University, but I don't live in Syracuse full-time. My husband and I live in Rhinebeck and I commute up on the train. Because I haven't got a car with me in Syracuse, I rent an apartment within walking distance of campus. This means I rent in a building on a block of buildings that caters primarily to students, mostly undergrads, whose parents probably pay their rent. (I say they're undergrads because when the school year started and everybody's windows were open, I found myself squeezed between Britney Spears on the left and death metal on the right; if they're not undergrads, something is very wrong.)

Because I walk a lot, I am perhaps more aware than some of my colleagues of the frequent "Crime Alert" bulletins that regularly appear via e-mail and posters—many of the muggings, snatchings, and assaults occur near my neighborhood. Most sound relatively harmless and inept; many sound very bold, occurring as they do in the middle of the day—for example, when a student was pulled off the sidewalk into an abandoned garage and raped this past July. Hearing about these attacks so regularly makes me very aware of my surroundings, which are, for some blocks, broken-down and poor—as are many of the people haunting those blocks, hitting passersby up for money, or trying to. In cold weather, they pretty much disappear, but when it's warm, they're always there. They are especially there in the park across the street from me, a park citizens avoid at night.

I've lived in large cities for most of my adult life—New York, San Francisco, and Houston—where large, sometimes volatile homeless populations are the norm, and where the comfortable and the wretched exist together, in some neighborhoods closely so. But to see the same opposites so thoroughly and baldly mixed together in a much smaller city makes me more aware of them, partially because I'm so dutifully informed of every crime that takes place anywhere near me and so am continually advised to use the university escort service whenever walking after dark. My awareness makes me feel freshly troubled by the disparity and, strangely, freshly amazed by it. I had been teaching at Syracuse for one semester when Katrina hit the Gulf Coast, and while on one hand the lack of government response was shocking to me, on the other it seemed absolutely congruent with what I saw around me every time I walked to work.

I was thinking of this when I taught Chekhov's "Gooseberries" to an undergraduate class during my second semester. I did not choose the story because I thought it was in any way topical, but the devastation wrought by Hurricane Katrina was fresh in my mind when I chose to read aloud this famous passage:

> Just look at this life: the insolence and idleness of the strong, the ignorance and brutishness of the weak, impossible poverty all around us, overcrowding, degeneracy, drunkenness, hypocrisy, lies. . . . Yet in all the houses and streets it's quiet, peaceful; of the fifty thousand living in a town, there is not one who would cry out, or become loudly indignant. We see those who go to the market to buy food, eat during the day, sleep during the night, who talk their nonsense, get married, grow old, complacently drag their dead to the cemetery; but we don't see or hear those who suffer, and the horrors of life go on somewhere behind the scenes. Everything is quiet, peaceful, and only mute statistics protest: so many gone mad, so many buckets drunk, so many children dead of malnutrition . . .

It was toward the end of class and I had to shout over the sound of a jackhammer outside—that may've been why about half the students seemed indifferent. I can imagine, too, that if they were indifferent (and sometimes it can be hard to know what students feel until they tell you), it was because the passage seemed hopelessly dated, not only in style but in content. After all, very little now seems to occur behind the scenes except for the exercise of power: Images of suffering people have become so routine (I'm thinking of Katrina again) that you can't help but see them even if you don't live in a neighborhood where you encounter them in the flesh. I think, though, that the students' very indifference, if that's what it was, indicates that Chekhov is still right, that no matter what we literally see, on television or in life, we nonetheless will ourselves not to see what we don't wish to see—or to feel. Sometimes, too, you don't know exactly what you feel.

The night that the car appeared in the air outside my apartment, I had earlier been hit up for money by a ragged middle-aged woman whom I'd seen a few days before, screaming obscenities at some students driving past in a car. I was walking home after having dinner and wine at a student joint, and I was feeling the wine as I opened my wallet. "You are so beautiful," I said a little too expansively. "I thought you were a student when I first saw you."

It was an inane comment; it was also true. Her large, wild eyes were hot blue, and her blond hair was sun-bleached and thick. Her face was regal, even with two front teeth knocked out. Inane or not, she didn't care—her eyes were glued to my wallet, which she might've snatched if it weren't for the students driving past. "Can I have another dollar?" she asked. "Not today," I said. "But next time. I know I'll see you again." She actually looked at me when I said that.

Because she looked at me I remembered her. I wondered if she knew the people who emerged from the park to watch the truck driver climb the ladder on the side of his rig and begin to unbolt the car from its fixed position. I couldn't see them clearly in the dark, and it's possible they were students—but I doubt it. The truck driver got into the car and drove it down the ramp and into the street, executing a sharp U-turn. One of the people in the park clapped; the others stared at him. The car, looking brand-new and fancy in the flashing light, pulled into my driveway. I said aloud, "You've got to be kidding me!" The driver got out with papers on a clipboard. He stood on the sidewalk for a moment, looking from house to house until a young woman of maybe nineteen came out of the building next to mine. She looked very pleased to see the car. The driver presented her with the papers on a clipboard; she signed.

"You little fucker," I said. I said it in wonder rather than anger, but I said it. I don't know exactly why. There was nothing horrible or outrageous about the sight of the car being delivered—but I found it ridiculous, irksome, and saddening at the same time. Did the girl who had just signed for the car know what a spectacle this was to the people in the park across the street? Did she even see them? Did it make any difference at all that I did?

When I read the speech from "Gooseberries" to my students, I did not finish it. I stopped before I got to the part that expresses an old idea, now very much out of fashion:

> At the door of every contented, happy man somebody should stand with a little hammer, constantly tapping, to remind him that unhappy people exist, that however happy he may be, sooner or later life will show him its claws, some calamity will befall him—illness, poverty, loss—and nobody will hear or see, just as he doesn't hear or see others now. But there is nobody with a little hammer, the happy man lives on, and the petty cares of life stir him only slightly, as wind stirs an aspen—and everything is fine.

The man who makes this speech is revealed by the end of the story to be an ineffectual, foolish, and perhaps envious person, who admits that he can do nothing about the state of the world and implores his younger friends to take action they've no interest in taking. By modern standards, the speech is too simplistic anyway. And yet, in spite of the simplicity and impotence, the reader feels the truth of what is said.

My nineteen-year-old neighbor may or may not have called herself happy; it seems that very few people call themselves happy now. Arguably, few live at such ease that "trivial daily cares faintly agitate" them. But to me, and I'm sure to the people across the street, she looked the picture of satisfaction as she got into the car and drove it into the small lot behind the building. I continued to watch, fascinated, as the trucker methodically refolded the ramp. By the time he drove away, the girl was back inside, and the people from the park were gone—or at least I couldn't see them anymore.

Stone Canoe, 2006

ENCHANTMENT AND CRUELTY

ON *PETER PAN* BY J. M. BARRIE

I recommend J. M. Barrie's *Peter Pan* to anyone who has seen only the Disney version, or no version at all. I recommend it as a book about enchantment and cruelty in very matter-of-fact language; I also recommend it as a book about mortality and gentleness in the face of mortality, the ruthlessness of youth, and the random nature of attraction. I recommend it as a book that doesn't condescend to young children, who (being human) know in their hearts every horrible thing that human beings are capable of, and every sadness that human life entails. What people who have seen only the Disney version don't know: In the real Peter Pan, murders and public hangings have the same entertainment value as chocolate pudding day, saying ninety-nine, and/or getting threepence for pulling your tooth yourself. These things aren't especially important, and they are also magic, or, rather ". . . are part of the island or they are another map showing through, and it is all rather confusing, especially as nothing will stand still."

That is the book in a few words—that nothing will stand still, not the most powerful of feelings nor the deepest of bonds. The importance of mothers and of mothering is a major theme in the book, and Mrs. Darling, the mother of the story, is a figure of longing, of romantic and familial love—but in the end, when the fates of her various children and husband are revealed in some detail, she is dismissed simply with the line "Mrs. Darling was now dead and forgotten." The love of Wendy and Peter is the ur-romantic love of preteens, but they forget each other, too, she in the service of biological function, he in the service of something more mysterious. When by some fluke he remembers her and returns to her nursery to find her a grown woman, she tries to hide her adulthood by curling herself into a little ball; "something inside her" cries "woman, woman, let go of me." But the woman cannot let go, and when she stands up to reveal her maturity, "for almost the first time in his life . . . Peter was afraid." He cries for her not to turn on the light, but after pausing to smile and play with his hair, she does turn it on: "He gave a cry of pain; and when the tall beautiful creature stooped to lift him in her arms he drew back sharply."

If you know the Disney version, you know he flies away with Wendy's daughter, Jane. But you probably didn't see Jane as an adult standing in the window, growing white-haired and stooped as Peter flies away with *her* daughter, having become as replaceable as her mother in the remorseless system that we call reality. In the playful and heartbroken version of reality called "Peter Pan," girls are as replaceable as flowers, and in general boys aren't even that interesting. But nonetheless, these little mortal creatures have adventures, fly, eat by snatching the food from the mouths of birds, build houses from leaves, bark, and roses, hire kindly dogs as nurses, and become doctors by saying that they are. They form alliances, try to kill one another, and sometimes do kill one another.

Captain Hook, by the way, doesn't get eaten by the crocodile by happenstance; he kills himself because Peter has "better form" than he does. His last act during their fight is to stick his rear out, inviting Peter to kick it, and when Peter makes that gesture, Hook cries out, "Bad form!" before jumping to his death. In other words, Hook wins by an act of aggression that is also an act of self-humiliation.

Tinker Bell, also by the way, is a busty, chubby slattern, not the elegant sylph-waisted creature of Disney. Though (speaking of Disney), it is strangely the case that Disney's *Pirates of the Caribbean* comes closest to the spirit of J. M. Barrie's *Peter Pan*—Johnny Depp's Jack Sparrow is a charming echo of Peter and Hook combined. But while the movie has much of the play and irreverent humor of the children's book, it has none of the gentleness—a quality that for all its sentimentality, popular culture seems no longer to understand.

Post Road, 2006

WORSHIPPING THE OVERCOAT

DAY ONE

When I saw Sarah Palin speak at the Republican National Convention, the hair on the back of my neck stood up. I had thought McCain's choice of running mate must mean that he was in a complete paranoid tailspin, the kind that comes before huge, humiliating defeats. But as I watched her, and the rabid, adoring response to her, I thought something else, which was: This woman is a sadist and she doesn't know it. And it's working for her; her people love her for that very reason, and they don't know it.

By "sadist" I don't mean a costume-wearing fetishist, and if I did, I wouldn't be as appalled. I mean something more basic, a person whose driving motive in life is to dominate, control, and inflict pain. Most people don't know what their driving motive is, and most people have more than one. But some people have one that is so unconflicted and so overwhelming that they fairly drip with it. What I was looking at onstage at the Republican Convention was somebody who dripped with highly charged, puerile cruelty; it was there in her sneering, aggressively charming voice, in her body, in the set of her mouth. It was there also in the roaring response to her, a response that comes from the body, while the head is thinking something else altogether, about loving America, standing up to terrorists, whatever.

When I said to people, "I think Sarah Palin is a sadist," they reacted like I was making a joke, or being provocative. I suppose that I was. But how far off was I? What do you call it when she incites crowds to threaten Obama with death by calling him a terrorist in that dripping, girlish voice? These are people who are looking to hurt someone, and their urge has just been legitimized, even idealized for them by an attractive woman whom some young men I know consider "hot."

DAY TWO

This election makes me remember Vladimir Nabokov's essay on Nikolai Gogol's "The Overcoat," in which he describes the short story as "a grotesque and grim nightmare making black holes in the dim pattern of life"; it is a beautiful, flexible, and fantastically broad phrase. "The Overcoat" is about a poor, half-crazy little clerk in pre-Revolutionary Russia who, when his thin coat rots off his back one freezing winter, spends his entire savings on having a new coat made for him. The new coat is magnificent, and it transforms his life. For the first time he is invited to a party, where he drinks too much; on the way home he is robbed of his coat; the robbery breaks his heart; he sickens and dies. The story is typically read as an allegory of "the little guy" in a socially unjust world, but Nabokov sees something more terrible, a story of "whirling masks," through which the tortured human protagonist must wander in desperate confusion, and in which the true plot, as opposed to the literal one, comes from "that secret depth of the human soul where the shadows of other worlds pass like the shadows of nameless and soundless ships."

How garish are these masks that talk to us nonstop every day, how huge they loom out of television and cyberspace! What

secret depths do they come from, what primitive forces are finding expression through them? What the fuck are they doing here?
John McCain, having unleashed insane Pandora, is now trying
to stuff her back in the box, probably because human beings are
horrified at seeing people at his rallies turn into prelynch mobs.
But when one of his supporters denounces Obama as "an Arab,"
and McCain responds like a person ("He's a decent family man"),
he's booed by his own. While one of his masks makes nice,
the others keep putting out the misinformation. Through it all
wanders the human voter—who, if he's Republican, bought the
overcoat years ago and, though it's been stolen from him, still
worships it on his knees.

DAY THREE

The most visible story of John McCain has been his "honor" and
how important it is to him, how key to the understanding of his
mind. The less visible story is his violent temper: how he yells
at people for nothing, nearly attacks people who frustrate him,
how he once called his wife a "cunt" in front of reporters. Now
the anger has come out in a hugely visible form, projected like a
demon into the screaming herds that accuse Obama of terrorism
as they run bellowing off a cliff.

A melancholy thought: McCain may once have had honor,
or at least a concept of it. If he still has enough decency to be
ashamed of losing it, he needs anger to hide his shame; without
his anger he would not be able to bear his shame.

DAY FOUR

When Hillary Clinton and Barack Obama were still fighting for
the nomination, I had a conversation with a woman who said she
supported Hillary because "any female" would be preferable to

"any male," and that she thought Obama was no different from anyone else in the male system. When Sarah Palin got nominated, I asked this woman if she supported her. "Of course not," she said. "Sarah Palin is not a woman, I don't care how many times she's given birth. She's totally bought into the male power system."

I thought, How ridiculous. Then my husband reminded me of Fritz Lang's *Metropolis* and the false Maria. In the movie, the real Maria is a working-class girl trying to help her fellows by pure-hearted means. The rulers then build a false Maria to sow division and hatred. It doesn't quite work as a comparison; Palin is more a combination of what the real Maria claims to be (evangelical) and what the false one is, proud and violent. But the film's logic is visual, and visually, it pictures America now as it once pictured Weimar Germany. The false Maria's dance is one of gluttony and power, and it has a demonic force that awakens ancient archetypes of chaos and destruction. And the damn thing even winks.

DAY FIVE

When Hillary was still running, I didn't support her because I preferred Obama, and because I didn't think she could win. Somebody asked me if I thought she couldn't win because she's a woman, and I said, "Not because she's a woman, but because she's not enough of a cunt." I meant that she didn't have a raw female presence equal to that of her husband, Bill. I went on to say that as a liberal (sort of) woman, I didn't think she'd dare go there, that the only woman who could do that would be a conservative. I was right, and I have never been more sorry. Sarah Palin has the kind of glandular force I was referring to, something that has nothing to do with her prettiness, but augments it immeasurably. Hillary Clinton was taunted for being strong—

privately, even liberals made her out as a castrator, which was brutally unfair: Like many professional women, Hillary never cut off anyone's nuts but her own. No one's taunting Sarah Palin like that, and no wonder: Hillary is accomplished verbally; her power comes from the part of the body with teeth. Palin can't talk her way out of a bag; she doesn't need to. That's not the source of her power.

DAY SIX

The language aspect of the Obama / McCain debate was the usual rote push-pull. When I turned down the sound, the picture was clearer and more alarming. McCain was malign, contemptuous, and very physical. Obama was weak, vague, and heady. McCain looked like a big, vicious dog, Obama like a smaller dog trying to avoid a fight by looking away and licking his lips a lot. It was very dispiriting to see.

DAY SEVEN

My sister has an eerie ability to look at people and read them very quickly in terms of their character; I have rarely known her to be wrong. She was the first person to tell me, years before the election, that Obama was great, that he needed to run for president. "He has white light glowing around his head," she said.

The second person to say anything to me about Obama was a writer friend. She said she liked him a lot but that she worried about him as a leader because she couldn't "feel his dick." She wasn't talking about sex. She meant that he didn't fully, on a bodily level, believe in himself, that his actions came totally from his head. I agree with her. That is what makes him look fragile sometimes, especially in contrast with John McCain, whose dick, like it or not, one *can* feel. McCain's confidence is ghastly, because it is so caught up in his violent righteousness—but it is there.

In a strange way, these two qualities, the powerful, glowing mind and the lack of full bodily presence, are part of what makes Obama a compelling and emotional figure. Whatever he has accomplished, it has been through the power of his mind, that almost otherworldly glow that has carried him through so many obstacles, especially vicious race prejudice. So many of us know what it is to lack confidence, yet to will yourself to go on, even though you don't quite feel the ground under your feet. People are calling McCain the "underdog" now, but this is bullshit. Obama, who's barely ahead in the polls, was always the underdog here—black people were scared to vote for him at first because they thought he'd be killed. And they had reason to fear. He has incredible courage to be where he is, up against that old bastard, especially if he got there without full confidence. My sister believes he can win. I hope she is right.

Libération, 2008

THIS DOUGHTY NOSE

ON NORMAN MAILER'S *AN AMERICAN DREAM*
AND *THE ARMIES OF THE NIGHT*

America needed the war. It would need a war so
long as technology expanded on every road of
communication, and the cities and corporations
spread like cancer; the good Christian Americans
needed the war or they would lose their Christ.

—*The Armies of the Night,* 1968

PRIVATE: *Gaitskill first encountered Mailer at the age of fifteen, when
she read Kate Millet's feminist polemic* Sexual Politics. *In a special
sexism-in-literature section, Millet quoted at length from Mailer's novel*
An American Dream, *a vivid comic-book story of society, magic,
music, murder, love, and sodomy, which in Millet's censorious context
seemed even more thrillingly dirty than it actually is. At fifteen, Gaitskill
had a complex streak of practicality that was both cheerful and dour,
and which allowed her to retreat into her private cave to thoroughly enjoy
Mailer's fantasy as presented by Millet, only to momentarily emerge full
of righteous outrage at it; she saw nothing questionable about this.*

When she heard that Mailer would be appearing on The Dick
Cavett Show *to discuss feminism with Gore Vidal, she watched, antic-
ipating a full complement of outrage and enjoyment. To her surprise,
she was surprised: Watching Gore Vidal was like watching a snake in*

a suit, all piety and fine manners, standing up on its hind tail to recite against the evils of sexism. Before this fancy creature, Mailer was nearly helpless, lunging and swiping like a bear trying to fight a snake on the snake's terms. At one point he spluttered, "You know very well I'm the gentlest person here," which made the audience laugh, while Cavett and guests made ironic faces—but (horribly enough) Gaitskill sensed that this was quite possibly true, even if Mailer did head-butt Vidal in the dressing room, even if, yes, he did foully stab his wife at a drunken party. For a gentle person who has been stung by clever, socially armored people adept at emotional cruelty may respond with oafish brutality; it is pre-cisely because he is gentle that he can't modulate his rage or disguise it the way a naturally cruel person can. Gaitskill watched the bearbaiting spectacle with a not unpainful sense of cognitive dissonance dawning in her, both sides of her peculiarly American schizophrenic self finally present and blinking confusedly. The only other person who had aroused such feelings in her before was Lyndon Johnson, whose ugly, profound, helplessly emotional face had made her feel like crying for reasons she could not understand.

PUBLIC: In 1967, Norman Mailer took part in a march on the Pentagon to protest the war in Vietnam. He marched along with writers Robert Lowell, Dwight Macdonald, and others whom he half-humorously called "notables"; he got arrested on purpose; he wrote a book called *The Armies of the Night,* which won both the Pulitzer Prize and the National Book Award.

The Armies of the Night is part memoir, part history, and as its protagonist, Mailer is like a tourist with a rude sense of humor, taking snapshot after snapshot of his grinning, waving, royally urinating self before every possible monument. Royally and literally: Close to the beginning of *Armies,* Mailer recounts the drunken, grandstanding speech he gave the night before the march, in which he tried to win back the audience (which, to his angry sorrow, had liked Lowell more than they had liked him) by telling them a story about trying to relieve himself in a darkened lavatory before the speech, where he missed the pot and pissed on the floor. Somehow it is key, this ridiculous speech, which, we understand, was buffoonish, inept, embarrassing—and yet which, in Mailer's mind anyway, was lovable precisely for those characteristics. Every turn of the speech, every nuance of its mood is lovingly recorded with sensitivity, intelligence, and wit. Even if you are a woman and so not apt to piss on the floor, it makes you warmly recall the times when, stuck in a dark, crowded lavatory, you considered relieving yourself in the sink for lack of an available pot. In its evocation of ego comedy and the commonality of bodily needs, the speech is a somehow poetic introduction to a historical moment of desperate, absurd, and whimsical heroism, an attempt by spoiled, life-ignorant, self-infatuated children in romantic revolutionary costume to end a war waged by experienced men of the world—men, as a matter of fact, of Mailer's generation.

Mailer wrote *The Armies of the Night* in the third-person style that became his trademark, a droll comment on his public persona, which had become so big that, like Gogol's Nose, it sometimes ran around town in fancy clothes, pissing on the floor, picking fights, and seducing ladies almost in spite of its (in this case) indulgent owner. "I'm as full of shit as Lyndon Johnson," cried the novelist, trying to work the crowd that night. "Why, man, I'm nothing but his little old alter ego. That's what you got right here working for you, Lyndon Johnson's little old *dwarf* alter ego." *Yes*. ". . . in the privacy of his brain, quiet in the glare of all that sound and spotlight, Mailer thought quietly, 'My God, that is probably exactly what you are at this moment, Lyndon Johnson with all his sores, sorrows and vanity, squeezed down to five foot eight." *Hell yes!* "This yere dwarf alter ego has been telling you about his imbroglio with the p*ssarooney up on the top floor, and will all the reporters please note that I did not talk of defecation commonly known as sheeee-it! . . . but to the contrary, speak of you-rye-nation! I p*ssed on the floor. Hoo-ee! Hoo-ee!"

DREAM: *Gaitskill was twenty-five when she read* An American Dream, *and by that time she was ready for it; that is, she was in a state of receptivity both dreamy and bruised, a receptivity that understood that life had a top layer with several layers under it, and that sometimes, one bled through the other in strange ways.* An American Dream *is not a diatribe against women or anything that logical; it is not even a realistic novel, but a fluid rendering of archetypal forces, personalized and then stuffed into the social costumes of the time. Kate Millet had, it seemed, crudely, blindly misread the book as a literal rendering, almost seeming to confuse a sexualized fantasy of murder with the real deal. Yet, Gaitskill could see how Millet had become confused. She really could.*

The novel's protagonist, a cock in a person suit named Rojack (or "Raw Jock"), is a war hero, author, and TV personality, an ex-congressman who meets his wealthy Great Bitch wife ("making love she left you with no uncertain memory of having passed through a carnal transaction with a caged animal") on a double date with "Jack" Kennedy. They are separated and he hates her guts, but still he goes to see her from time to time, and on one of these times she taunts him by reminding him that she does rim jobs for other men. He slaps her; she charges him ("like a bull"); he strangles her and tosses her bitch ass out the window. Feeling great, feeling sexy, Rojack finds and screws his wife's maid, going back and forth between Love's mansion and the place of excrement. ("I do not know why you have trouble with your wife. You are absolutely a genius, Mr. Rojack.") Thus refreshed, he goes outside, where he meets a nightclub singer (named Cherry) at the traffic pileup caused by his wife's corpse going splat; Cherry can tell at a glance that he killed his wife, and maybe that's why it's love at first sight.

Yes, the book is driven by outsized fear of and rage at women—for Christ's sake, after the damn wife is dead and lying in her own shit,

Rojack is still pissed off at her for being violent and wishes she would come back to life so that he can smash her nose, kick her ribs in, "kill her again, kill her good this time, kill her right." But even more, the book is driven by a desire to ecstatically swim in the lava of essential forces flowing beneath human life, the raw unknowns of sex and death that animate the endless social masks which charm, blur, and bedevil our existence; it wants to catch the winking demon peeping out from between the masks and personalities as they cascade through each and every strange and singular human form. Its attempts to do this— especially the successful ones—are joyous, alive, and filled with charged motion even in the stasis of cliché. The different faces he gives to the German maid ("that mobile, mocking, know-the-cost-of-every-bargain Berlin face, was loose and independent of her now, swimming through expressions, a greedy mate with the taste of power in her eyes and her mouth") and Cherry ("a clean tough decent little American boy in her look: that gave charm to her upturned nose tip-tilted . . . at the racy angle of a speedboat skipping a wave, yes that nose gave character to the little muscle in her jaw and the touch of stubbornness in her mouth") are the visions of a faceted eye that enjoys illusions but seeks to pen- etrate the core beneath them.

REALITY: The lava of sex and violence does not run through *The Armies of the Night*, at least not so opulently. This book is about actual people and events that don't lend themselves so easily to archetypal conversion; the shrewd, rational facet of the novelist's mind was thus called upon, and that must have been a grounding factor. In *The Armies of the Night*, Mailer turns his piercing eye on the antiwar movement, especially Dave Dellinger's tortured strategic unification of middle-class pacifists, old-school Com- munists, New Left college kids, and hippies chanting to levitate the Pentagon, and/or blow smoke up the country's rear. He ana- lyzes the uniquely American wisdom of obscenity and humor, the rhetoric of hawks and doves ("He knew the arguments for the war, and against the war—finally they bored him") and flexes his prescient intuition in real-world terms: "There was nothing to fear—perhaps there never had been. For the more Communism expanded, the more monumental would become its problems, the more flaccid its preoccupations with world conquest. In the expansion of Communism, was its own containment. The only force which could ever defeat Communism, was Communism itself."

The novelist's eye is also richly turned on people, and the book fairly pops with characters: lawyers in Mad Hatter dialogue with a Jehovahic commissioner; cops trembling with suppressed emotion; National Guardsmen who are scared to use their clubs but break girls' bones with them; jailers harried by working overtime and college boy prisoners giggling as they taunt them; signifying Yippie monkeys; pure good boys (especially one with the "small bright snubbed features of a cat" who made "the most spectacular arrest . . . breaking through the line of MPs . . . outrunning them, crossing the field on them, doubling back, stopping short, sprinting, loping, teasing them"); a Nazi counterdemonstrator and a marshal with leather testicles in psychic communion: (Nazi) "Join me where the real war is. Already the strongest and wildest men in America wear our symbol on their motorcycle helmets." (Marshal) "Next to strong wild men, you're nothing but a bitch." All of these are full characters, but they are also homunculi, big, small, dignified, ridiculous, jabbering, contemplative, fine or coarse textured bits of a whole called America, the book's greatest character, a character rendered half in the rational words of public discourse and half in the language of images and dreams: "The love of the Mystery of Christ, however, and the love of no Mystery whatsoever, had brought the country to a state of suppressed schizophrenia so deep that the foul brutalities of the war in Vietnam were the only temporary cure possible for the condition—since the expression of brutality offers a definite if temporary relief to the schizophrenic. So the average good Christian American secretly loved the war in Vietnam. It opened his emotions. He felt compassion for the hardships and the sufferings of American boys in Vietnam, even the Vietnamese orphans."

And then there is that fuggin Nose, scheming to get arrested and get out in time to make the red-eye back to New York for a glam party with wicked chicks, worrying about the state of his suit, or what the press will say about him, or ruminating obsessively on his first drink of water in prison: "he took a drink of water. It was characteristic of him to make such a move, and he hardly knew if he did it for the best or worst of reasons, did it because in recognizing the value of thirst he had a small panic to destroy the temptation to search such a moral adventure further, or did he do it precisely because he was now aware of the value of thirst, and so thirst by such consciousness had lost its value since the ability to suffer drought was, by this logic, valuable only if water were not available. Or did he take a drink because he wished to study his new state after satisfying thirst? He noticed only that he was a trifle sad on the first sip, and couldn't stop going to the sink for more and more water afterward, which declared the result of the experiment: between the saint and the debauchee, no middle ground seemed tenable for his appetites."

How bittersweet to read them now, the ramblings of this doughty Nose. They are precious, annoying, and narcissistic, and yet as such, they are artifacts from narcissism's golden age, when the revelation of the self, the man behind the curtain of Art, was a refreshing surprise rather than an especially dull convention. Compared to today's relentlessly small-focus self-blathering (*of which Gaitskill may herself on occasion be not unguilty!*), Mailer's self-reporting flexibly (a little *too* flexibly in the case of that interminable drink of water) changes the lens of his vision from large to small in a way that mimics individual perception as it moves from moment to moment, and defuses some of his natural pomposity. It is also (intentionally or not) comically honest about its low motives, its need to dominate and to be loved—especially to be loved by those whom he dominates—for example, the audience of demonstrators whom he called "one big collective dead ass," jeered at for not being black, and generally harangued with drunken nonsense in order to make them—force them—to like him as much as they liked Lowell.

MASTURBATION: *It was not the first time Gaitskill had noticed it, this sore, conspicuous need. In* An American Dream, *the evil wife is evil mostly because she does not love the hero, and he is justified in killing her for it; her own daughter from a previous marriage is good in part because she hates her mother for failing to be a good wife to Rojack, and Cherry is an angel for knowing he killed his wife and loving him anyway. When Cherry's previous lover—a black jazz singer insanely named Shago—unexpectedly comes to visit, Rojack must prove himself by beating the man until he vomits blood—after which beating, Shago gives it up, the validating approval only a black man can give: "Tell Cherry, her and you, I wish you luck . . . I swear. Yes, I swear. Luck, man." To which Rojack (the gentlest man there!) replies, "Thank you, Shago."*

Gaitskill must pause here to recall a conversation she once had with a middle-aged female writer, a paragon of dumpy feminism whom Mailer might've been expected to despise, who claimed, with not uncertain contempt, that Mailer had once not unplaintively asked her, "Why don't you like me?" How embarrassing, this need to be liked in a man so free with his fists! How nakedly it appears in An American Dream! *And yet, Gaitskill sensed something more serious embedded in Mailer's maudlin quest and question. If* An American Dream *expresses a wish to be loved by those one beats and kills, it more deeply expresses a desire for union between forces that, in life on earth, must pit themselves against each other, sometimes to the death.*

———

INTERCOURSE: This impulse toward union is more fully developed in *The Armies of the Night* as a wish not only to be liked but to like; the book is full of emotional turnarounds in which Mailer will start out dismissing someone, or even loathing him, and then will notice something about him that completely changes his mind: He is able to tell the story of the Nazi kook and the marshal who subdues him because even though they both appear to loathe Mailer, Mailer is able to align himself with them through a convincing preternatural empathy. He considers arguing with a Marxist pedant who is driving him crazy with his incessant lectures, and then decides not to on the grounds that if he won, he would merely "depress the one source of energy in the room."

Mailer's vision of the event is itself a unifying one; as a war veteran, and a hero to a generation that, at least in 1968, largely supported the war in Vietnam, he is someone you might expect to empathize with the marshals and jailers—and he does. You feel his compassion as he imagines how the jailers "were here to work out the long slow stages of a grim tableau—the recapitulation of that poverty-ridden rural childhood which had left them with the usual constipated mixture of stinginess and greed, blocked compassion and frustrated desires for power," and how the insouciant protestors had not only "left such careful slow and overcautious work of reconstruction in a shamble" but were completely unaware that they had done so. And yet he is also able to connect (though not effortlessly; one feels the effort) with the "tender drug-vitiated jargon-mired children" who mounted the offensive on the Pentagon, and finally to respect their rite of passage.

Mailer is able to work this way partly because the same quality that sometimes made *An American Dream* unintentionally funny appears as a strength in *The Armies of the Night*. The problem with *An American Dream* is not primarily Mailer's attitude toward women; it is that it insists on taking its big, forceful metaphors and making them literal and physical. It is one thing to create a woman who is emotionally dangerous and verbally cruel, who thus appears intimidating to her husband. However, these emotional qualities are treated as if they are physical threats, and under these circumstances, the beleaguered hero *must* kill this woman who is magically made so powerful by malice that he is afraid that, while she is being strangled, she is, from a kneeling position, going to rise up and lift his entire body off the floor. In a novel, this is not a ruinous problem—after all, one of the book's subthemes is magic, and anyway a novel is bound only to obey its own rules. But Mailer stubbornly literalizes his metaphors in essays and interviews, too; he says he does not address female writers in *Cannibals and Christians* because a writer can only be judged by whether or not he is able to make the Great Bitch of literature cum like a house on fire—and a woman, of course, isn't going to be sleeping with another woman!!! He is also well known for insisting at length in an interview with Paul Krassner that masturbation is equal to suicide, though millions masturbate and live.

(Gaitskill cannot help but note here that it is odd for Mailer to react so strenuously to masturbation. For onanism bears the same relationship to intercourse that dreams bear to reality; in each case, the two activities are not comparable and do not compete with each other. If Mailer the artist seems to confuse the private dream world with prosaic reality, it may be because the dream world, with its layering of symbol, archetype, and metaphor, its fluid boundaries between life and death, is where his genius shines most luminously. He sounds like a kook only when he tries to make his poetic, prophetic dreams literal.)

But in *The Armies of the Night*, despite the best efforts of his Nose, he does not overall sound like a kook. This is in part because he seems, in all sanity, to have embraced his kook status, and repeatedly, shamelessly refers to himself as a fool. This is also because 1968 was a historic moment for kooks. It was a moment when a door opened between the worlds of dream and reality, literal and metaphor, and in the strange light that came through that door, the most sober, serious, world-wise, experienced men in power were revealed as kooks—morally wrong kooks. The forces of the preposterous, the romantically costumed, the poetic, and the mad were for once right, magnificently right, about the ultimately real question of whether or not a war should be fought. And in that moment, Norman Mailer was the ideal witness, journalist, and poet to record their victory in a truer-than-life dream world only he could create.

A New Literary History of America,
EDITED BY GREIL MARCUS AND WERNER SOLLORS, 2009

LOST CAT

A MEMOIR

Last year I lost my cat Gattino. He was very young, at seven months barely an adolescent. He is probably dead, but I don't know for certain. For two weeks after he disappeared, people claimed to have seen him; I trusted two of the claims because Gattino was blind in one eye, and both people told me that when they'd caught him in their headlights, only one eye shone back. One guy, who said he saw my cat trying to scavenge from a garbage can, said that he'd "looked really thin, like the runt of the litter." The pathetic words struck my heart. But I heard something besides the words, something in the coarse, vibrant tone of the man's voice that immediately made another emotional picture of the cat: back arched, face afraid but excited, brimming and ready before he jumped and ran, tail defiant, tensile, and crooked. Afraid but ready; startled by a large male, that's how he would've been. Even if he was weak with hunger. He had guts, this cat.

Gattino disappeared two and a half months after we moved. Our new house is on the outskirts of a college campus near a wildlife preserve. There are wooded areas in all directions, and many homes with decrepit outbuildings sit heavily, darkly low behind trees, in thick foliage. I spent hours at a time wandering around calling Gattino. I put food out. I put a trap out. I put hundreds of flyers up. I walked around knocking on doors, asking people if I could look in their shed or under their porch. I contacted all the vets in the area. Every few days, someone would call and say he had seen a cat in a parking lot or behind his dorm. I would go and sometimes glimpse a grizzled adult melting away into the woods, or behind a building or under a parked car.

After two weeks, there were no more sightings. I caught three feral cats in my trap and let them go. It began to snow. Still searching, I would sometimes see little cat tracks in the snow; near Dumpsters full of garbage, I also saw prints made by bobcats or coyotes. When the temperature went below freezing, there was icy rain. I kept looking. A year later, I still had not stopped.

Six months after Gattino disappeared, my husband and I were sitting in a restaurant, having dinner with some people he had recently met, including an intellectual writer we both admired. The writer had considered buying the house we were living in and he wanted to know how we liked it. I said it was nice but that it had been partly spoiled for me by the loss of our cat. I told him the story and he said, "Oh, that was your trauma, was it?"

I said yes. Yes, it was a trauma.

You could say he was unkind. You could say I was silly. You could say he was priggish. You could say I was weak.

A few weeks earlier, I had an e-mail exchange with my sister Martha on the subject of trauma—or rather, tragedy. Our other sister, Jane, had just decided not to euthanize her dying cat because she thought her little girls could not bear it; she didn't think she could bear it. Jane lives in chronic pain so great that sometimes she cannot move normally. She is under great financial stress and is often responsible for the care of her mother-in-law as well as the orphaned children of her sister-in-law, who died of cancer.

But it was her cat's approaching death that made her cry so that her children were frightened. "This is awful," said Martha. "It is not helping that cat to keep him alive; it's just prolonging his suffering. It's selfish."

Martha is in a lot of pain, too, most of it related to diabetes and fibromyalgia. Her feet hurt so badly, she can't walk longer than five minutes. She just lost her job and is applying for disability, which, because it has become almost impossible to get, she may not get, and which, if she does get, will not be enough to live on, and we will have to help her. We already have to help her because her COBRA payments are so high that her unemployment isn't enough to cover them. This is painful for her, too; she doesn't want to be the one everybody has to help. And so she tries to help us. She has had cats for years, and so knows a lot about them; she wanted to help Jane by giving her advice, and she sent me several e-mails, wondering about the best way to do it. Finally she forwarded me the message she had sent to Jane, in which she urged her to put the cat down. When she didn't hear from Jane, she e-mailed me some more, agonizing over whether or not Jane was angry at her, and wondering what decision Jane would make regarding the cat. She said, "I'm afraid this is going to turn into an avoidable tragedy."

Impatient by then, I told her that she should trust Jane to make the right decision. I said, "This is sad, not tragic. Tragedy is thousands of people dying slowly of war and disease, injury and malnutrition. It's Hurricane Katrina; it's the war in Iraq; it's the earthquake in China. It's not one creature dying of old age."

After I sent the e-mail, I looked up the word *tragic*. According to *Webster's College Dictionary*, I was wrong; their second definition of the word is "extremely mournful, melancholy or pathetic." I e-mailed Martha and admitted I'd been wrong, at least technically. I added that I still thought she was being hysterical. She didn't answer me. Maybe she was right not to.

I had found Gattino in Italy. I was in Tuscany, at a place called Santa Maddalena, run by a woman named Beatrice von Rezzori, who, in honor of her deceased husband, a writer, has made her estate into a small retreat for writers. When Beatrice learned that I love cats, she told me that down the road from her, two old women were feeding a yard full of semiwild cats, including a litter of kittens who were very sick and going blind. Maybe, she said, I could help them out. No, I said, I wasn't in Italy to do that, and anyway, having done it before, I know it isn't an easy thing to trap and tame a feral kitten.

The next week, one of her assistants, who was driving me into the village, asked if I wanted to see some kittens. Sure, I said, not making the connection. We stopped by an old farmhouse. A gnarled woman sitting in a wheelchair covered with towels and a thin blanket greeted the assistant without looking at me. Scrawny cats with long legs and narrow ferret hips stalked or lay about in the buggy, overgrown yard. Two kittens, their eyes gummed up with yellow fluid and flies swarming around their asses, were obviously sick but still lively—when I bent to touch them, they ran away. But a third kitten, smaller and bonier than the other two, tottered up to me, mewing weakly, his eyes almost glued shut. He was a tabby, soft gray with strong black stripes. He had a long jaw and a big nose shaped like an eraser you'd stick on the end of a pencil. His big-nosed head was goblinish on his emaciated potbellied body, his long legs almost grotesque. His asshole seemed disproportionately big on his starved rear. Dazedly, he let me stroke his bony back; tentatively, he lifted his pitiful tail. I asked the assistant if she would help me take the kittens to a veterinarian, and she agreed; this had no doubt been the idea all along.

The healthier kittens scampered away as we approached and

hid in a collapsing barn; we were able to collect only the tabby. When we put him in the carrier, he forced open his eyes with a mighty effort, took a good look at us, hissed, tried to arch his back, and fell over. But he let the vets handle him. When they tipped him forward and lifted his tail to check his sex, he had a delicate, nearly human look of puzzled dignity in his one half-good eye, while his blunt muzzle expressed stoic animality. It was a comical and touching face.

They kept him for three days. When I went to pick him up, they told me he would need weeks of care, involving eye ointment, ear drops, and nose drops. Beatrice suggested I take him home to America. No, I said, not possible. My husband was coming to meet me in a month and we were going to travel for two weeks; we couldn't take him with us. I would care for him, and by the time I left, he should be well enough to go back to the yard with a fighting chance.

So I called him Chance. I liked Chance, as I like all kittens; he liked me as a food dispenser. He looked at me neutrally, as if I were one more creature in the world, albeit a useful one. I had to worm him, deflea him, and wash encrusted shit off his tail. He squirmed when I put the medicine in his eyes and ears, but he never tried to scratch me—I think because he wasn't certain of how I might react if he did. He tolerated my petting him but seemed to find it a novel sensation rather than a pleasure.

Then one day he looked at me differently. I don't know exactly when it happened—I may not have noticed the first time. But he began to raise his head when I came into the room, to look at me intently. I can't say for certain what the look meant; I don't know how animals think or feel. But it seemed that he was looking at me with love. He followed me around my apartment. He sat in my lap when I worked at my desk. He came into my bed and slept with me; he lulled himself to sleep by gnawing softly on my fingers. When I petted him, his body would rise into my hand. If my face was close to him, he would reach out with his paw and stroke my cheek.

Sometimes, I would walk on the dusty roads surrounding Santa Maddalena and think about my father, talking to him in my mind. My father had landed in Italy during World War II; he was part of the Anzio invasion. After the war, he returned as a visitor with my mother, going to Naples and Rome. There is a picture of him standing against an ancient wall, wearing a suit and a beret; he looks elegant, formidable, and at the same time tentative, nearly shy. On my walks I carried a large, beautiful marble that had belonged to my father; sometimes I took it out of my pocket and held it up in the sun, as if it might function as a conduit for his soul.

My father died a slow, painful death of cancer, refusing treatment of any kind for as long as he was able to make himself understood, gasping, "No doctors, no doctors." My mother had left him years before; my sisters and I tended to him, but inadequately, and too late—he had been sick for months, unable to eat for at least weeks before we became aware of his condition. During those weeks, I thought of calling him; if I had, I would've known immediately that he was dying. But I didn't call. He was difficult, and none of us called him often.

My husband did not like the name Chance, and I wasn't sure I did, either; he suggested McFate, and so I tried it out. McFate grew stronger, grew into a certain one-eyed rakishness, an engaged forward quality to his ears and the attitude of his neck that was gallant in his fragile body. He put on weight, and his long legs and tail became soigné, not grotesque. He had strong necklace markings on his throat; when he rolled on his back for me to pet him, his belly was beige and spotted like an ocelot's. In a confident mood, he was like a little gangster in a zoot suit. Pensive, he was still delicate; his heart seemed closer to the surface than normal, and when I held him against me, it beat very fast and lightly. McFate was too big and heartless a name for such a small fleet-hearted creature. *"Mio Gattino,"* I whispered, in a language I don't speak to a creature who didn't understand words. *"Mio dolce piccolo gatto."*

One night when he was lying on his back in my lap, purring, I saw something flash across the floor; it was a small sky blue marble rolling out from under the dresser and across the floor. It stopped in the middle of the floor. It was beautiful, bright, and something not visible to me had set it in motion. It seemed a magical and forgiving omen, like the presence of this loving little cat. I put it on the windowsill, next to my father's marble.

I spoke to my husband about taking Gattino home with us. I said I had fallen in love with the cat, and that I was afraid that by exposing him to human love I had awakened in him a need that was unnatural, that if I left him, he would suffer from the lack of human attention that he never would have known had I not appeared in his yard. My husband said, "Oh no, Mary . . ." but in a bemused tone.

I would understand if he'd said it in a harsher tone. Many people would consider my feelings neurotic, a projection onto an animal of my own need. Many people would consider it almost offensive for me to lavish such love on an animal when I have by some standards failed to love my fellow beings—for example, orphaned children who suffer every day, not one of whom I have adopted. But I have loved people; I have loved children. And it seems that what happened between me and the children I chose to love was a version of what I was afraid would happen to the kitten. Human love is grossly flawed, and even when it isn't, people routinely misunderstand it, reject it, use it, or manipulate it. It is hard to protect a person you love from pain, because people often choose pain; *I* am a person who often chooses pain. An animal will never choose pain; an animal can receive love far more easily than even a very young human. And so I thought it should be possible to shelter a kitten with love.

I made arrangements with the vet to get me a cat passport; Gattino endured the injection of an identifying microchip into his slim shoulder. Beatrice said she could not keep him in her house, and so I made arrangements for the vet to board him for the two weeks Peter and I traveled.

Peter arrived; Gattino looked at him and hid under the dresser. Peter crouched down and talked to him softly. Then he and I lay on the bed and held each other. In a flash, Gattino grasped the situation: The male had come. He was friendly. We could all be together now. He came onto the bed, sat on Peter's chest, and purred thunderously. He stayed on Peter's chest all night.

We took him to the veterinarian the next day. The kennel there was not the quiet, cat-only quarters one finds at upscale American animal hospitals. It was a common area that smelled of disinfectant and fear. The vet put Gattino in a cage near that of a huge enraged dog that barked and growled, lunging against the door of its kennel. Gattino looked at me and began to cry. I cried, too. The dog raged. There was a little bed in Gattino's cage, and he hid behind it, then defiantly lifted his head to face the gigantic growling; that is when I first saw that terrified but ready expression, that willingness to meet whatever was coming, regardless of its size or its ferocity.

When we left the vet, I was crying absurdly hard. But I was not crying exclusively about the kitten, any more than my sister Jane was crying exclusively about euthanizing her old cat. At the time I didn't realize it, but I was, among other things, crying about the children I once thought of as mine.

Caesar and his sister Natalia are now twelve and sixteen, respectively. When we met them, they were six and ten. We met him first. We met him through the Fresh Air Fund, an organization that sends poor urban children (nearly all of whom are black or Hispanic) up by bus to stay with country families (nearly all of whom are white). The Fresh Air Fund is an organization with an aura of uplift and hope about it, but its project is a difficult one that, frankly, reeks of pain. In addition to Caesar, we also hosted another little boy, a seven-year-old named Ezekial. Imagine that you are six or seven years old and that you are taken to a huge city bus terminal, herded onto buses with dozens of other kids, all of you with big name tags hanging around your necks, driven for three hours to a completely foreign place, and presented to total strangers with whom you are going to live for two weeks. Add that these total strangers, even if they are not rich, have materially more than you, that they are much bigger than you, and, since you are staying in their house, you are supposed to obey them. Add that they are white as sheets. Realize that even very young children "of color" have often learned that white people are essentially the enemy. Wonder: Who in God's name thought this was a good idea?

We were aware of the race-class thing. But we thought we could override it. I fantasized about serving them meals, reading to them at night, tucking them in. Peter fantasized about sports on the lawn, riding bikes together. You could say we were idealistic. You could say we were stupid. I don't know what we were.

We were actually supposed to have only one, and that one was Ezekial. We got Caesar because the FAF called from the bus as it was on its way up, full of kids, and told us that his host family had pulled out at the last minute due to a death in the family, so could we take him? We said yes because we were worried about how we were going to entertain a single child with no available playmates; I made the FAF representative promise that if it didn't work out, she would find a backup plan. Of course it didn't work out. Of course there was no backup plan. The kids hated each other, or, more precisely, Ezekial hated Caesar. Caesar was younger and more vulnerable in every way: less confident, less verbal, possessed of no athletic skills. Ezekial was lithe, with muscular limbs and an ungiving facial symmetry that sometimes made his naturally expressive face cold and masklike. Caesar was big and plump, with deep eyes and soft features that were so generous, they seemed nearly smudged at the edges. Ezekial was a clever bully, merciless in his teasing, and Caesar could only respond by ineptly blustering, "Ima fuck you up!"

"Look," I said, "you guys don't have to like each other, but you have to get along. Deep down, don't you want to get along?"

"No!" they screamed.

"He's ugly!" added Ezekial.

"Oh dry up, Ezekial," I said; "we're all ugly, okay?"

"Yeah," said Caesar, liking this idea very much, "we're all ugly!"

"No," said Ezekial, his voice dripping with malice, "*you're* ugly."

"Try again," I said. "Can you get along?"

"Okay," said Caesar. "I'll get along with you, Ezekial." And you could hear his gentle, generous nature in his voice. You could hear it, actually, even when he said, "Ima fuck you up!" Gentleness sometimes expresses itself with the violence of pain or fear and so looks like aggression. Sometimes cruelty has a very charming smile.

"No," said Ezekial, smiling. "I hate you." Caesar dropped his eyes.

We were in Florence for a week. It was beautiful but crowded and hot, and I was too full of sadness and confusion to enjoy myself. Nearly every day I pestered the vet, calling to see how Gattino was. "He's fine," I was told. "The dog isn't there anymore. Your cat is playing." I wasn't assuaged. I had nightmares; I had a nightmare that I had put my kitten into a burning oven and then watched him hopelessly try to protect himself by curling into a ball; I cried to see it, but I could not undo my action.

Peter preferred the clever, athletic Ezekial, and Caesar knew it. I much preferred Caesar, but we had made our original commitment to Ezekial and to his mother, whom we had spoken with on the phone. So I called the FAF representative and asked her if she could find another host family for Caesar. "Oh great," she snapped. But she did come up with a place. It sounded good: a single woman, a former schoolteacher, experienced host of a boy she described as responsible and kind, not a bully. "But don't tell him he's going anywhere else," she said. "I'll just pick him up and tell him he's going to a pizza party. You can bring his stuff over later."

I said, "Okay," but the idea didn't sit right with me. So I took Caesar out to a park to tell him. Or rather, I tried. I said, "You don't like Ezekial, do you?" and he said "No, I hate him." I asked if he would like to go stay at a house with another boy who would be nice to him and where they would have a pool and— "No," he said. "I want to stay with you and Peter." I couldn't believe it—I did not realize how attached or at least how used to us he had become. But he was adamant. We had the conversation three times, and none of those times did I have the courage to tell him he had no choice. I pushed him on the swing set and he cried, "Mary! Mary! Mary!" And then I took him home and told Peter I had not been able to do it.

Peter told Ezekial to go into the other room and we sat Caesar down and told him he was leaving. "No," he said. "Send the other boy away." Ezekial came into the room. "Send him away!" cried Caesar. "Ha-ha," said Ezekial, "you go away!" The FAF woman arrived. I told her what was happening. She said, "Why don't you just let me handle this." And she did. She said, "Okay, Caesar, it's like this. . . . You were supposed to go stay with another family, but then somebody in that family *died* and you couldn't go there."

"Somebody *died*?" asked Caesar.

"Yes, and Peter and Mary were *kind* enough to let you come stay with them for a little while and now it's time to—"

"I want to stay here!" Caesar screamed, and clung to the mattress.

"Caesar," said the FAF woman. "I talked to your mother. *She* wants you to go."

Caesar lifted his face and looked at her for a searching moment. "Lady," he said calmly. "You a liar." And she was. I'm sure of it. Caesar's mother was almost impossible to get on the phone and she spoke no English.

This is probably why the FAF woman screamed, actually screamed: "How dare you call me a liar! Don't you ever call an adult a liar!"

Caesar sobbed and crawled across the bed and clutched at the corner of the mattress; I crawled after him and tried to hold him. He cried, "You a liar, too, Mary!" and I fell back in shame.

The FAF lady then made a noble and transparently insincere offer: "Caesar," she said, "if you want, you can come stay with me and my family. We have a big farm and dogs and—"

He screamed, "I would never stay with you, lady! You're gross! Your whole family is gross!"

I smiled with pure admiration for the child.

The woman cried, "Oh I'm gross, am I!" And he was taken down the stairs screaming, "They always send me away!"

Then Ezekial did something extraordinary. He threw his body across the stairs, grabbing the banister with both hands to block the exit. He began to whisper at Caesar, and I leaned in close, thinking, If he is saying something to comfort, I am going to stop this thing cold. But even as his body plainly said, *Please don't do this,* his mouth spitefully whispered, "Ha-ha! You go away! Ha-ha!"

I stepped back and said to Caesar, "This is not your fault!" He cried, "Then send the other boy away!" Peter pried Ezekial off the banister and Caesar was carried out. I walked outside and watched as Peter put the sobbing little boy into the woman's giant SUV. Behind me, Ezekial was dancing behind the screen door, incoherently taunting me as he sobbed, too, breathless with rage and remorse.

If gentleness can be brutish, cruelty can sometimes be so closely wound in with sensitivity and gentleness that it is hard to know which is what. Animals are not capable of this. That is why it is so much easier to love an animal. Ezekial loved animals; he was never cruel with them. Every time he entered the house, he greeted each of our cats with a special touch. Even the shy one, Tina, liked him and let him touch her. Caesar, on the other hand, was rough and disrespectful—and yet he wanted the cats to like him. One of the things he and Ezekial fought about was which of them Peter's cat Bitey liked more.

On the third day in Florence, I called Martha—the sister I later scolded for being hysterical about a cat—and asked for help. She said she would psychically communicate with Gattino. She said I needed to do it, too. "He needs reassurance," she said. "You need to tell him every day that you're coming back."

I know how foolish this sounds. I know how foolish it is. But I needed to reach for something with a loving touch. I needed to reach even if nothing was physically there within my grasp. I needed to reach even if I touched darkness and sorrow. And so I did it. I asked Peter to do it, too. We would go to churches and kneel and pray for Gattino. We were not alone; the pews were always full of people, old, young, rich, and poor, of every nationality, all of them reaching, even if nothing was physically there. "Please comfort him, please help him," I asked. "He's just a little thing." Because that was what touched me: not the big idea of tragedy, but the smallness and tenderness of this bright, lively creature. From Santissima Annunziata, Santa Croce, and Santa Maria Novella, we sent messages to and for our cat.

I went into the house to try to comfort Ezekial, who was sobbing that his mother didn't love him. I said that wasn't true, that she did love him, that I could hear it in her voice—and I meant it; I *had* heard it. But he said, "No, no, she hates me. That's why she sent me here." I told him he was lovable, and in a helpless way I meant that, too. Ezekial was a little boy in an impossible situation he had no desire to be in, and who could only make it bearable by manipulating and trying to hurt anyone around him. He was also a little boy used to rough treatment, and my attempts at caring only made me a sucker in his eyes. As soon as I said "lovable," he stopped crying on a dime and starting trying to get things out of me, most of which I mistakenly gave him.

Caesar was used to rough treatment, too—but he was still looking for good treatment. When I went to visit him at his new host house, I expected him to be angry at me. He was in the pool when I arrived, and as soon as he saw me, he began splashing toward me, shouting my name. I had bought him a life jacket so he would be safe in the pool, and he was thrilled by it; kind treatment did not make me a sucker in his eyes. He had too strong a heart for that.

But he got kicked out of the new host's home anyway. Apparently, he called her a bitch and threatened to cut her. I could see why she wouldn't like that. I could also see why Caesar would have to let his anger out on somebody if he didn't let it out on me.

Ezekial was with me when I got the call about Caesar's being sent home. The FAF woman who told me said that Caesar had asked her if he was going back to his "real home, with Peter and Mary." I must've looked pretty sick when I hung the phone up, because Ezekial asked, "What's wrong?" I told him, "Caesar got sent home and I feel really sad." He said, "Oh." There was a moment of feeling between us, which meant that he had to throw a violent tantrum an hour later in order to destroy that moment—a moment that could scarcely have felt good to him.

After Ezekial left, I wrote a letter to Caesar's mother. I told her that her son was a good boy, that it wasn't his fault that he'd gotten sent home. I had someone translate it into Spanish for me, and then I copied it onto a card and sent it with some pictures I had taken of Caesar swimming. It came back marked "Moved, address unknown." Peter told me that I should take the hint and stop trying to have any further contact. Other people thought so, too. They thought I was acting out of guilt, and I was. But I was acting out of something else, too. I missed the little boy. I missed his deep eyes, his clumsiness, his generosity, his sweetness. I called the Fresh Air Fund. The first person I talked to wouldn't give me any information. The next person gave me an address in East New York; she gave me a phone number, too. I sent the letter again. I prayed the same way I did later for Gattino: "Spare him. Comfort him. Have mercy on this little person." And Caesar heard me—he did. When I called his house nearly two months after he'd been sent back home, he didn't seem surprised at all.

When Peter and I returned to the veterinary hospital to claim Gattino, he purred at the sight of us. When we went back to Santa Maddalena, his little body tensed with recognition when he saw the room we had lived in together; then he relaxed and walked through it as if returning to a lost kingdom. My body relaxed, too; I felt safe. I felt as if I had come through a kind of danger, or at least a kind of complex maze, and that I had discovered how to make sense of it.

The next day, we went home. The trip included a two-hour ride to Florence, a flight to Milan, a layover, an eight-hour Atlantic flight, then another two-hour drive. When we reached Florence, Peter was told that because of an impossible bureaucratic problem with his ticket, he had to leave the terminal, get his bag, and recheck it for the flight to Milan. The layover wasn't long enough for him to recheck the bags and make it onto the flight with me, and the airline (Alitalia) haughtily informed him that there was no room on the next flight. I boarded the plane alone; Peter had to spent the night in Milan and buy a ticket on another airline; I didn't find this out until I landed in New York with Gattino peering intrepidly from his carrier.

And Gattino *was* intrepid. He didn't cry in the car, or on the plane, even though he'd had nearly nothing to eat since the night before. He settled in patiently, his slender forepaws stretched out regally before him, watching me with a calm, confidently upraised head. He either napped in his carrier or sat in my lap, playing with me, with the person sitting next to me, with the little girl sitting across from me. If I'd let him, he would've wandered up and down the aisles with his tail up.

The first time I called Caesar, he asked about Bitey; he asked about his life jacket. We talked about those things for a while. Then I told him that I was sad when he left. He said, "Did you cry?" And I said, "Yes. I cried." He was silent; I could feel his presence so intensely, like you feel a person next to you in the dark. I asked to talk to his mother; I had someone with me who could speak to her in Spanish, to ask her for permission to have contact with her son. I also spoke to his sister Natalia. Even before I met her, I could hear her beauty in her voice—curious, vibrant, expansive in its warmth and longing.

I sent them presents—books, mostly, and toys when Caesar's birthday came. I talked more to Natalia than to her brother; he was too young to talk for long on the phone. She reached out to me with her voice as if with her hand, and I held it. We talked about her trouble at school, her fears of the new neighborhood, and movies she liked, which were mostly about girls becoming princesses. When Caesar talked to me, it was half-coherent stuff about cartoons and fantasies. But he could be suddenly very mature. "I want to tell you something," he said once. "I feel something, but I don't know what it is."

I wanted to meet their mother; I very much wanted to see Caesar and meet his sister. Peter was reluctant because he considered the relationship inappropriate—but he was willing to do it for me. We went to East New York with a Spanish-speaking friend. We took board games and cookies. Their mother kissed us on both cheeks and gave us candles. She said they could visit us for Holy Week—Easter. Natalia said, "I'm so excited"; I said, "I am, too."

And I was. I was so excited, I was nearly afraid. When Peter and I went into Manhattan to meet them at Penn Station, it seemed a miracle to see them there. As soon as we got to our house, Caesar threw a tantrum on the stairs—the scene of his humiliation. But this time I could keep him, calm him, and comfort him. I could make it okay, better than okay. Most of the visit was lovely. We have pictures in our photo album of the kids riding their bikes down the street on a beautiful spring day and painting Easter eggs; we have a picture of Natalia getting ready to mount a horse, an expression of mortal challenge on her face; we have another picture of her sitting atop the horse in a posture of utter triumph.

On the way back to New York on the train, Caesar asked, "Do you like me?" I said, "Caesar, I not only like you; I love you." He looked at me levelly and said, "Why?" I thought a long moment. "I don't know why yet," I said. "Sometimes you don't know why you love people; you just do. One day I'll know why and then I'll tell you."

When we introduced Gattino to the other cats, we expected drama and hissing. There wasn't much. He was tactful. He was gentle with the timid cats, Zuni and Tina, slowly approaching to touch noses, or following at a respectful distance, sometimes sitting near Tina and gazing at her calmly. He teased and bedeviled only the tough young one, Biscuit—and it's true that she didn't love him. But she accepted him.

Then things began to go wrong—little things at first. I discovered I'd lost my passport; Peter lost a necklace I'd given him; I lost the blue marble from Santa Maddalena. For the sixth summer in a row, Caesar came to visit us and it went badly. My sister Martha was told she was going to be laid off. We moved to a new house and discovered that the landlord had left old junk all over the house, the stove was broken and filled with nests of mice, one of the toilets was falling through the floor, and the windowpanes were broken.

But the cats loved it, especially Gattino. The yard was spectacularly beautiful and wild, and when he turned six months old, we began letting him out for twenty minutes at a time, always with one of us in the yard with him. We wanted to make sure he was cautious, and he was. He was afraid of cars; he showed no desire to go into the street, or really even out of the yard, which was large. We let him go out longer. Everything was fine. The house got cleaned up; we got a new stove. Somebody found Peter's necklace and gave it back. Then late one afternoon I had to go out for a couple of hours. Peter wasn't home. Gattino was in the yard with the other cats; I thought, He'll be okay. When I came back, he was gone.

Because he had never gone near the road, I didn't think he would have crossed the street—and I thought if he had, he would be able to see his way back, since across the street was a level, low-cut field. So I looked behind our house, where there was a dorm in a wooded area, and to both sides of us. Because we had just moved in, I didn't know the terrain and so it was hard to look in the dark—I could see only a jumble of foliage and buildings, houses, a nursery school, and what I later realized was a deserted barn. I started to be afraid. Maybe that is why I thought I heard him speak to me, in the form of a very simple thought that entered my head, plaintively, as if from outside. It said, I'm scared.

I wish I had thought back, Don't worry. Stay where you are. I will find you. Instead, I thought, I'm scared, too. I don't know where you are. It is crazy to think that the course of events might've been changed if different sentences had appeared in my mind. But I think it anyway.

The next day I had to go into Manhattan because a friend was doing a public reading from her first new book in years. Peter looked for Gattino. Like me, he did not look across the street; he simply didn't think the cat would've gone there.

The second day we made posters and began putting them up in all the dorms, houses, and campus buildings. We alerted the campus security people, who put out a mass e-mail to everyone who had anything to do with the college.

The third night, just before I went to sleep, I thought I heard him again. I'm lonely, he said.

The fifth night we got the call from a security guard saying that he saw a small, thin, one-eyed cat trying to forage in a garbage can outside a dorm. The call came at two in the morning and we didn't hear it because the phone was turned down. The dorm was very close by; it was located across the street from us, on the other side of the field.

I walked across the field the next day and realized something about it that I had not noticed before: From a human perspective, it was flat enough to easily look across; from the perspective of a creature much lower to the ground, it was made of valleys and hills too big to see over.

Something I didn't say correctly: I did not lose the blue marble from Santa Maddalena. I threw it away. When Peter lost his necklace, I decided that the marble was actually bad luck. I took it out into a field and threw it away.

A friend offered to pay for me to see a psychic. He hadn't seen her—he doesn't see psychics. But a pretty girl he was flirting with had seen this psychic, and been very impressed by her; my friend wanted me to tell him what the psychic was like, I guess in order to get some sideways knowledge of the girl. So I made the appointment. She told me that Gattino was "in trouble." She told me he was dying. She couldn't tell me where he was, except that it was down in a gulley or ditch, someplace where the ground dropped down suddenly; water was nearby and there was something on the ground that crunched underfoot. Maybe I could find him. But maybe I wasn't meant to. She thought maybe it was his "karmic path" to "walk into the woods and close his eyes," and, if that was so, I shouldn't interfere. On the other hand, she said, I might still find him if I looked in the places she described.

I told my friend that I was not impressed with the pretty girl's choice of psychics. And then I went to the places the psychic had described and looked for Gattino. I went every day and every night. At the end of one of those nights, when I was about to go to sleep, words appeared in my head again. They were, *I'm dying* and then *Good-bye.* I got up and took a sleeping pill. Two hours later I woke with tears running down my face.

Who decides which relationships are appropriate and which are not? Which deaths are tragic and which are not? Who decides what is big and what is little? Is it a matter of numbers or physical mass or intelligence? If you are a little creature or a little person dying alone and in pain, you may not remember or know that you are little. If you are in enough pain, you may not remember who or what you are; you may know only your suffering, which is immense. Who decides? What decides—common sense? Can common sense dictate such things? Common sense is an excellent guide to social structures—but does it ever have anything to do with who or what moves you?

After that first Easter visit, Caesar and Natalia came up for two weeks during the summer. We went biking and swimming and to the movies and the Dutchess County Fair. Natalia started taking horseback-riding lessons. At night she and I had a ritual of "walking at night," during which we would stroll around the neighborhood and talk intimately. She told me she was having trouble at school with the work and the other kids. I asked if she would like me to help her with her homework on the phone at night, and she said yes.

Peter was primarily in charge of Caesar, but they did not have a bond. Peter didn't like the boy's combination of neediness and aggression. The kid would hang on Peter and always want his attention—and if he didn't get it, which he often did not, he would say something like "When I get older, I'm going to knock your teeth out." He said it like a joke, and he was, after all, a small child. But psychically he wasn't small; neither he nor his sister were small in that sense, and one took what they said seriously because of it. I took Caesar's aggression seriously—but for a long time I forgave it. I forgave because for me the aggression and need translated almost on contact as longing for the pure affection he had been denied by circumstance, and outrage at the denial. His father had left the family; his mother—who was in her mid-forties—worked long hours at a factory and so left the children alone often. When she got home, she was usually too tired to do more than cook dinner; Caesar said she cursed him regularly. Both children believed she preferred her four grown kids, who lived in the Dominican Republic, to them.

But nonetheless she loved them, especially Caesar. You could see it in their bodies when they were together, see it in the way she looked at him when she greeted him as "my beautiful son." She loved both children, and she beat them. She beat them rationally as punishment, and irrationally, seemingly just as a way of relating. Once when I was on the phone with Natalia, helping her write an essay, she said, "Just a minute, I need to get another pencil." She put the phone down, said something to her mother in a light, questioning voice, and was answered with violent shouts that turned into crashes and scuffling and Natalia sobbing before the phone was slammed into its cradle. The mother sometimes attacked the children as if she were a child herself, pulling Natalia's hair or scratching her. She demeaned Natalia continually. Caesar, she infantilized, bathing him and brushing his teeth for him even when he was nine years old.

Two social workers at the children's school told us they already knew about the beatings, or thought they did; Natalia would report having been beaten, and then take it back, saying she'd been lying. If she had bruises, she refused to show them. One of the social workers believed the kids were being abused and thought they should be taken away from their mother; the other thought Natalia was a liar and felt sorry for the mother, whom she had known for years. "She loves those kids," said the woman. "She works her ass off for them."

And they loved her, passionately; their self-esteem was completely bound up with her. And so we bit our tongues and tried not to speak critically to the children of their mother. We found a person who could speak Spanish to translate for us, and we tried to consult her about the kids whenever possible (her advice was usually something like "Just punch him in the mouth"), to show respect for her in front of them, to work with the situation. We had the kids up for Christmas, Easter, sometimes on their birthdays, and always for at least a few days in the summer. We occasionally met them in the city, too. I worked with Natalia on the phone, helping her read assigned books and write reports on them. I also hired a tutor for Natalia, paying a college student to go out to Brooklyn once a month to give her math lessons. Her teacher said she was improving. Then other kids began to jeer at her for it, and she got into fights. But she didn't talk about that. She would call me and cry and say she couldn't do well in school because of her mother beating her. I said, "You don't have control over your mother. You have control over yourself." I said, "Please keep trying." She was quiet for a moment. She said very calmly, "Mary, I don't think I can." I said, "Just try." But I could hear that she could not. I could hear it in her voice. I can't put into words why she could not. But I could hear it.

She kept doing her homework on the phone with me. She kept meeting the math tutor. But even though she did the assignments, she didn't turn them in. She would say she had, that the teacher was lying, that the teacher had torn them up, that the teacher hated her. The teacher said she never saw the work.

I kept looking for Gattino. I didn't think in particular about the children while I looked for him. I barely thought at all. I tried to feel the earth, the sky, the trees, and the wet, frozen stubble of ground. But I couldn't feel anything but sad. Once when I was driving to a shelter to check if he had been turned in, I heard a story on the radio about Blackwater contractors shooting into a crowd of Iraqi civilians. They killed a young man, a medical student, who had gotten out of his car. When his mother leapt from the car to hold his body, they killed her. We all hear stories like this every day, and I realize they are terrible stories. But I don't feel anything about them, not really. When I heard this one, my heart felt so torn open, I had to pull off the road until I could get control of my emotions.

It was the loss of the cat that had made this happen; his very smallness and lack of objective consequence had made the tearing open possible. I don't know why this should be true. But I am sure it is true.

It was true not just of my heart; my mind also tore. I called another psychic, a pet psychic, and asked her about Gattino. She told me he had died, probably of kidney failure after drinking something toxic. She said he had suffered. I called another one. She said he had died but that he hadn't suffered, that he had "curled up as if he were going to sleep." I began asking random people if they had any "psychic feeling" about the cat; I am still amazed at how many claimed that they did. Some of them were friends, some were acquaintances, and some were complete strangers. A stranger, an innkeeper in Austin, told me that he had been sicker than I'd realized, and that he had gone away to die in order to spare me any suffering; she said that he'd loved me. An acquaintance, a taciturn and generally unfriendly woman who works in a stable, and whom I would not have thought to ask for psychic input, looked at the poster I showed her and her partner, then remarked in a low voice, just as I was about to walk away, "For whatever it's worth, I don't think your cat's dead." She thought he was living in or under a white house with a lot of walkways around it. It sounded like a description of half the dorms on campus.

And so, in the middle of January, I put another round of posters up on campus and in mailboxes. I started getting calls almost immediately from people who said that they had seen a small one-eyed cat. I began leaving food in the places he was supposed to have been, to keep him there. I also left scraps of my clothes near the food, so he might catch my scent and remember me. I left food in our backyard. I collected turds and piss clumps from the litter boxes and scattered them in our yard so that he might catch the scent of our other cats and be guided home by it. I collected a whole shopping bag of turds and piss and then went out late one night to make a trail of it from the far edge of the field to our house. The snow was up to my calves and it took me almost an hour to get through it, diligently strewing used litter in the path of my footsteps.

I asked Peter if he thought I was crazy. He said that sometimes he did think that. But then he thought of friends of his whose twin daughters had recently died of a rare skin disease called recessive dystrophic epidermylosis. When the girls were born, their parents were told they should put them in an institution. When they insisted on taking them home, the doctors just shrugged and gave them some bandages. Nothing was known about home care; the parents had to learn it all themselves. They devoted themselves to the care of their children, and they gave them nearly normal lives; in spite of excruciating pain involving almost every ordinary activity, including eating, the girls played sports, went to college, flirted online, and had boyfriends. Although they continued to hope for a cure, they died at twenty-seven. Their parents worked right up until the end to make their lives as good or at least as unpainful as possible. "We would've done anything," said their mother. "If someone had told us it would help to smear ourselves with shit and roll in the yard, we would've done it." "But they didn't actually do it," I said. "Well," said Peter, "no one told them to."

Because Natalia said she was afraid to go to the public junior high school, we paid for her and her brother to go to Catholic school. Caesar did okay; she got kicked out in a couple of months. Her mother laughed bitterly. She said, "Natalia will always cause trouble." I said, "I still believe in her." There was incredulous silence on the other end of the line.

That summer, we sent them to a camp that was supposed to be great for troubled kids, and it *was* great, especially for Natalia. She excelled; the counselors loved her and invited her to participate in their yearlong Teen Leadership Program, which provided group phone calls with counselors and other kids, tutoring in school, and weekend trips up to the camp every month. Natalia was thrilled, and when we returned her to her mother, we showed her the pictures of Natalia at camp, getting along with everybody and not causing trouble. Her mother looked at the pictures and literally dropped them on the ground.

Natalia made the first two trips to camp and then stopped showing up. She stopped participating in the group phone calls.

She stayed out all night and skipped school. She said it was because her mother beat her. Her mother said it was because she wanted to have sex and do drugs.

When she came up to visit for Christmas, we had a fight; afterward I tried to talk to her. She said, "I don't care. I don't care about nothing." I said I doubted that was true. She said, "It is true. It's always been true." And I felt her relief in saying it. "All right," I said. "It might be true sometimes, but not all the time; almost everybody cares about something, sometime." She looked at me sullenly; she did not disagree. "But," I said, "if you walk around acting like you don't care for long enough, people will start to believe you. If you really don't care, then people who do care will leave your life and people who don't care will come into it. And if that happens, you will find yourself in a very terrible place." As I spoke, her face slowly opened; slowly, her sullenness revealed fear. I kissed her and said, "It doesn't have to be that way." A few months later she ran away from home.

Caesar was nine when his sister ran away, and I could sense him metaphorically watching her with very wide eyes. He joined his mother in condemning her, but even when he did, I could still hear affection for her in his voice. He loved his family—but he loved me, too. I could talk to him about anything—about dreams, heaven and hell, what made a person evil, and why a picture was good or bad. When he noticed the picture of my father in the glassed-in cabinet that functions as a sort of shrine, he wanted to know about him. I told him that my father was an orphan by the age of ten; his mother died when he was nine, followed by the death of his father a year later. Then his dog died. Still, when the world war broke out, my father wanted to enlist. He joined the war at Anzio, one of the most terrible battles. Caesar said, "I feel bad for your father. But I don't feel sorry for him.

Because he sounds like a terrific person." Later, when Peter asked if Caesar had ever had an imaginary friend, he said, "I didn't before, but I do now. My imaginary friend is Mary's father."

When my father was dying, I asked him something. I did not really ask him; I don't think he was conscious, and I whispered the question rather than spoke it. But nonetheless it was a serious question. "Daddy," I said, "tell me what you suffered. Tell me what it was like for you." I could never have asked him this earlier in life. But I believed that on the verge of death he could "hear" my whispered words. And slowly, over a period of time, I believe I have been answered, at least in part. I felt that I was hearing part of the answer while I was out looking for my cat, when it was so cold and so late that no one else was around. It occurred to me then that the loss of the cat was, in fact, a merciful way for me to have my question answered.

Both my sisters and I sat with my father when he was dying; we all took care of him with the help of a hospice worker who stopped by every day. But Martha was alone with him when he died. She said that she had felt death come into the room. She said that death felt very gentle. Later she told us that she felt and even saw terrible things before he died. But she seemed at peace about witnessing his death.

When Martha returned home, she had to go right back to work. She was not close to the people she worked with and they were not ideal confidants. But she needed to talk, and so she did. When she described my father's life to a coworker, he found it absurd that Martha seemed to place as much emphasis on the death of my father's dog as she did on the death of his parents, and he spoke to her coolly. "I love dogs," he said. "I'm sad when a dog dies. But no dog should ever be compared to family."

When I was out looking for the cat, I remembered this story, and I wished I had been with my sister when her coworker spoke to her that way. I would have said, "Imagine you are a nine-year-old boy and you have lost your mother. You are in shock, and because you are in shock you are reduced to a little animal who knows its survival is in danger. So you say to yourself, Okay, I don't have a mom. I can deal with that. And then the next year your father dies. You think, A'ight. I don't have a dad, either. I can deal with that, too. Then your dog dies. And you think, Not even a dog? I can't even have a dog?" I would've said, "Of course the dog didn't mean as much to him as his parents did, you moron. His parents meant so much to him, he could not afford to feel their loss. The dog he could feel, and through the door of that feeling came everything else." My sister *did* say a more polite version of this. But I wish that I had been there and able to speak, too.

The figurative loss of "my" children and the loss of my cat were minor compared to what my father lost. That is why it was a merciful loss; it was enough to give me a taste of what my father felt, and a taste was all I could bear. I had not understood this before. The family myth was that my father was weak, neurotic, a little boy unable to grow up emotionally. There was some reality to this perception. But the bigger reality is this: My father was strong, much stronger than I am. If I had experienced what he had experienced by the age of ten, it would've broken me several times over. What happened to him hurt him, and badly. It did not break him. He raised a family and held a job. He was brutally unhappy and sometimes he behaved miserably toward his wife and children. But he never stopped. He never broke. Until the very end.

———

Caesar once asked me if he could come live with us. I said I didn't think he really wanted that; for one thing, we would make him do his homework constantly. He replied that he would. I said I thought he would miss his mother too much. He hesitated, then replied that maybe he would. I said, "Besides, we wouldn't hit you when you were bad, and then you wouldn't know what to do."

He was silent for a moment. Then he said, "You're right."

"Why do you think that is?" I asked.

He thought for a long time; I could tell that he was thinking hard. Finally he said, "I don't know. Why do *you* think that is?"

"Honey," I said. "I don't know the answer to that. Nobody knows the answer to that. If you could answer that, you would make a million dollars."

Maybe it was a strange conversation to have with a ten-year-old. But I wanted him to think about it even if he would never find the answer. If he could think about why he needed to be hit, then he would know that the need to be hit wasn't *him,* but something separate, about which he might have thoughts. I'm not sure this would have made any difference. Once, during a fight with him about his throwing rocks at some ducks, I said, "Do you want me to treat you like that, just because I'm bigger? Do you want me to hit you?"

He said, "Yeah, hit me, go on." He said it a couple of times.

I didn't. I turned and walked away. But for a moment I was tempted. I was tempted partly by frustration. I was also tempted by the force of his need.

These children, you see, were not weak people. They were troubled, at risk, disadvantaged; they suffered from racism, from low self-esteem—anything you like. Socially—that is, in terms of money and privilege—I was their superior in every way. But in a bigger, harder to articulate way, they were, in spite of their youth, at least my equals, if not superior to me. Superior not because of anything innate, but because of their exposure to brutal, impossibly complex social forces that they were made to negotiate every day of their lives. Sometimes, when Natalia and I were watching a movie together, she would lean against my shoulder and I would acutely feel that my smaller body, my bony shoulder, was not big enough to bear her weight. I would think, I am simply not big enough to give this girl what she needs. I had moments of great joy with them—watching them unwrap their presents under the Christmas tree, making them sandwiches, watching Natalia on a horse or Caesar learning how to swim. But I often felt inadequate, wrong, unable to affect them, frustrated, mismatched—at best like a well-intentioned mouse crazily trying to chew two lion cubs out of a massive double net cast upon them by vast powers beyond its tiny vision.

They knew this, I'm sure. They no doubt sometimes felt scorn for my feelings of ineptitude, and also for my attempts to act confident in spite of them, to be inspiring and optimistic when I barely knew how. But they were also supportive and, on occasion, very kind. When I or Peter was trying to do something and it wasn't working out easily—put dinner on the table, find the petting zoo, get our erratic VCR to play—the kids would sometimes get very quiet and we could feel them unite in their appreciation of our efforts, subtly throwing their goodwill behind us. Sometimes, I felt their generosity even when they weren't there, as if they were standing behind me, their hands on my shoulders. I am afraid of flying, and I remember one panic-stricken moment at an airport, when my own mind became too much for me to bear; the only way for me to calm myself was to remember Natalia riding a horse, sitting up straight in the saddle and smiling.

———

After Gattino had been gone almost two months, I visited a woman whose husband had died three years earlier. She was still deep in grief, and her grief accentuated her propensity for mysticism; I wondered aloud if the blue marble that had so magically appeared to me in Italy, and which I then threw away, might have something to do with the cat's disappearance. Instead of trying to talk common sense to me, the grieving woman said she knew of a great psychic who might be able to answer that question. I said no, I did not want to pay any more psychics. The woman said that this psychic was a friend of hers, and that she would just ask her the question, that it need not be a full reading.

A few weeks later I received an e-mail from this psychic that said the blue marble was not a curse or an omen of any kind. However, its physical movement across the floor had been the by-product of a deliberate psychic energy directed toward me by a young man at Santa Maddalena; this young man was a practitioner of magic, and he had recognized me as a kindred spirit, a person in need of love and capable of fully expressed love. He had wished me well, and it was the force of his wish that had set the marble rolling. It had nothing to do with Gattino, but it became bound up with the circumstances of the cat, which was interesting to the psychic because the marble was to her symbolic of an eye, and the kitten was missing an eye.

She added that Gattino was not dead; she said that he had been picked up by a "traveler" who was well acquainted with the system of cat shelters and havens all over the state. This traveler had taken my cat to one of these shelters, where he was at this moment being well cared for. If I wanted to find him, she suggested that I contact every such shelter within a fifty-mile radius.

This information would, she said, cost me one hundred dollars.

If someone had told me to smear shit on myself and roll in the yard, if that person was a cat expert and made a convincing case that, yes, doing so *could* result in the return of my cat, I probably would've done it. I did not consider this pathetic susceptibility "magical thinking." I didn't consider it very different from any other kind of thinking. It was more that the known, visible order of things had become unacceptable to me—senseless, actually—because it was too violently at odds with the needs of my disordered mind. Other kinds of order began to become visible to me, to bleed through and knit together the broken order of what had previously been known. I still don't know if this cobbled reality was completely illusory, an act of desperate will, or if it was an inept and partial interpretation of something real, something bigger than what I could readily see. In this way, my connective symbols—the marble, the things various psychics said to me—were similar to religious statues and icons that people pray to, or parade through the street with, or wear around their necks. Except that the statues and icons are also artful creations, sometimes beautiful ones. My symbols were not beautiful; they were stupid and trite. They were related to the symbols of religion as a deformed and retarded child might be the distant cousin of a beautiful prince. But they were related nonetheless.

I paid the money. I called, and Peter helped me call, all the cat shelters within a fifty-mile radius. Many of the shelters I contacted asked me to send them a picture of Gattino along with my contact information, which they posted on their Internet sites; I immediately began getting responses from people who thought they might've seen him. I also got responses from businesses devoted to the rescue of hopelessly lost cats, one of which included a private detective willing to fly to your state with his tracking dogs, a smiling pit bull and a vigilant poodle depicted nobly flanking their owner on the site. The superior quality of these businesses was attested to by customer after satisfied cus-

tomer on each of the sites: "At first I was skeptical. But as soon
as I opened my front door and saw Butch and his gentle tracking
dogs, I knew . . ."

I also received an e-mail from someone who appeared barely
able to write English but who claimed to have seen someone
named "Samuel" find a cat outside of a "community center," to
have talked with Samuel about seeing an ad for my cat online,
and to have gotten an e-mail address from Samuel, if I wanted
to contact him. "Samuel," of course, wanted to see a picture of
Gattino to be sure he had the right cat; on receiving a photo, he
said that, yes, he definitely had my cat. He went on to say that,
like me, he had fallen in love with Gattino and taken him home
to Nigeria, but if only I would send the airfare, he would return
my darling. Upon Googling the first few lines of his note, I found
an outraged warning about him from someone who had paid the
fee and never saw her cat.

> This world is the only reality available to us, and if we do
> not love it in all its terror, we are sure to end up loving the
> "imaginary," our own dreams and self-deceits, the utopias
> of politicians, or the futile promises of future reward and
> consolation which the misled blasphemously call "reli-
> gion."

This is Leslie Fiedler, writing about Simone Weil. When I read
it, I thought, Yes, that is me: deep in dreams of marbles, omens,
and psychics, hoping that something will take pity on me and my
cat. But can one always tell what is imaginary and what isn't? To
be sentimental is scorned by intelligent people as false, but the
word is one short syllable away from *sentiment*—that is, feeling.
False feeling is so blended with real feeling in human life, I wonder if anyone can always tell them apart, or know when one may
be hiding in the other. When my father was dying, he cried out

for people who were not there, in a voice that we did not recognize as his. One of these times he said, "I want my mama." When we heard this, Jane and I froze; both of us were asking ourselves, Should we pretend to be his mother? It was Martha who knew what to do; she held his hand and sang to him. She sang him a lullaby, and he calmed. He thought his mother was there. Was this a dream, a self-deceit?

I called the three young men who had been at or near Santa Maddalena with me, to find out if any of them practiced magic. The first one I called was a medical student who had also written an internationally acclaimed book about a child soldier in West Africa. I had e-mailed him first and asked if we could talk on the phone. I wonder what he thought was coming. It could scarcely have been what came: "I know this is a peculiar question," I said. "But do you practice anything that anyone could call magic?"

There was a long silence. "Do you mean literally?" he asked.

I thought about it. "Yes," I said. "I think I do."

The silence that followed was so baffled that I broke down and explained why I was asking.

"Well," he said, "I pray. Do you think that counts?"

I said, "To me, it could. But I don't think that's what the lady meant." He was very sympathetic about Gattino. He said he would pray for me to find him. I thanked him and called someone else.

When my father was alive, he and Martha were distant, uncomprehending, nearly hostile. He was cold to her, and she felt rejected by him. As he became more and more unhappy with age and was eventually rejected by my mother, he tried to reach out to Martha. But the pattern was too set. During one of our last Christmas visits to him, I saw my father and Martha act out a scene that looked like a strange imitation of a cruel game between a girl who is madly in love with an indifferent boy and the boy himself. She kept asking him over and over again whether he liked the present she had gotten him. Did he really, really like it? Would he use it? Did he want to try it out now? And he responded stiffly, irritably, with increasing distance. She behaved as if she wanted to win his love, but she was playing the loser so aggressively that it was almost impossible for him to respond with love, or to respond at all. What was the real feeling here? What was the dream or the self-deceit? Something real was happening, and it was terrible to see. But it was so disguised that it is hard to say what it actually was.

Still, as he lay dying, she was the one who knew to hold his hand, to sing to him.

The second young man I called, a Hungarian writer I had met outside of Santa Maddalena, answered quite differently from the first. "I have powers," he said intensely, "but I have never been taught how to use them very well. If I made something move, it would be something big, like a building. But a marble—I'm not that good. To move something that small would require more refinement than I possess."

At least this conversation made me smile; when I repeated it at a party, I meant to amuse people, but it actually offended someone. "He sounds like an idiot!" said a film producer who happened to overhear me. "There's nothing charming in that; he just sounds really, really stupid." And then the producer, the voice of normalcy and intelligence, began describing to me his latest idea for a comedy: A man who married very young is, at thirty, full of wanderlust. His wife goes off for a trip alone, and he finds himself in the presence of a beautiful young woman who wants him. "Finally, she gets him alone and she takes off her shirt, and she's got incredible tits, really big tits, and they're perfect, the most beautiful big tits you've ever seen! But he says no and—"

I laughed, almost hysterically. Yes, it was a comedy, and a deeper one than its creator knew, to have at its dramatic center the rejection of beautiful naked breasts. Of course the hero rejects these breasts in the name of faithfulness, and rationally all is well. But if one mutes the trite music of the story and watches the action as sketched by the producer, one sees a different, more stark film. Whether it's a comedy or a drama, a titillating image or a perverse one depends on what you feel about naked breasts, which, in the most fundamental symbolic language, translate as nurture, love, and vulnerability. My sister was offering my father love, in a form he could not accept, just as he, with increasing desperation, offered my mother love she could not accept or even recognize. In each offering, purity and perversity made a strange pattern; each rejection made the pattern more complete.

If my father had acted differently toward Martha, it is possible that he could've broken this pattern. Because he was the parent, it's possible that the burden was on him to do so. But I don't think he could have. He wasn't sophisticated when it came to his emotions. His emotions were too raw for sophistication.

When I was thirty-two, I tried to break the pattern. I was visiting home and my father was having a temper tantrum, which meant on this occasion that he was yelling at my mother about her failings. He had done this for years, and normally the entire family would be silent and wait for him to tire himself out. This time I did not. I yelled at him. I told him I was tired of listening to him complain and blame everything on someone else. I expected him to yell back at me; in the past, I might've expected him to hit me. But he didn't. He turned and walked away. I followed him, still yelling. Finally I yelled, "I am sorry for talking to you this way. I'm doing it because I want to have a real relationship with you. Do you want a real relationship with me?"

He said, "No," and shut his bedroom door in my face.

I felt bad. I also felt vindicated. I had been right and he had been wrong. Even so, I apologized the next day, and we talked, a little. He did not take back his words. That made me even more right. It made me right to shut the door on him emotionally.

I repeated this conversation to an older man, a friend who was also a father. He laughed and said, "I would've said no, too, if I were him."

I asked why. I don't remember what he said. I came away with the impression that my friend found the language I used too corny or therapeutic. And it was. Certainly my father would've found it so. But I don't think that's the only reason he walked away. If my language was a cliché, it was also heartfelt and naked. That kind of sudden nakedness, without even a posture of elegance, would've been a kind of violence to my father. It would've touched him forcefully in a place he had spent his life guarding. To say yes would've allowed too much of that force in too deeply. Saying no was a way of being faithful to the guarded place.

My father continued to throw tantrums and blame people for his suffering. A little while after I asked him if he wanted a real relationship with me, I wrote a letter telling him how angry I was with him for acting that way. Before I sent it, I told my mother about it. She said it would really hurt him. She said, "He told me, 'Mary and I have a real relationship.'" At the time I tore the letter up and thought, How sad. Now I think he was right. Our relationship *was* real. What I wanted it to be was ideal.

Because a security guard named Gino claimed to have seen Gattino months after he disappeared, both Peter and I began to believe that he had somehow found a place to survive, even though the temperatures had sometimes gone down to freezing, even though it must've been hard to get enough to eat. I began draping the bushes of our house with sweaty clothes, hoping that the wind would carry the scent to him and that he would be able to find his way back. We continued to put food out in sheltered places near parking areas; in addition, we began to stake out these areas at night, sitting in our car with the headlights trained on the food. We saw at least two cats come to eat—both were gray tabbies, but big ones that surely no one could mistake for the delicate cat depicted on our poster. Only once, Peter saw a very small, thin cat who could've been ours, but he couldn't get a good look because it was slinking under parked cars. It was about to emerge into the open, when a noisy crowd of students came by and it darted away back under the cars.

The very act of doing these things—waiting in the parking lots, draping the bushes with clothing—made me feel that Gattino was still there.

Before I met Gattino, before I went to Italy, I talked with Caesar on the phone, and during that conversation he asked why I sent his mother money. I should have spoken from my heart. If I had, I would've said, "Because I love you and I want to help her take care of you." Instead, for some crazy reason, I went sociological on him. I said, "Because when I first met your mother and she told me she made six dollars and forty cents an hour, I felt ashamed as an American. I felt like she deserved more support for coming here and trying to get a better life."

He said, "What you're saying is really fucked up."

I said, "Why?"

He said, "I don't know, it just is."

I said, "Put words on it. Try."

He said, "I can't."

I said, "Yes you can. Why is what I'm saying fucked up?"

He said, "Because it's good enough that she came here to get a better life."

I said, "I agree. But she should be acknowledged. I have a hard job and sometimes I hate it, but I get acknowledged, and she should, too. And somebody besides me should do it, but nobody is, so I am."

He said, "People are acknowledging her. She makes more money now."

I said, "That's good. But it still should be more."

He said, "You act like you feel sorry for her."

I said, "I do, so what? Sometimes I feel sorry for Peter; sometimes I feel sorry for myself. There's no shame in that."

He said, "But you talk about my mom like she's some kind of freak."

I said, "I don't think that."

He said, "You talk about her like you think you're better than her."

And for a moment I was silent. Because I do think that—rather, I feel it. Before God, as souls, I don't feel it. But socially, as creatures of this earth, I do. I'm wrong to feel it. But I do feel it. I feel it partly because of things Caesar and Natalia have told me.

He heard my hesitation and he began to cry. And so I lied to him. Of course he knew I lied.

He said, "For the first time I feel ashamed of my family."

I said I was sorry; I tried to reassure him. He asked me if I would take money from someone who thought they were better than I was, and I said, "Frankly, yes. If I needed the money, I would take as much as I could, and I would say to myself, Fuck you for thinking you're better than I am."

Passionately, he said he would never, ever do that.

I snapped, "Don't be so sure about that. You don't know yet."

He stopped crying.

I said, "Caesar, this is really hard. Do you think we can get through it?"

He said, "I don't know." Then: "Yes."

I asked him if he remembered the time on the train when he was only seven, when he asked me why I loved him and I said I didn't know yet. "Now I know why," I said. "This is why. You're not somebody who just wants to hear nice bullshit. You care. You want to know what's real. I love you for that."

This was the truth. But sometimes even loving truth isn't enough. He said he was sorry he'd bothered me, and that he was tired. I asked him if he still felt mad at me. He hesitated and then said, "No. Inside, I am not mad at you, Mary."

For months after Gattino disappeared, I still dreamed of him at least once a week. I would dream that I was standing in the yard calling him, like I had before he'd disappeared, and he'd come to me the way he had come in reality: running with his tail up, leaping slightly in his eagerness, leaping finally into my lap. Often in the dream he didn't look like himself; often I blended him with other cats I have had in the past. In one dream I blended him with Caesar. In this dream, Caesar and I were having an argument, and I got so angry that I opened my mouth, threatening to bite him. He opened his mouth, too, in counterthreat. And when he did that, I saw that he had the small, sharp teeth of a kitten.

When we came back from Italy, Caesar came to visit. We were tired and packing to move. We did not have as much energy as we usually have for him; he felt that immediately and resented it. He said, "You've changed." And he became volatile and hostile, behavior that had a very different quality at the age of twelve than it had had when he was seven. The second day he was with us he told Peter, "I want to cut off your nuts"; I thought Peter would knock him down the stairs. Some days later he told me I didn't have any kids because I went to the vet and "got fixed"; I answered rationally, but inside, for the first time, my feelings for him went dead. That night after he went to bed, he started screaming that he couldn't breathe. I gave him his inhaler and rubbed his chest. For over an hour he continued to scream and to force himself to cough, loudly and dramatically. I went in the room and sat with him. I told him I knew he was faking the asthma, and that I also knew it was hard to be with us and that the visit wasn't going right. I told him I was having a hard time sleeping, too, and that I was really tired, which was part of why I couldn't be as present as I'd like. I put my hand on his stomach and told him to breathe there. He did. We talked about the Harry Potter movie we had seen the night before. We talked about the idea of an alternate universe, and what might be going on in it right now. I felt connected to him again. He closed his eyes and began to breathe evenly. I left his room at one o'clock. He woke me up at six the next morning, demanding that I get up and help him turn on the shower.

In March, four months after Gattino disappeared, I got a call at three in the morning from Gino, the security guard, who said he had just seen him in one of the parking lots. I put my coat on over my pajamas, got in the car, and was there within minutes. Gino and another guard were excitedly pacing around with flashlights, pointing at the dim figure of a cat under the last car at the end of a row of cars. When I appeared, the cat bolted. "There he goes!" cried Gino. And he shined his flashlight on the obese tabby we had been seeing for months. "That can't be him," said the other guard. "That cat has two eyes." "No he doesn't!" insisted Gino. "I shined my light on him and I saw!"

A few nights later I spoke to another security guard, a reticent older man who had once told me that he'd seen my cat. I asked him when he had last seen Gattino. He said it had been three months ago—maybe longer. "I haven't seen many cats lately," he said. "I'll tell you what I have seen, though. There's a huge bobcat, all over campus late at night. That and a lot of coyotes."

His meaning was clear. I didn't say much of anything. I thought, At least it's a death an animal would understand.

Caesar did not behave badly the whole visit. He loved Gattino; he loved the story of his illness and his dramatic flight from Italy. When he knew that a friend of Peter's was coming for dinner, he spontaneously spent his own money to buy four cannolis at a pastry shop at which we'd stopped to buy a soda. "I want to go all out for us," he said. When it came time to have the dessert, he said, "Wait, let me get it ready!" And he served the pastry garnished with blueberries, which must've been a last-minute inspiration. But when Peter's friend e-mailed Caesar a poem to thank him for the cannoli, his response was "What a stupid bitch. What kind of stupid bitch would write this for someone she doesn't even know?" His school had assigned him three book reports over the summer, and he hadn't done any. I knew he had read *Call of the Wild,* and I knew he had loved it. So I made him write a book report about it. He moaned, "Aw man . . ." But he worked on it for nearly an hour. When he finished, I went over it and pointed out the errors, and the places where he needed to be clearer or more specific. He spent at least a half hour revising it. He showed it to me proudly, and rightly so—it was excellent. A few weeks later I learned that he never turned it in.

———————

I talked to Natalia after Caesar's visit; she asked how it went. I said I was angry at him for not turning in his homework. There was a beat of silence on her end, and then she said, "I would be mad, too." She said it with a slight smile in her voice. It was two kinds of smile in one—mocking and relieved at having a conventional adult response to mock. She may also have been simply pleased to be on my team for the instant it took to say the sentence; we had not been on the same team for quite a while.

Two years earlier she had been taken away from her mother and sent to live in a group home; she was deemed too wild for foster care. The year before we had managed to get her once more into the camp she had loved, and we had hope that it would work out better now that she wasn't living with her mother. At first, it seemed to. Again the counselors got excited about her; again she was accepted into the Teen Leadership Program. After a few months, she blew it off. She started going AWOL, skipping school and running the streets. Every weekend, she went home to stay with her mother, even though they fought violently.

Finally her mother said that if Natalia behaved herself for three months straight, stopped violating curfew, and went to school, she could return home. Natalia did this for the entire three months. The court date was set. It was expected to be a walk-through. Formally, the judge asked Natalia's mother if she would allow her daughter to return home. And her mother laughed. She laughed and said, "I would never let that girl come live with me again." The social worker told me Natalia screamed like an animal. She said she had to be held back by court officers. She said that Caesar had been there, and that he had laughed along with his mother. She said she had never seen anything like it.

The social worker who told me what had happened in court

repeated to me what she had said to Natalia: that she "has to accept her mother for what she is because she will never change." What heavy knowledge for a young girl. If Natalia actually absorbed such deep knowledge at fifteen—and I suspect that she absorbed it much younger—how can the more refined knowledge of reading and writing and math problems ever seem like anything but trivial to her? What will it do to her to accept a woman who mistreats her? She is sixteen now, and she is finally about to be transferred to a foster home. She still goes back to stay with her mother every weekend except for the weekends she is with us. She will go back there again and again. My guess is that she will continue to do so in some form long after her mother is dead.

How stupid to think I could break this pattern when I could not break my own. I can't say offhand how many times, during the decades before I got married, I asked for or demanded some sort of relationship with someone who shut the door in my face, then opened it again and peeked out. I would—metaphorically—pound on the door and follow the person through endless rooms. Sometimes the door opened and I fell in love—before losing interest completely. I thought then that my feelings were false and had been all along, but the pain that came from rejecting someone or being rejected was real and deep. It did not help when I realized that I was as much to blame for the result as the people I pursued, that I often "played the loser" so aggressively that I scarcely gave the person opposite me much choice in their response.

When I talk about my relationship with the children and how frustrating it is, some people say, "But you're showing them another way." Am I? Deeper than my encouraging, ideal words is my experience of the closed door and the desperate insistence that it open—emotional absence, followed by a compulsive reaction that becomes its own kind of absence. Even if they don't identify it, I'm sure the children feel it.

I'm also sure that they feel the true, live thing trapped somehow inside the false game—if, in fact *game* is the right word for what I have described. A game is something conscious, with clear rules and goals that everyone agrees to. What I experienced too often, inside myself or with another, was a half-conscious, fast-moving blur of real and false, playfulness and anguish, ardent affection and its utter lack. More than a game, it was as if I were stumbling, with another person or alone, through a labyrinth of conflicting impulses and complex, overlaid patterns, trying to find a way to meet, or to avoid meeting, both at the same time. In spite of everything, sometimes I did meet with people, and lovingly. I met my husband in that way almost by accident. And sometimes, after ten years, he and I nonetheless find ourselves wandering apart and alone.

And so I take the kids to movies and to plays; I send them books, listen to them talk, and lecture them about their homework, still sometimes try to help them do it. I dedicated a book to Natalia and sent it to her so she could see her name written in it. I don't think I will ever fully know how any of it affects her or Caesar, for good or ill. I act almost blindly and hope that most of it will be to the good.

This, too, my father experienced.

When I was about forty, my father called me to tell me that he had found a picture that I had drawn when I was seven, and that it "showed real talent." He said that he had planned to frame it but then he lost it; he looked everywhere, he was frantic. Then he realized it could've gotten mixed up with some magazines that he had taken to a recycling bin—he went to the bin, which was full of sticky crap and swarmed by bees, and he spent at least an hour looking for the picture. He didn't find it. But now, a month later, he had discovered it under another pile of papers. He was happy and relieved and he wanted me to know. I don't remember how I reacted. I remember that the tone of his words was the same to me as if he had called to once again announce that he was going to kill himself, or to try to persuade me to talk our mother into coming back to him, or to tell me that having children had ruined his life, or to rage about the noise a neighbor was making.

The family myth was that our father was crazy, compulsive, obsessed with things like bargains on toilet paper or coupons. And he was. It was hard to hear feeling in his words because his voice and his words were habitually agitated, obsessed, so tight that the feeling of them was lost.

After he died I found the drawing he was talking about. It was framed and hanging on his wall; I must've seen it before when I'd come to visit. But I had not registered it. My feelings had become as lost as his had been. I sat with the picture and cried.

At the end of Caesar's last visit, we drove him back to the city. While I thought he was asleep in the backseat, I had a conversation with Peter about human love, how perverted and cruel it can be on one hand, how bluntly, functionally biological on the other. Flippantly, I said, "Maybe it actually doesn't even exist." Right after I said that, a stuffed animal bounced off my head and into my lap; it was a smiling little cow that Caesar had won for me at the county fair the previous day. "What do you call that?" he asked. I laughed and thanked him.

Love as a cheap stuffed toy bounced off your head—it's a brilliant metaphor and a true one. But the metaphor for love that I feel more deeply is a lost, hungry little animal dying as it tries to find its way back home in the cold. It isn't truer. But I feel it more.

Maybe, though, it is wrong to put the weight of such a metaphor onto the memory of something so small and light as a kitten. Maybe it was wrong to chase my father through his house, shouting about "a real relationship"; maybe it is even worse to keep analyzing and questioning what his experience was and what it meant, in public no less. It was certainly wrong to use people to repeatedly replay this drama, whether they willingly participated or not, whether I knew what I was doing or not. It may be wrong to feel like I have lost Caesar and Natalia because they aren't doing what I want them to do. It's also possible that if they choose to hurt themselves by deliberately failing and rejecting much of what I can give them, I *should* lose them; I'm not sure.

I once read a Chekhov story that described a minor character as "trying to snatch from life more than it can give"; maybe I have turned into such a person, unable to accept what is given, always trying to tear things up in order to find what is "real," even when I don't know what "real" is, unable to maintain the respect, the dignity of not asking too much or even looking too closely at the workings of the heart, which, no matter how you look, can never be fully seen or understood.

The thought makes me look down in self-reproach. Then I think, But life can give a lot. If you can't see inside the heart no matter how you look, then why not look? Why not see as much as you can? How is that disrespectful? If you are only given one look, shouldn't you look as fully as you can? A lost cat would not ask itself if food and shelter were too much to expect, or try to figure out how much food and shelter were enough or who was the right person to give those things. It would just keep trying to get those things until the moment it died.

During the time I was beginning to lose hope of finding Gattino, I went to Montana to do a reading at a university there. My hotel room overlooked a river, and one day as I was staring out the window, some people with a dog came walking along the riverbank. The dog got excited, and his owner let him off his chain. He went running and made a wild leap into the water, his legs splayed ecstatically wide. I smiled and thought, Gattino; for once, the thought was comforting, not sad. I thought, Even if he is dead, he's still here in that splayed, ecstatic leap.

This idea was no doubt an illusion, a self-deception. But that dog was not. That dog was real. And so was Gattino.

Granta, 2009

I SEE THEIR HOLLOWNESS

A REVIEW OF *COCKROACH* BY RAWI HAGE

"We are all outlaws in the eyes of America / In order to survive we steal cheat lie forge fuck hide and deal . . ." The Jeffer-
son Airplane wrote these cheerfully absurd words for "We Can
Be Together," their 1969 anthem for a largely middle-class teenage audience playing at being revolutionaries; the lyrics would
be a fitting epigraph for Rawi Hage's second novel, *Cockroach*.
Hage is a highly esteemed forty-five-year-old Beirut-born writer
now living in Montreal. His first book, *De Niro's Game,* won the
2008 IMPAC Dublin Literary Award given for the best English-
language book published anywhere in the world. *Cockroach* was
a finalist for the Governor General's Award and other Canadian
prizes. Yet the Airplane anthem of teenage "revolution" is the
perfect sound track for it.

Cockroach is so titled because the narrator, a morally correct
thief who targets hypocrites and the undeserving rich, is able to
turn into a bug when he needs to gain entry, sparing the thief
(and the writer) the technical difficulties of, for example, getting
into the backseat of a car in plain sight of its rotten bourgeois
owners. He has survived war and domestic violence in his home
country, including the murder of his sister; he is in love with a
beautiful, high-spirited Iranian woman named Shoreh, who loves
sex but has no interest in being anyone's girlfriend; he becomes
entangled in a revenge plot against a onetime secret policeman

who raped and tortured her in Iran. When we meet him in his therapist's office, we learn that he has just tried to commit suicide.

This dramatic material, however, is not dramatically realized. Most of it develops as told to the narrator's unbelievably stupid and credulous therapist in language like this: "I had attempted suicide out of a kind of curiosity, or maybe as a challenge to nature, to the cosmos itself, to the recurring light. I felt oppressed by it all. The question of existence consumed me." It is hard to take such language seriously, and indeed the character stops being suicidal after the first few pages. The story of past suffering and revenge is jumbled together quickly and with a strange lack of emotional weight; most of the narrator's energy goes into descriptions of various petty thefts and petty conversations, "existential" thoughts ("what really fascinates me is the bits of soap foam floating down the drain, swirling and disappearing. Little things like that make me think") and contempt for the loathsome phonies around him. This means pretty much everyone, except for Shoreh and a few of her friends. It *especially* means anyone who is French, or who has French affectations; a line of French dialogue or a mention that a character is eating French food is a signal to the reader that said character is a complete pig.

It is possible, of course, to tell a dramatic story mainly through flashbacks, in the form of thoughts about what has happened rather than what happens. But to do this effectively, a writer has to be a master stylist, and Hage's style here is mannered, preening, and clumsy: "I peeled myself out from under layers of hats, gloves, and scarves, liberated myself from zippers and buttons, endured the painful tearing Velcro that hissed like a prehistoric reptile, that split and separated like people's lives, like exiles falling into cracks that give birth and lead to death under digging shovels that sound just like the friction of car wheels wedging snow around my mortal parts."

It is also possible—and sometimes a lot of fun—to have a central character who loathes everyone around him. But the loathing eye is most effective when it sees precisely the unique and baroquely mixed quality of a character's evil, the worm safely nesting in the beautifully built personality—especially when the voice that accompanies the eye inadvertently reveals its own secret worm.

Such revelation may be what Hage intends, but his negative characterizations are broad clichés, much too easy and too flattering to the narrator and the reader. He spends pages describing a brainless French Canadian woman he took monetary advantage of, along with her uniformly brainless friends, whom he easily seduces (they are automatically thrilled to be screwing an "exotic"), then robs them during dinner at a French restaurant, which thrills them even more, especially their boyfriends, who are excited to be in the company of a "noble savage." He goes on to describe how these disgusting decadents use drugs, wave guns around to impress him, and eat their own shit out of boredom, concluding in all seriousness: "I see people for what they are. I strip them of everything and see their hollowness."

These portrayals are laughably inept, and strangely so considering that when he wants to, Hage can actually write. *De Niro's Game,* despite its silly title, had depth, passion, and emotional nuance; you believed the characters and cared about what happened to them. At a French book fair (!) I heard Hage read a passage from it that struck me as extraordinary: It was about a petty criminal being tortured by a militia goon who nearly drowns him again and again. As the criminal comes to expect and accept death, he thinks lovingly of how his mother used to smoke while she stole water from a neighbor's reservoir. The scene has power not only because of the subject but because of the art with which it is told.

At its best, *Cockroach* has moments that recall, albeit dimly, the power of this scene. Its best quality however, is a sort of whimsical, earthy charm. When the narrator breaks into people's homes, he rarely does more than raid the fridge, sleep in their bed, and watch TV; he's prone to pranks like turning the classical station to hard rock and cranking the volume. Some of the cockroachian imagery is funny and sharp. He admires the gallantry of bar waitresses; his sexual devotion to Shoreh and her bodily fluids is playful and erotic. Shoreh is a potentially great character, made tragic by her degraded past, but also fiercely up for a good time, sexy clothes, and good food. The portrayal is vivacious but finally shallow; we don't fully feel the depth of her tragedy or the greatness of her spirit. This is not for lack of trying—Hage clearly means to honor her—but his language is too hackneyed to create the kind of portrait she deserves.

Having read both of Hage's books, I see his talent. However, I wonder at how extravagantly he's been praised, and at how fast he's been elevated to the status of an internationally important author. One of the people Hage's cockroach looks down on is a fellow immigrant, a musician who manipulates the naïve sympathies of well-meaning Canadian women with his stories of hardship and oppression by religious fundamentalists: "Gullible heads would nod, compassionate eyes would open, blankets would be extended on sofas and beds, fridges would burp leftovers, and if the rooster was lucky, it would all lead to chicken thighs and wings moistened by a touch of beer or wine." Yet the cockroach happily does the same, describing himself as "the fuckable, exotic, dangerous foreigner" who gives Canadian fools "a sense of the real." I doubt he intends it, but this could be Hage talking about some of his adoring critics; if so, contempt would be the proper response. To overpraise is a subtle form of disrespect—and everybody knows it.

I don't mean to suggest that everyone who has responded to Hage's work has done so insincerely. But when I see *Cockroach* being compared in papers of note to Dostoevsky, Kafka, Genet, Rimbaud, and Burroughs, it is hard for me to imagine who believes that. In making such overblown comparisons, these "admiring" critics have respected Rawi Hage far less than I have.

The New York Times Book Review, 2009

LIVES OF THE HAGS

A REVIEW OF *BABA YAGA LAID AN EGG*
BY DUBRAVKA UGRESIC

Baba Yaga Laid an Egg, by Dubravka Ugresic, is on the simplest story level about the adventures of four old hags, plus their families and friends, adventures seen through the palimpsest of Baba Yaga, ur-witch, "evil, horror, nightmare"—in other words, the greatest hag of 'em all. I don't use the word *hag* impudently here. The author not only invites the term; in this book, she *owns* it.

Ugresic starts out warning readers about the omnipresent armies of creepy old ladies who "roll by you like heaps of dried apples," ride mass transit like "abandoned luggage," heads all bumpy and bulldoggy, skin hanging "like a turkey's wattle." Don't exchange more than a few words with them, warns the author, because if you do, you will enter their terrible world, and "your time has not yet come, your hour, for God's sake, has not come." Yet she ends with a passionate evocation of mysterious old-lady majesty and mojo, ardently willing that it may one day find its rightful worldly place. In the context of the novel, these points of view are prismatic rather than oppositional.

The book comes in three parts, starting with a mundane story about a difficult mother-daughter relationship that, as it continues, hints at something eerie hidden in the folds of its plain skirt. The story is located in Zagreb, which, we learn from the daughter (who is the narrator and happens to be an author), is suffering a plague of birds gone wild, taking over parks, subway stations, and restaurants, where they snatch food from people's hands and "strut brazenly" on tables. This invasion coincides with the mother's mind gone wild from cancer of the breast spread to the brain, resulting in scrambled language (when a doctor asks her name, she replies "vacuum cleaner"), compensatory rigidity, and territorial wars with her daughter over cupboards, pictures, food, and clothes. Then there are the usual indignities—incontinence, lost beauty, and social invisibility.

Wanting to help, the daughter makes a trip to her mother's childhood home in Croatia, in order to take photographs so that Mom might have one more look at the place. Here she meets a weird and annoying young Bulgarian woman anagrammatically named Aba Bagay, a folklorist and overenthusiastic fan of the author's books who has also managed to insert herself into the mother's affections. Although Bagay is supposedly there to visit friends, she follows the author everywhere, staying in hotel rooms with her, quoting her books, even ordering the same food at restaurants; the narrator seethes inside, but outwardly complies, seemingly out of unclear obligation and guilt.

This minor, muddy, and vaguely awful encounter culminates in a tale told by the folklorist, called "The Tsar-Maiden," in which a young man must journey across the sea to find a girl's heart in a four-times hidden egg, which he then must trick the girl into eating. The narrator is charmed by the story, but she soon sees in the tone of its telling a "hunger for attention; a blind hunger which sought to be led by the blind; a crippled hunger which sought an ally in the crippled, the hunger of a deaf mute cooing to a deaf mute." The girl is desperate for attachment and approval, and that makes her an emotional tar baby for the author, who thinks, with a kind of despair, "Yes, love is on the distant shore of a wide sea. A large oak tree stands there, and in the tree there is a box, in the box a rabbit, in the rabbit a duck, and in the duck an egg.

And the egg, in order to get the emotional mechanism going, had to be eaten."

At this point, in the mood for some more dramatic evil or nightmare, I skipped ahead, looking for Baba Yaga. I found her in the third section, where instead of wreaking havoc, she was serving as a subject for the annoying Aba Bagay, who somehow got the job of providing a study guide for Ugresic's book! I rolled my eyes at this piece of clumsy cleverness and then got so engaged by it, I couldn't stop reading.

Baba Yaga, Slavic yet international, is a hideous old woman with a skeleton leg who eats kids and flies around in a giant mortar, or hypertrophied pussy. She lives in a hut atop live chicken legs, which is made of human bones and surrounded by skulls on fence posts. The door latch is made of human hands; the lock is a mouth with sharp teeth. It's an abode that's also a body, human and animal, dead and alive. Inside lurks Baba, "her nose touching the ceiling, her slobber seeping over the doorstep . . . she tosses her breasts onto the oven or hangs them 'over a pole,' or even 'shuts the oven door with her breasts,' while snot trails out of her nose and she 'scoops up soot with her tongue.' "

Sometimes she has a daughter, sometimes actually forty of them, and sometimes she eats them—sometimes by mistake, sometimes not. In one account, she drinks too much seawater after gobbling flour and salt, then bursts and gives "violent birth to frogs, mice, snakes, worms and spiders." She is the "aunt of all witches," a villain, avenger, sentry between worlds, donor, adviser, and, if you play your cards right, of great help. She is unpredictable and amoral. She is associated with time and weather. She has hordes of lesser sisters who eat hearts, who knead dough with their breasts, who shape-shift, who come back from the dead to give suck to their babies. She has a special relationship with birds, which Ugresic calls "symbolic postmen" between heaven and earth. Like birds, Baba may produce and traffic in eggs, and her eggs are magic. She is obscene but rarely sexual; in the spirit of Baba Yaga, "old women in southern Serbia" run naked around their family homes during storms, shouting, "Don't you dragon, / fight my monster, / it's devoured lots like you! / Flee you monster, from my monster! / They can't both be master here."

And so, with heightened interest, I flipped back to the second section, which opens with three much more genteel hags from Zagreb checking in at an expensive spa in Czechoslovakia for a vacation together. They are Beba, a former nurse with exhausted blond hair and monster breasts, who nervously quotes entire poems she has never learned, and mixes phrases—for example, "See you, die!" instead of "Good-bye"; Kukla, a tall, elegant, elderly virgin widowed multiple times; Pupa, an ancient, acerbic gynecologist who resembles a "piece of crackling" and who must be wheeled about by her friends because both her deformed legs are perpetually wedged into a giant boot.

There are several colorful bit players: a kindhearted old playboy; a crass American with a dumb, sexy daughter; a longevity salesman named Dr. Topolanek ("Dr. Bullshit" to the hags); and Mevludin, a beautiful young man whose giant dick is permanently erect yet insensate due to an explosion during the siege of Sarajevo. There is colorful action bordering on the zany: Beba goes to the spa casino and wins thousands without realizing what's happened (incidentally defeating a mobster who called her "hippopotamus tits"); Kukla turns out to be the anonymous and completely indifferent author of an acclaimed book; Pupa flies home in a gigantic wooden egg, decorated to look like "the garden of Eden painted by an amateur." There are huge surprises from the past, last-minute revelations, and unexpected bounty. If the first section was rather gray, the second is drenched in Technicolor, and because I skipped ahead, Baba Yaga's leering face peered through it all, giving depth and weight to what otherwise might've been a too-kooky, too-cute tale insistently peppered with rhymes like "While life gets tangled in the human game, the tale hastens to reach its aim!" The book is ridiculously overladen with eggs and birds, the mystical meaning of which Aba Bagay belabors to pieces—even Baba Yaga can't take the tedium out of that.

Yet, the book is affecting and eloquent, in part because running alongside the quirky, aggressively sweet plot are moments of depth and the stoicism it brings: These hags are also gallant women who have survived wars, displacement, death, estrangement from their families, and political brutality on an epic scale. Some *have* devoured their children emotionally; some have magically benefited men who beat them.

Truthfully, I'm not even sure that in the context of *Baba Yaga Laid an Egg* Ugresic's lapses in literary taste are lapses at all. For Baba Yaga's hut seems to be, among other things, a place of slippage and in-betweenness, where life lives in death, beauty nests inside pestilence, and mothers suck their daughter's breasts. In such a place, kitsch and cuteness are on equal speaking terms with refinement, intellect, and all manner of suffering and joy; Ugresic moves freely from one state to the other.

At the very end of the book, Ugresic—or that pesky Aba Bagay—tries to turn Baba Yaga into a feminist symbol, a sword-wielding matriarch ready to avenge centuries of brutality against women. I understand the impulse, but it is pure Hollywood. As Ugresic describes Baba Yaga, she is neither good nor evil; she is raw primal force paradoxically housed in a decaying body. She is a mythic version of what any old woman is: a sacred meeting place of life and death. Only a fool would fail to have reverence for this place; only a fool would fail to be afraid of and repelled by it. Most of us feel both—and what a weight for an old lady to bear, along with everything else. What strange powerless power, this involuntary embodiment of root forces, this wisdom so often beyond the strength of the body or the mind to express. Such power does not make itself felt through a sword, but through the soul. And not every soul is receptive to it.

While I was reading the book, I had an e-mail conversation with a friend, who compared Baba Yaga to "another angry goddess," the fierce Tantric Kali. "Kali isn't angry," I wrote back. "She's just doing her job. Baba Yaga isn't angry, either. She is just being herself. Yes, she may or may not eat children, some of whom happen to be her relations. But not because she's angry. Just hungry, at the time."

Bookforum, 2009

LEAVE THE WOMAN ALONE!

ON THE NEVER-ENDING POLITICAL
EXTRAMARITAL SCANDALS

When the Eliot Spitzer scandal erupted a year and a half ago, I found myself more than usually irritated at the lavish sympathy directed at Silda Spitzer, who was presumed to be deeply humiliated by people who had no way of knowing what she was feeling; this sympathy was *so* lavish that at times it bore a striking resemblance to gloating. It was the way Hillary Clinton was talked about (though the gloating was more up front in that case) and the way Elizabeth Edwards would be talked about, at least until her book *Resilience* came out, when with quite remarkable speed that outsize sympathy turned to outsize contempt—suggesting to me that it had been contempt all along.

Indeed, the way Elizabeth Edwards was attacked was extraordinary; the attacks included everything from accusing Edwards of conspiring with her wicked husband to mislead the public to her attitude toward his mistress, culminating in a magnificently nasty piece written by Kathleen Parker for the online publication *The Daily Beast*, in which she remarked that "wise women know that the world's Elizabeths owe the world's Hunters a thank-you note." In the wildly vituperative context of Parker's essay, the comment was almost a non sequitur, and message-board commenters could make no sense of it. On the face of it, I think Parker flippantly meant to say that women married to cads ought to be thankful to the single predators out there for taking the worthless bastards off their hands—but on a more murky visceral level, it felt like a particularly hard slap in Elizabeth's face: As the "good woman," she was actually being instructed to thank the "bad woman," who traditionally would be pilloried in the public square while the wife looked on with satisfaction. In this case, not only was the mistress getting a free pass—I saw nothing criticizing Rielle Hunter—but for God's sake, the damn *wife* was in the stocks. As I read Parker's screed, along with dozens like it, I asked myself, What is going on here?

Perhaps it should be obvious: Adultery is a social threat that arouses raw anger and fear, which the bellicose then need to discharge rather than merely feel, traditionally most savagely on the adulteress or the home-wrecker. Monogamy is the religiously undergirded ideal for nearly every culture on the planet (even polygamous cultures expect monogamy from women), and yet for centuries, men were unfaithful and tolerated as such, as long as they kept it quiet, and respected their wives, as opposed to the mistresses or prostitutes they dallied with. It is a good thing, or at least a fair thing, in modern life that fidelity is expected on both sides. It is good, too, or at least realistic, that sexually independent women have been given a degree of acceptance in the form of playfully sexual pop icons, respect for unmarried single moms, and acknowledgment of women's sexual feelings in portrayals such as those in, say, *Sex and the City*.

But fair and realistic can also be confusing. If men are expected to be monogamous, too (even if it seems they still are less likely to be), that means everybody has to be good all the time, and that is hard, especially in a floridly sexual and permissive climate. Monogamy is desirable for many reasons, especially in terms of creating a stable, emotionally connected home for children. But judging from centuries of human behavior, it is also a very difficult standard to meet. Women seem to be more inclined to it than men, but I doubt that is because we are more moral. I think it is because if women have children, their erotic/emotional energy is very taken up by that in a way that men's traditionally is not. And it seems to me that morality is not always the issue. Or rather, that total fidelity can come with a moral price tag of its own.

What is faithfulness anyway? Can you be unfaithful to your own feelings and be faithful to someone else? Is it faithful to lie in bed night after night with someone you love but no longer desire, while ardently dreaming of someone else? Is it faithful to make love to your wife while lewdly fantasizing about someone else again and again? Is it faithful to be monogamous if that means deadening your own nature, constantly, in order to be genitally true to someone you may love but no longer have physical passion for? For two people to satisfy everything each needs for their entire lives is a tall order. Some couples may be equipped to do this. Some are not.

In *The Marriage of Heaven and Hell*, the poet William Blake said, "Sooner murder an infant in its cradle than nurse unacted desires." Maybe he meant, Don't nurse it, kick it to the curb! But given the poem's joyous mash-up of hellish and holy, it seems more likely that Blake meant to honor desire and its many forms of expression; whatever he meant in terms of action, the line speaks eloquently of the tension between the pure quality of desire and the forces of propriety that would contain it.

And how great that tension when you live in a society where well-bred teenagers with words like *juicy* written in pink script across their butts drive around in the car Daddy bought them, with PORN STAR stamped on their license plates, with Lady Gaga on the radio singing about "bluffin' with my muffin." In other words, a society that is sexually hyperstimulated all the time, yet fiercely values monogamy and fidelity in marriage. Adultery causes heartbreak—and yet men and women do it every day because they feel it would break their spirit not to. It's a problem, and everybody knows it. That is why Anna Karenina and Madame Bovary are great heroines, and why adultery is a soap opera staple. That is also why adultery in high-profile people, especially elected officials whose job it supposedly is to be good all the time, brings out an especially nasty asexual desire—that is, the desire to stone someone in the public square, or to at least pillory their hypocritical ass.

This desire is acted out on adulterers most vigorously: Eliot Spitzer lost his job and his honor, and Mark Sanford is in danger of losing both; Bill Clinton, an exception all his life, barely squeaked by with both sort of intact, even if he was impeached. The much-despised John Edwards will never make a successful run for higher office. "Cad," "heel," "hypocrite," and "narcissist" were some of the nicer things said about these men in papers of note; limitless and merciless scorn was heaped upon them via the Internet, where it was suggested by an anonymous poster that Edwards ought to be "hung up by his mistress's favorite part of him."

I feel an impulse to defend these men on the perhaps lax grounds that none of us know why they acted as they did, what their personal circumstances really are, or what anguish they experienced—it's hard for me to imagine they experienced none. Their crimes were ordinary crimes of the heart, which many everyday people commit without being subject to such punishment. Their hypocrisy is practically a job requirement, which we, in our hypocrisy, demand of them.

And yet my impulse to defend them is tempered by the above-mentioned obvious: They broke a centuries-old moral code and in some cases used taxpayers' money to do it. If one wants to do that, one must be prepared to take the consequences, including vicious public scorn. But why have their wives been punished, too? Think of it: Would you want to be described, in print, over and over again, as "humiliated" by people—strangers, actually—who are supposedly taking your side? Even Jenny Sanford, who didn't attend her husband's press conference confession, and who read to me as more pissed off than shamed, was criticized by Tina Brown for failing to "rip off her burqa and revolt on behalf of all the other downtrodden political wives called to genuflect before their husband's outsize egos." In other words, I guess, because she didn't chase Mr. Sanford down the street with a rolling pin.

What is humiliation, exactly? People often use the word as if it is merely a particularly potent form of embarrassment, but to me it is something more extreme. By it, I mean that a person's image of him- or herself has been debased, not only before others but in his or her own heart. The first dictionary definition is perhaps less dire: the loss of pride, self-respect, or dignity. These words in their most authentic sense refer more to internal states than to how one is seen by others. Using any of these definitions, is it right to *automatically* describe the wives of adulterers as humiliated? Why? The wrongful act was committed by their husbands, not them. Why must they be said to have lost pride or self-respect because of the actions of someone close to them? It isn't surprising if they are embarrassed; anyone might feel that way about the kind of scrutiny they have been subjected to. But why should we announce that a woman has lost her dignity because her husband slept with someone else? Shouldn't she be the judge of that? Or do we actually believe that her dignity is entirely dependent on how men or even one man relates to her? Is she "humiliated" because she has failed to be all things to her husband, all the time, in perpetuity, at least as far as he is concerned—in other words, because she has failed to do the impossible? (Or simply because she has failed to be beautiful enough; America Online posted a picture of Tiger Woods's gorgeous blond wife with the caption "Who would cheat on *her*?"—a piece of stupidity that needs no comment.) It seems a curious form of emotional brutality to insist that a person must feel a certain way and then to repeatedly define her that way in public—if everyone is insisting that you are humiliated, how much harder to know what you actually feel.

Elizabeth Edwards was, of course, subjected to worse than this punitive definition: The real outrage came when she published her book—that is, when she tried to define herself. The anger was supposedly because (1) Mrs. Edwards had supported her husband's run for the presidency even though she knew about the affair; (2) she said that, aside from the affair, she had a "perfect marriage"; (3) she was "cashing in" on the whole thing. But it seems to me that, like any loyal and ambitious wife, she'd been pointed at her husband's goal for decades and that it would've been hard to change direction with any speed, especially if she was feeling exhausted from living with a deadly illness. Yes, "the perfect marriage" sounds ridiculous—but doesn't anyone recognize in it a sort of stunned gallantry? Can anyone really think she needs the money all that badly? I believe her real motive for writing the book and speaking about it was to show the world and her children that her misfortune had *not* defined her. Of course, the more you say that *whatever* doesn't define you, the more it does. But can she be blamed for trying?

It is necessary to remember in all this that the cuckold has also been a traditional object of snickering sympathy—unless he does the "manly" thing and physically punishes his wife, possibly by murdering her, which is sanctioned by law in some countries. I wonder if we will ever see a high-profile female adulterer in politics, and if so, how *that* would be dealt with in the public square. I imagine that while the tenor of it would be different, the husbands, too, would be endlessly described as "humiliated" and that instead of committing murder, they, too, would content themselves with writing books. But do they *have* to be described that way? Who made this a rule of the game? Do all of us have to play by it, all the time? What is in it for us?

There *is* such a thing as humiliation through sexual betrayal, of course, and I don't mean to pretend otherwise. When passion is alive and joined with love, it is the closest thing to sacred on earth, whether it takes place in marriage or not. When one lover loses this passion, it feels shocking and belittling to the one still engaged. And yet . . . I can't prove it, but it seems to me that most of the time in marriage when one partner loses that passionate engagement, it's mutual, or quickly becomes that way. Sexual passion of the kind I have just described is short-lived by nature. Phrases like "You have to work to keep it going" are commonplace now. But while passion may reignite, it seems to do so on its own terms; it doesn't come when you call. Even more difficult: Certain kinds of passion don't flourish in the dailiness of domestic life, but depend on mystery, illusion, and risk. Passion is sometimes completely incompatible with politeness or dignity in the normal *social* sense of the words.

This kind of passion may be called immoral or immature, but passion doesn't care—it doesn't come *where* you call it, either. And if it doesn't, how can it be surprising if, after years or decades of its absence, one spouse, longing to feel that powerful life force again, not only gets interested in someone else but gives him- or herself over to it? The danger is anguish for everyone involved, and morality exists in part as protection against that kind of pain. However, there is such a thing as being so protected that your life begins to feel lifeless and rote.

Maybe we are so eager to seize on public figures who have been caught "cheating" and hold them up for outraged examination because we are secretly hoping for some kind of insight as to how we might avoid their fate. But the emotional truth of what they've done and why they've done it can't be said in the crude language of public discourse—language like "If you take out this piece . . . I have a perfect marriage." Language like that is suitable for the public world of politics, not for what goes on between married people during the intimate, vulnerable realities of adultery and its aftermath—one possible reality being that working through the infidelity and the reasons it happened may bring them closer. Or not. In any case, they have to figure it out in their own way just as we do, in private. No matter how many interviews we read or see, how many pictures or videos, how many tell-alls get written, we will never see into the private circumstances of the Edwardses, the Sanfords, or the Spitzers, nor should we. We have enough to do trying to understand and know ourselves, if we could only stop bellowing about other people long enough to try.

And if we can't stop bellowing about the adulterers, can we at least maybe lay off their wives?

Elle, 2010

MASTER'S MIND

A REVIEW OF *AGAAT* BY MARLENE VAN NIEKERK

Agaat is the second novel and fifth book by South African writer Marlene van Niekerk; it is a stunning work. Set in the apartheid era of the 1950s through the 1970s, on a dairy farm contentiously run by a desperately unhappy white couple and their half-adopted, half-enslaved colored maid Agaat, it is about institutional racial violence, intimate domestic violence, human violence against the natural world, pride, folly, self-deception, and the innately mixed, sometimes debased, nature of human love. It is especially about how this mixed nature is expressed through the deep and complex language of the body; I don't believe I've ever seen a book that so powerfully translates this physical language into the form of printed words.

Agaat is narrated almost entirely by Milla de Wet, a strong-minded, verbally sophisticated, emotionally bereft Afrikaans woman paralyzed in old age by a motor-neuron disease, unable to communicate except with her eyes, and only then to her caregiver Agaat, with whom she has an anguished and loving bond, and who cares for her on an all-too-intimate level—for example, cleaning out her mouth:

> Say "ah" for doctor, says Agaat. I close my eyes. What have I done wrong? The little mole hand nuzzles out my tongue. The screw has squashed it in my mouth. . . . My

tongue is being staked out for its turn at ablution. The sponge is rough. With vigorous strokes my tongue is scrubbed down. It tastes powerfully of peppermint. Three times the sponge is recharged before Agaat is satisfied. My tongue feels eradicated. . . .

Then:

Her fingers move more gently, more kindly on my gums. Then it becomes caressing. Forgive me, ask the fingers, I also have a hard time with you, you know.

And then:

More passionate the movement becomes. Agaat curses me in the mouth with her thumb and index finger. Bugger you! I feel against my palate, bugger you and your mother. . . . She takes her hand from my mouth. . . . She wipes my face, the tears from my cheeks. Thank you, I signal briefly. You're welcome, says Agaat.

The relationship is loaded not only because it is mutually dependent and (at least socially) unequal but also because Milla has, as a charity project, rescued Agaat from a violently abusive family and nurtured her with methods both harsh and kind: Against the scornful judgments of her husband and everyone else, Milla falls in love with the child, whom she raises as a daughter. But there is simply no place in the world of apartheid for such a relationship to exist, a reality that Milla finally cedes to by gradually teaching her beloved girl her "place"—that is, reducing her to a kind of privileged servant. When Milla gets pregnant, she ruthlessly cuts Agaat out of her heart (or tries), all the while believing that her behavior is noble.

Agaat's servitude is made complete by her own instinct for love, and when Milla compels her, at the age of twelve, to deliver the new baby when they can't make it to Milla's family in time, we feel this servitude being driven into her core—and paradoxically joined with what will become her power over Milla, particularly Milla's body:

You talked fast, emphasised the main points. Water. Breath. Push. Head. Out. Blood. Slippery. Careful. Slap. Yowl. Bind. Cut. Wrap. Bring to. Wash. Hitch-hike. That was the easy scenario. If the little head can't get out, she has to take the scissors and cut, you said, to the back, do you understand? towards the shitter, she had to cut through the meat of your arse, so that he can get out. Saw if necessary, she mustn't spare you. If he's blue, she has to clean his nose and wipe out his drool, out from the back of his throat and from his tongue and blow breath into him over his nose and mouth until he makes a sound. As we do with the calves when they're struggling. She can leave you, you said, even if you're bleeding something terrible, it doesn't matter. And that again is different from the cows, you said.

These instructions to a young girl who has been so severely raped before her "white stepmother" found her that she can't have her own child.

But it is also Agaat's instinct for love that allows her not only to survive but to enact a revenge that is equal parts tenderness and rage, and that is as lifelong, exacting, and daily as her servitude—the emotional theft of Milla's only son, Jakkie, who grows to love Agaat more than his brutal father or convoluted mother.

Then there is a more subtle revenge, subtle because it comes about accidentally and in part out of a simple desire to understand and communicate: While Milla lies paralyzed and dying, Agaat finds and begins to read aloud the diaries that her foster mother/mistress kept largely to chronicle what she thinks of as "the covenant" between herself and the abused girl whom she sought to "make human." Milla cringes to hear her "unconsidered writing" forced "down [her] gullet," and with reason: She is thus made to confront the self-flattery, dishonesty, and heartlessness to which she was able to blind herself when young, and which she is now too broken to deny. She is so overcome with shame that she fails to see that the diaries also reveal a good, even ardent woman warped by a twisted society, a cold family, and an abusive marriage, a woman whose impulses toward love are simply no match for the internalized pathology of her environment.

That Agaat *does* see only makes it worse for her. For it is difficult to say which is more terrible, that Milla's love is warped by her enmeshment in the social system around her, or that it is on a private level true and pure, especially during the time that she is first earning the little girl's trust:

Then I bent down and whispered in her ear. What did I say to her? I'm so hungry, I'm so thirsty, I said, because you don't want to talk to me and I know you can talk. . . . Perhaps you can say your new name for me? I blinked with my eyes to ask, big please! Why is it taking me so long to write it up? I'd rather just think about it again and again. It's too precious! Too fine! Words spoil it. Who could understand? . . . I imagined the tip of her will as the rolled-up tip of a fern. Did I say it out loud? That she should also imagine it? A tender green ringlet with little folded-in fingers? I bent it open with my attention. Then it came into my ear, like the rushing of my own blood, against the deep end of the roof of her mouth, a

gentle guttural-fricative, the sound of a shell against my
ear, the g-g-g of Agaat. . . . Then we said her name at the
same time. Sweet, full in my mouth, like a mouthful of
something heavenly. Lord my God, the child You have
given me.

Yet it is this child whom she will later describe as a "little snot
skivvy," whom she will as a matter of course betray to the cruelty of white outsiders, whom she will humiliate both deliberately and indifferently, and at least once physically punish to the
extent that even her viciously racist husband remarks that he's
sick of being an "extra in [her] concentration camp movie." This
behavior is especially grotesque because of the extreme social
circumstances that shape it. But far from being exclusive to South
Africa or anyplace else, it is all too recognizable as the way human
beings treat each other in every context imaginable.

At the book's end, we finally get out of Milla's tortured head
and hear from her son, Jakkie, now grown and living in Canada,
in a state of "mourning [as] a life-long occupation." As close as
he once was to Agaat, he has come to see her as an "Apartheid
Cyborg. Assembled from loose components plus audiotape,"
ruined as his parents have been by his country's inhuman system.
After the intense emotionality of his mother's narrative, this cold,
sorrowing assessment is welcome. Yet . . . he calls this "cyborg"
his "brown mother," and it is through him that we finally hear
Agaat's voice telling him the secret story she told every night, the
story Milla was never allowed to hear.

In revealing this much of the plot, I am scarcely giving away
the story, because it is the telling of this story that makes it
extraordinary, and because there is so much else going on that
I simply do not have space to cover. But this terrible entwining
of deep feeling and its total lack—the tension between the will

to cruelty and the will to love, between the social machine and the small beings that must live within its strictures—cycles relentlessly through the story, taking us to a more devastating place of understanding with each turn. In *Agaat*, each dichotomy—love, cruelty, purity, shame, betrayal, fidelity, goodness, and brute political will—is equally and tragically real.

Bookforum, 2010

IMAGINARY LIGHT

A SONG CALLED "NOWHERE GIRL"

I don't know why this song touched me. I heard it at a small Manhattan club in 1981; it came tingling through the crowded dark and lightly touched me with an indefinable feeling that was intense almost *because* it was so light—and then disappeared into whatever song followed. It was in no way the best song I heard during that time; it did not "save me." I did not even go out and buy it, though if I'd been able to afford anything to play it on, I might've. *Might've.* I am not a fan by nature, and it was a slight, slightly ridiculous song. But it touched me in a way I could not quite forget. I heard it randomly maybe three more times; I didn't go out that much, and apparently it wasn't hugely popular. But each time I heard it, it touched me in that peculiarly light and emotional way, with the quality of something small that is trying to get your attention, though unconfidently, from somewhere off in a corner. Or from nowhere.

"Nowhere girl in self-imposed exile / Nowhere girl a martyr-like denial." Part of what touched me was the word *nowhere,* and the idea of someone living there, a picture of mysteriously seductive loneliness, a delicate and melancholy thing expressed in manic synthpop. (Maybe it unconsciously reminded me of a fantasy story I'd written when I was fifteen, in which some space-traveling teenagers come across a beautiful woman confined in a transparent false world that moves fluidly with her movements, in which she lives a hallucinatory nonlife, unaware of "real world" people who can watch her delusional existence but who cannot help her.) "Nowhere girl, you've never gone outside / Nowhere girl cause you prefer to hide / Every day, every night / In that old familiar light": The words *every day* and *light* activated this phrase, and, put together with the music, made multiple pictures that blended and flashed through me. Everyday light: light in a basement, streetlight, club light, imaginary light; something as mundane as a lamp and as sinister as the glow of a hypnotizing dream that the girl has become lost in, yet which is at the same time the only thing keeping her alive. The music evokes delight, longing, urgent melancholy, and fun: "And I try to get through / And I try to talk to you / But there's something stopping me from getting through." The sincere, slightly exasperated, actually pretty happy voice is that of a guy in cheap, fashionable clothes that look good as long as it's dark; he's no prince, and he's more bemused than ardent—still, the song has the enchanted feeling of Sleeping Beauty, though in this case the enchantment will not break.

So much association and imagery is a lot of weight to put on such a small song, and I didn't think any of that at the time, I just felt it sort of speeding past. But the wistful sound that translated as a kind of emotional touch entered my system with all of that somehow encoded, and it bloomed in my subconscious imagination like the artificial seashell somebody gave me when I was a kid, which, when dropped into a glass of water, opened and bloomed into an elaborate flower.

This is a quality that many, maybe all, good pop songs have, this deceptively light ability to touch and awaken multiple associations that blend with the wordless, innocent, and completely nonhierarchical sense of dreams. (For someone else's fantastically rendered dream of this song, in a more tarted-up and sentimental version than the one I first heard, see the video posted by somebody called "davidapa" on YouTube; it's a beautiful mash-up with the mad scientist scene in Fritz Lang's *Metropolis,* in which the theme of awakening is demonically moving.) It's a quality that I felt more complexly in many other songs from the same time, which I find better and more delicious, songs by Crime & the City Solution, Talking Heads, Joy Division, Roxy Music, Patti Smith, Sonic Youth, and the Psychedelic Furs, among others. It is a quality that can make pop music appear ephemeral to the point of cheap, exceptionally vulnerable to changes in fashion, attachable to dumb things like ads for cars or pizza, dependent on its period of time for its language of shared associations to make sense. It is also a quality that makes pop music exceptionally powerful in its ability to enter a person's most private schema and whisper to that person in secret.

It makes sense if this song wasn't popular; what nightclubber in NYC wants to identify with some retard sitting by herself in the basement, staring into space? At the same time, it also makes sense that this retard and the guy trying to get her out of the basement appeared in NYC in 1981, a time of costuming, pretense, fancy-shaped, Day-Glo-colored hair. Costuming is a romantic way of giving shape to something previously inchoate inside you, of trying to discover, to become. It can also be a way of obnoxiously parading the self while simultaneously hiding it, especially if the costume is socially agreed on. The song is about a person who "prefers to hide" in a physical place, such as a room, but also perhaps in the self, in a construction of personality in which something essential and vulnerable remains hidden and undeveloped. When I heard "Nowhere Girl," I was lost in a self-created nightmare that had become a terrible reality I was trying desperately to get out of, and instead was getting more lost in by the moment. I think the song in its quick passing gave me a strange glimmer of hope just because in it I could hear that other people saw and felt this lostness, too, and rather than despising it, someone had considered it worth writing a song about.

By 1986, I was starting to find my way. I could sort of talk to people. I remember, though, a particular moment when I couldn't. I was spending an afternoon with this guy I liked, and we were walking around doing something I no longer recall. I do remember that at one point we sat down outside somewhere and he said, "I really like you and I want to get to know you. But it feels like there's all these obstacles and I don't know what they are and I don't know how to get around them." I was so astonished that I could not reply. I knew exactly what he meant. At the same time, I didn't know what the obstacles were, either. I crossed my hands over my lap and looked down. I have no idea what I was thinking. Maybe I was trying to come up with something smart to say and realizing that it was beyond me. Probably I thought he was saying there was something wrong with me. He put his hand on my arm, then took it away. The moment passed. We talked about something else, then said good-bye.

Because I knew I was going to write about this song, I told this anecdote to someone recently, and she said, "It just sounds like he was coming on to you." My mind snagged on the word *just;* I seldom think that anyone "just" comes on. I don't know what he wanted or what he was doing. I remember the moment because I felt he was trying to get through, trying to talk to me, and that something was stopping him—and that despite this, he succeeded. It is still moving to me that he saw something real that most people wouldn't bother to see, and that he said something about it; that he helped me, in a tiny way, to wake up.

By 1987, I had gotten somewhere in the social sense; I had sold a book and it was about to be published. I remember going to a club for the first time in a while and being kind of appalled. There were no costumes, no sense of discovery or romance;

there were mostly a lot of expensive clothes, and I was wearing them, too. The best thing was the DJ, who for some reason made me remember a song I hadn't heard in years; I went up to her and asked, "Do you have 'Nowhere Girl' by B-Movie?" She did. She played it, and for a moment the room was drenched in feeling from the past: the feeling of something unknown trying to get your attention, of not quite being able to see what it is; of somebody trying to awaken somebody else; of trying to wake. Banal somewhere was suddenly and beautifully infused with mysterious nowhere. It was a very small moment, but it was a lovely one. As this is a small but lovely song.

How to Write About Music,
EDITED BY MARC WOODSWORTH AND ALLY-JANE GROSSMAN, 2015
(COMPOSED IN 2011)

FORM OVER FEELING

A REVIEW OF *OUT* BY NATSUO KIRINO

Out, by Natsuo Kirino, is a murder mystery even though you know who the killer is in the first fifty pages, which is when the first crime gets committed. There are a number of crimes after that, and you know who commits them, too. Kirino's characterizations aren't mysterious; you know who is weak, who is strong, who is stupid, and who is shrewd, and you know—indeed, you keep being reminded—that these four classifications are apparently all that matters in terms of the author's moral empathy. As you read, you deduce that Kirino detests weakness, is suspicious of emotionality, particularly if it is related to weakness, and that she admires strength and intelligence above all else, even when it is combined with ruthlessness and cruelty. *Compassion* is a term of sometimes complacent approbation in mainstream American literary culture, and if compassion for weak or unappealing characters is a primary standard of value, *Out* flunks. But here is a mystery: Although Kirino is near pitiless in her depiction of her characters, especially the weakest and dumbest one, whom she bathes in contempt before sadistically killing off, the book is saturated with an intense, anguished pity that makes the American literary ideal of "compassion" look insubstantial.

The plot of the book centers on four discontented middle-aged women who work the late shift at a dismal lunch-box factory. Masako and Yayoi are stuck in loveless marriages, Masako to

a bore, Yayoi to an abusive fool who gambles away their life savings. Yoshie is a widow trapped taking care of ungrateful kids and
a bedridden mother-in-law. Kuniko is a fat, vain dullard, in hock
to loan sharks because she can't control any of her appetites. It's
not giving away much to reveal that Yayoi snaps and kills her
worthless husband, and that, because she is too weak to handle
the aftermath of the crime, she turns to the tough, resourceful
Masako for help. Masako decides that dismemberment is the way
to go and she doesn't so much ask for help as extort it from the
relentlessly practical Yoshie, who owes Masako for a loan. The
idiotic Kuniko bumbles onto the crime scene because she's looking for a loan, too, and so gets enlisted in cutting up the corpse.
Kuniko, being fat and weak, is naturally too incompetent to get
anything right, including the proper disposal of the body parts,
which are discovered. The murder gets pinned on a nightclub
owner and pimp named Satake, an elegant, intelligent man with
a grim and, in the sensibility of this book, alluring secret. That is
when things start to get interesting.

Part of what is mysterious about Kirino's novel is the way that
the crudeness of characterization and moral outlook (strength:
good, weakness: bad), rather than being merely ham-fisted,
translates as visceral depth and a kind of ferocious allegiance to
harsh reality. An American literary writer—myself, for example—
would want to reveal something surprising about Kuniko, some
redeeming charm or secret intelligence; some integrity or hidden
strength—at the very least, an ordinary goodness that would give
her death dignity and/or pathos. This is a contemporary idea of
complexity and it is realistic to be sure; few people *are* definable
by three or four traits, and even when three or four traits are
paramount in a person, they can be dynamically related to their
opposites.

However, this "idea of complexity" can become a convention, a duty to be done for the comfort of the reader as much

as anything, and it is curiously bracing to read a writer of clear intelligence and depth who has no interest in such conventions or comfort. Why does Yayoi kill her husband? She is angry because he hit her and spent their money. Why do her coworkers agree to cut him up? They need money. Simple motives, blunt and powerful—yet Kirino plays against the simplicity and the power with subtle notes, such as her brief description of the oldest of the women, Yoshie: "All she had was her pride, goading her to keep working no matter how hard it was. Yoshie had wrapped up everything personal that mattered in a tight package and stored it away somewhere far out of sight, and in its place she had developed a single obsession: diligence. This was her trick for getting by." In this way, she shares something with the pimp Satake, a sort of brutal devotion to form that makes him particularly hard on a client he sees behaving aggressively with his "top girl": "Yamamoto was way out of his league by any standards . . . just as there were rules in gambling there were rules in this game as well; and it made Satake, who was himself so scrupulous, furious to see someone like Yamamoto ignoring them."

This hewing to form over feeling comes to seem like a kind of violence itself—yet, it is that fanatic dignity, rather than sentiment, that connects the characters to something beyond their desperation and venality. It is Yoshie (called "the Skipper" at work because she's so efficient) who says, after the women have systematically chopped up the corpse, "But I can't help thinking . . . that he might even be glad that we did this to him. I mean, when I used to read about these dismemberings, I thought it sounded terrible. But it's not really like that, is it? There's something about taking somebody apart so neatly, so completely, that feels almost respectful." And in the context of their bickerings, jokes about saws, and decisions about what to do with the victim's head, what she says makes total sense. As they prepare to put it all into "city-approved garbage bags" and drop it off in various locations to be "incinerated along with the rest of the garbage in Tokyo," murder gets blended with daily life in a way that is both matter-of-fact and reverent.

But it is through her protagonist Masako that Kirino reveals her depth of feeling most. Even more than the others, Masako is a woman who cares about rigor, dignity, and strength—form over feeling. Yet she chooses the forms she cares about, and that does not include her family, the most socially approved form of all in every culture. She decides to help Yayoi not because she needs money, but finally because she is bored and restless to the point of despair. She is sarcastic about Yoshie's reverence when speaking of the victim's head, yet it is she who returns to the place she buried it: "A small mound of fresh earth was visible in the undergrowth, the only sign of what she'd done. Summer was reaching its peak and the woods smelled of life, richer and fuller even than when she'd been here ten days ago. She pictured Kenji's head turning to pulp in the ground, becoming part of the earth. Becoming food for worms and insects. It was a gruesome thought, but also somehow comforting—she had given the head to the creatures underground."

It is in this moment of impersonal emotion that a kind of mercy is allowed, not particularly for the small, flawed person who was Kenji, but for existence, the unknowability of it that Kirino's characters each in their own way (except for the sloppy and therefore reprobate Kuniko) try to honor. This will to honor the large forces that compel us will find its most dramatic expression in the final scene between Masako and Satake. It is a violent and, for all its squalor—indeed, in part because of its squalor—a romantic scene, drawing heavily on the fantasy erotics of murder a bit *too* romantically for a book built on such a grim devotion to commonsensical reality.

Yet, while you are reading it, you don't care if it's too romantic; you don't even care if it's realistic, psychologically speaking.

It feels real beyond psychology, beyond the formal constraints of life that Kirino and her characters have obeyed humbly or proudly, real in the way that the creatures who will eat Kenji's head are real and always with us regardless of who we are and what we think we are doing. By the time we get to the last scene, we are longing for form, longing for all feeling to be broken—and it will be. Masako has longed for freedom and she will have it, at the expense of everything else. It is Kirino's great gift that she makes us believe in her heroine's willingness to pay this expense, and to walk mysteriously, triumphantly into nothingness.

Asymptote Journal, 2011

BEG FOR YOUR LIFE

ON THE FILMS OF LAUREL NAKADATE

I am getting into this by going the long way around.

Once when I was driving in my car, I heard a story by Ira Sher read on the radio. I don't know if I remember it accurately, because I was driving and it was a long time ago. It was an amazing story, but still, it was just a story, and so for a long time I forgot it. It came back with a lot of force when I saw Laurel Nakadate's 2009 video *Exorcism in January*. I am not sure why.

Ira Sher's story is about a bunch of restless kids who live somewhere in a small town in a desert. The narrator's home life is screwed up in some way—I don't recall exactly how, maybe divorce. For fun, he goes with his friends to explore in the desert, and one day they discover something dramatic: a guy trapped at the bottom of a dry well. He pleads with them to get help, and instead, they go home and make up a basket of food with water for him. He is very thankful and asks when help is coming. They are noncommittal. This goes on for a few days. The man starts to get desperate. He says, "You told your parents, right? Help is coming, right?" They don't really answer. It's not that they don't care. It's more that it's very exciting to have him as their special thing.

————————

There is no literal connection between Nakadate's video and Sher's story. *Exorcism in January* is not about kids or abandonment; the film is, in a strange way, about friendship. In the film, Nakadate plays a girl in a hot-pink bra who wakes up in a near-empty room of light, puts on cowboy boots, and goes to visit an old guy who lives in a dark, dirty apartment lit like a Dutch masterpiece. She asks him how he is and he says he's pretty down. She asks why and he says it's a chemical imbalance in his brain. Or maybe a demonic possession; maybe an exorcism would help, he says, maybe she could pray over him and shake rattles and drive the spirits away. She asks when he wants to do it and he says tomorrow. She says okay and she leaves; his eyes follow her out. The next day she wakes again in her room of light and puts a pink shirt over her pink bra and puts on her boots. He is lying on his bed in his dark, chaotic room. You hear her voice, and it is the voice of a child; she is saying, "Go away, spirits, go away," and he is repeating her words and shaking his hands while his cat licks itself. "Shake them out," she says. "Lick them out. Bad spirits, go away." "I don't want you here," he says, "go away." She kneels by his bed and says, "Go away." The next day she wakes again in underwear, in bright light. She goes into his dark apartment and asks if he's better. He says yes, he is. He thinks the exorcism worked. She says he should give an acceptance speech "about how great it is." He does, sort of.

The kids in the story keep bringing the man food and water, but they never tell their parents. They don't tell because they are afraid they will get into trouble for not telling. Eventually he realizes what is going on. Eventually he asks, "What are your names?" One of them answers without thinking and the others go "Shhh!" And they go away.

The man in the movie is named Larry. He is a friend of Laurel's; he wrote the script for *Exorcism in January*.

Laurel Nakadate wrote and directed *The Wolf Knife*, which is about two sixteen-year-old girls named Chrissy (Christina Kolozsvary) and June (Julie Potratz), who decide to go to Nashville to find Chrissy's father. They decide to do this after Chrissy's mom tells them there is a rapist in the neighborhood with a gun; immediately after she tells them this, the mom's boyfriend proposes. The boyfriend pulls a diamond ring out of his shirt pocket, the same pocket from which he earlier pulled a pair of underpants, which he gave to Chrissy. He says he wants Chrissy's mom to be his princess forever. He keeps saying princess, not queen, even though Chrissy's mom is not young. The girls get up and leave in disgust. Later they lie in twin beds, and Chrissy tells June that she's heard her mom and the boyfriend having sex and that they say gross, aggressive things; the boyfriend says, "Beg for your life." June laughs and Chrissy snaps at her. Chrissy decides they should go to Nashville to look for her dad; they flee in the dead of night.

Nakadate does not act in this film, but the actress who plays Chrissy is a dead ringer for how we might imagine Nakadate at sixteen. (I don't know why this seems to matter, but it does.) She is an intensely physical person, this girl, and it's a willful, *intelligent* physicality, like her body came into the world knowing things, not specifically carnal things, but deep, complicated things. Her dark, thick-lashed eyes, though, have the questing, hurt look of someone who *knows*, yet still doesn't quite want to believe what she knows, and is looking to find something less . . .

well, less insane. It's the expression of someone whose socialized mind isn't prepared for what the rest of her is taking in.

June is less powerfully physical, with more question than knowledge in her limbs. Her eyes are beyond questing; they are yearning, blindly, with no idea what for. Chrissy is clearly the dominant of the two, with far greater will and imagination. What the two have in common, what makes them seem like sisters, is the beautiful way they inhabit the fecund density of adolescence in bloom. Nakadate drenches the viewer in this quality with her close-ups; through the intensity of her gaze, the girls bodily express vital, amoral goodness, good as a plant or animal is good just by being what it is. Done up in wet, shiny lipstick, heavy eye makeup, and tight neon-colored clothes, the girls radiate, in their skin, lips, and eyes, the abiding purity of a primary impulse seeking to find a shape in the bizarrely shaped landscape of twenty-first-century humanity. It's not just the girls. Grass, trees, animals, people—everything in Nakadate's world is burstingly alive and bright with the need to be what it is. There is an almost tragicomical tension between this ferocious, innocent need and the perversity of the human culture / character through which it must come; it is a tension that at some point, and repeatedly, will become anguished.

As it turns out, Chrissy isn't looking for her father. She's going to visit her retired third-grade teacher, who she says is a really nice guy. When June discovers this, she is angry and wants to go back home. But without Chrissy, she is simply not resourceful enough. So they go see Mr. Dews. Nearly an old man now, Mr. Dews is living with his elderly father; he looks a louche ruin, as though years of crushing disappointment have crushed him into the shape of an elegant troll. And yet, within this shape, he still wants and seeks to be. His voice is a nightmare of nuance, full of humor and horror, and with it he croaks at Chrissy as from the bottom of a well. And then he pulls her in. Their dialogue is a masterpiece of misshapen, mixed-up emotion, crashing from tenderness to rapacity to loathing to longing to pity to remnants of real affection and respect that pathetically shimmer—and then are violated all in the tonal changes of the wretched man's voice. The visit ends with Chrissy squashed up against a mirror, confessing something that June did that she wishes she could've done. Her third-grade teacher is devouring what he thinks is her innocent shame, and she is feeding it to him. As awful as this is, it may be preferable to what she really feels, for her shame is in being unwanted and hating June for it.

But it is June who cries. She cries and won't say much to Chrissy, who feels guilty and so begins to bully her friend with cruel little gestures, like forcing a straw into her mouth and commanding her to "drink more." June finally fights back—and then the wolf knife comes out. And still the girls' skin and eyes and lips continue to seek, to yearn, to be. As does the earth and grass and sky around them, with heartbreaking amoral goodness.

In her 2006 film *Beg for Your Life,* Nakadate is a girl who points guns at old guys and says, "Beg for your life!" She does this for laughs. A lot of other stuff happens; old guys kidnap the girl and she kind of makes one of them kill her, except she's not dead. Music plays; the last song is about "making love out of nothing at all." But because the film is called *Beg for Your Life,* I'm thinking that's the highlight. The girl seems to really like saying it, and the old guys seem to really like it, too. One of the men starts cracking up in the middle of it, and how could he not? It's ridiculous funny, weird sweet, and also a little bit horrible. These old guys aren't actors professionally. They are old guys she met in places like the Home Depot parking lot, who came up and talked to her because she's pretty. Some of them are mentally ill. Many of them, like Larry, she came to know well.

I never got to hear the end of Ira Sher's story because I had to get out of the car. The last part I did hear—the narrative had shifted away from the man in the well to the protagonist's problematic home life. So I don't know what happened. My guess is that they left him down there. Maybe at the end the narrator went back and shouted down and got no answer. But I don't know. It was a great story anyway.

Someone I know who saw *The Wolf Knife* before I did described it as being about "girls making bad choices." Which is true. Except that in the world of *The Wolf Knife*, there really don't seem to be good choices. In the world of *The Wolf Knife*, there are swimming pools full of lapping light and soft plapping sounds; there are peacocks and flowers and bright blue lawn chairs, and unless you are perfect, you will need an ass-lift when you are twenty-six; your sweating, blank-eyed mother dances joylessly in the attic and her boyfriend pulls panties from his pocket. There is ice cream, and giant wooden pictures of water and sky; white prisoners are more glamorous than black prisoners and the cute guy you like only wants a hand job from you and then you never talk again, but the other cute guy fucks your friend and she doesn't even tell you; the light turns your friend's skin orange and yellow and you are orange and yellow, too, and her eyes are all occluded. You make her lie on her back on a dinosaur statue in public so her crotch bone sticks out and take her picture. Mr. Dews says, "Legs and hips and shoulders and eyes and lips and ankles and hair and eyebrows and nose" in the dirtiest voice you ever heard and you can see what he means, even though he is talking about you. Your mother's engagement ring comes out your mouth. Somebody is down in a hole and people know and no one knows. Sometimes you think you know who it is: Sometimes it is someone else. Sometimes it is you. It is horrible. And it is amazing.

SAN FRANCISCO FILM SOCIETY ONLINE: SF360.org, 2011

THE CUNNING OF WOMEN

ON *ONE THOUSAND AND ONE NIGHTS*
BY HANAN AL-SHAYKH

One Thousand and One Nights is about worlds underground, where jewels are embedded in darkness and a beautiful woman may love a devil; it's about powerful slaves and foolish demons, secret spirits hidden in jars; it's about truth living in the treacherous heart like an abiding and holy law waiting to be revealed in the words of a story told by a porter, a tailor, a concubine or lady—all told through the lips of the lady Shahrazad to an enraged, cuckolded king on a revenge mission against womankind. If she stops telling stories, he will kill her like every other woman he sleeps with.

Shahrazad isn't a character in the usual sense, as her voice disappears in the stories, which seem to exist without a narrator; she appears only at the very beginning and very end of *One Thousand and One Nights*. Yet she is an icon of feminine force, both submissive and powerful, invisible and generative. Traditionally, *One Thousand and One Nights* ends when Shahrazad presents the king with three children and, because she has proven herself, he decides to marry, rather than kill, her. Perhaps the most refreshing thing about Hanan al-Shaykh's delightful translation is that it does not end with Shahrazad's transformation from storyteller to wife and mom; instead, al-Shaykh chooses to keep her in the realm of invisibility and magic.

Shahrazad's stories are on every theme and subject, from

con artistry to justice to love; they are surreal and grimy-real, and they express powerful oppositions: male/female, union/dis-union, love/hate, nature/society. The theme of betrayal and/or trickery runs through many of them: A brokenhearted woman helps her gullible fiancé to win the love of a murderous beauty while protecting him with talismanic poems that will save his life—even as he destroys their lives. A woman traps five amorous fools inside a cabinet (which she has tricked one of them into building), where they eventually, to avoid bursting their bladders, pee on each other's heads. An impoverished elderly widow disguised as a holy woman and concerned mother goes on a rampage of fraud and theft, tricking one of her victims into yanking out another's teeth—and is rewarded for her crimes with a government position. A husband chops his beloved wife to pieces because, at market, a slave, who in truth has never met her, brags that he's the wife's lover as he flaunts a rare fruit the husband gave her. Two sisters who betray another sister because they are jealous that she has found love are turned into dogs and must be savagely beaten every day by the sister they wronged for the rest of their lives—even though she has long ago forgiven them and sobs as she strikes them.

The action of the stories in *One Thousand and One Nights* is dark and full of cruelty—especially toward women, who are constantly being accused of adultery and then murdered or beaten up. But the animating spirit here is light and full of play, *especially* on the part of the female characters, who are consistently resourceful and witty. The supposedly enslaved mistress of a demon taunts and commands two cuckolded kings to "make love" to her; they obey and then dance and cheer, "How great is the cunning of women!" Both cunning queens are murdered, but the demon's mistress lives on to triumphantly declare, "I have slept with one hundred men under the very horns of this filthy demon as he snored happily, assuming that I am his alone . . . he is a fool, for he does not know that no one can prevent a woman from fulfilling her desires, even if she is hidden under the roaring sea, jealously guarded by a demon."

This apparent fear of and admiration for triumphant female lust keeps popping out against the theme of vengeance against said lust, and it is *not* al-Shaykh's invention; it is intrinsic to the complex soul of the original. But how to refer to the "original"? The stories in *One Thousand and One Nights* were told orally for centuries, coming out of India and Persia in the sixth century, and carried by traders and travelers all over the world; they were first written in Arabic in 1450. Through subsequent translations, disparate versions became folded into one another, as minor characters become major players and events were transformed, revealing the original themes differently, yet faithfully. For if the characters telling the stories within the stories are, like Shahrazad, pleading for their lives, they are also pleading for an aspect of truth to be revealed, and this desire for revelation is profoundly heartfelt. Shahrazad is not just out to save her skin; she wants to heal. She is asking for forgiveness, not only for women's sexual infidelity but for men's violent possessiveness, for human boobishness in general. She also acknowledges that certain things cannot be tolerated. In her stories, foolishness, lust, greed, jealousy, lying, cruelty, cowardice, and vanity are exposed and readily forgiven; rape and cold-blooded murder are *not* forgiven. The moral codes are honored sincerely—but then there is that lewd demon's mistress, a consistent narrative mischief, a respect for pure, life-force passion that runs through the tales, which reminds me of what William Blake said about *Paradise Lost:* that Milton, being a poet, was of the Devil's camp whether he liked it or not.

Al-Shaykh's translation has special beauty in that it emphasizes this mischievous aspect alongside the expansive, revelatory, and forgiving nature of the tales. With so many versions of the

Nights, it's hard to compare, but many of the older versions I've seen have a tight, convoluted quality that, while dreamishly, brilliantly inventive, can have the random feel of the Grimms' least interesting fairy tales, a sort of then-this-happened-and-then-this-happened action-based narrative style. In contrast, al-Shaykh's style foregrounds structure and character. She pays little attention to the famous voyage of Sinbad, and Ali Baba (who was apparently invented by the first Western translator, Antoine Galland) doesn't even get a mention. Instead, the narrative pivots around a grand party at the sumptuous home of three beautiful and independent sisters who are hosting several men—dervishes, merchants, and a porter, all of whom are unexpected guests. They eat, drink, and sing, but mostly they talk and tell stories that take them around the world and beyond it. The classic *Nights* features these ladies and their guests in passing, but al-Shaykh returns to them again and again, rooting her stories in the mysterious underground of male-female relations.

Many of the classic stories have long, literally underground, sequences where major action takes place: One story starts with a prince agreeing to entomb his cousin and his cousin's beautiful sister in a fabulous crypt, where they will consummate their love and be burned to cinders doing so. Another prince follows a beautiful young man down into the gorgeous underground chamber, in which the boy's father has hidden him and discovers his fate—that he must kill the boy—while doing everything possible to avoid it.

Al-Shaykh features some of these stories, but she stresses the secret underworld we experience every day, in which emotional truth is expressed in strange actions that have somehow become normal. The story of the two sisters turned into bitches, who are compulsorily whipped by their unwilling sister in the middle of a civil gathering, is a story of cruelty that is secret and mechanical even as it happens in plain sight. It is a physical metaphor for the invisible violence that goes on between people everywhere (especially in families), while civil words are being spoken and daily life goes forward.

When we first see the dogs being beaten, we don't know who they really are or why this is happening. The sisters demand that their guests ask no questions, and when one of them breaks the rule, the truths underlying the beautiful party are revealed. The very slave who caused an innocent woman to be hacked to death with his trivial marketplace bragging is exposed and pardoned by a suddenly revealed king; much later the slave reveals himself as a powerful healer with magic strong enough to lift the curse and return the dogs to their human form. Whipped dogs are also dignified women; a stupid slave is also a wise healer. The truth of this night is ugly, then beautiful, then finally mysterious because of the way these qualities are linked.

But *how* such truth is revealed is as important as *what* is revealed: Delicacy and attention to propriety are present in the stories, even if sometimes comically so. The first guest of the three glamorous ladies, the besotted porter, is allowed to stay, feast, and bathe with them because he shows himself discreet by quoting poetry: "Guard your secrets closely / When they're told they fly / If unable to keep treasures in our own heart / Who then can forbid another, yours to impart?" As the night goes on, they each cuddle up in his lap and ask him what they've got between the legs—by which they mean, he's got to guess the exact name they've given it or else be pummeled—and each lady has a different private name. In the story of the woman (Aziza) who helps her fiancé (Aziz) to woo another woman who also happens to be a killer, Aziza instructs Aziz on exactly what verses to say to the lady every night, and asks how the lady replies:

He: Lovers, in the name of God
     Tell me how one can relieve this endless desperation?
She: He should conceal his love and hide
     Showing only his patience and humility.
He: He tried to show fair patience but could only find
     A heart that was filled with unease.
She: If he cannot counsel his patience to conceal his secrets
     Nothing will serve him better than death.
He: I have heard, obeyed and now I must die
     Salutations to she who tore us apart.

In fact, Aziz has failed completely to conceal his love or to be patient, but he is nonetheless saved from death by reciting these lines. At the same time, the fiancée is speaking to her rival through the words, congratulating her on her victory; ironically, it is Aziza, who *has* restrained her love and shown infinite patience, who will die. The story (and there is more to it than I have described) is essentially a fight between sacred and profane love; it is bloody and no one can really win. It doesn't make sense that reciting his poem should save Aziz; none of it makes "sense"—and yet in a deeply fascinating way it does, for the ritual nature of the incantatory words stands as a dramatic counter to the raw power of sexuality and emotion, and expresses the protective quality of propriety, discretion, and order.

These stories of intense opposites are rich and flashing in combination, a skein of words that glimmers like a net of fast-darting fish that are also jewels. They make unity of chaos and take joy from suffering. Before he meets the demon's mistress, the brother of the cuckold Shahrayar, King Shahzaman (a cuckold, too!) sulks about their wives doing it with slaves and kitchen boys, lamenting, "What treacherous world is this which fails to distinguish between a sovereign king and a nobody?" (Note to king: A playful, generous kitchen boy will nearly always be better than an egomaniac, murderous king.) It's a question that asserts propriety, discretion, and social hierarchy, and, over the course of *One Thousand and One Nights*, Shahrazad, with her loving plenitude and subtlety, replies by revealing the entire world, with all its chaos and abiding order. He asks, "What kind of a world is this?" And she replies, "Why, king, a very wonderful world indeed." Finally, he believes; so do we.

INTRODUCTION TO *One Thousand and One Nights: A Retelling*, BY HANAN AL-SHAYKH, 2013

PICTURES OF LO

This love was like an endless wringing of hands,
like a blundering of the soul through an infinite
maze of hopelessness and remorse.

—*Pale Fire*

This could be Humbert Humbert agonizing over Lolita after he
has ruined her life and his, but it is not; it is Charles Kinbote, king
of fabulous Zembla, musing with wistful offhandedness about
his young, beautiful, unloved, and undesired wife, Disa. In waking hours, he feels nothing for her but "friendly indifference and
bleak respect"; in his dreams, these dry sentiments are saturated
and swollen until they "[exceed] in emotional tone, in spiritual
passion and depth, anything he had experienced in his surface
existence." In life, he casually, *near accidentally* tortures her; in his
dreams, he remorsefully adores her.

In *Pale Fire*, Disa is a minor character who receives only a
pathetic handful of the book's 214 pages. But with the poignancy
and plangency of sorrow, she illumines *Pale Fire*'s core; the delusional dream, the preposterous poem, the crumbling bridge
between mundane reality and fantastic ideal, the tormenting
ideal that insists on bleeding through to the surface ("all peach
syrup, regularly rippled with pale blue") even as it sinks in the

mud below. If Kinbote, though king, can't have the one he really wants, Humbert Humbert can: In *Lolita,* the dreamer is in the driver's seat, reality is broken, and it is the raving dream that broke it. Humbert "seldom if ever" dreams of Lolita, even when he has lost her. Except that he does. In his grossly unbeautiful dreams, Lolita appears as Charlotte, her disgusting mother, and as Valeria, Humbert's equally disgusting former wife, both of whom disgustingly loved him:

> ... she did haunt my sleep but she appeared there in strange and ludicrous disguises as Valeria or Charlotte, or a cross between them. That complex ghost would come to me, shedding shift after shift, in an atmosphere of great melancholy and disgust, and would recline in dull invitation on some narrow board or hard settee, with flesh ajar like the rubber valve of a soccer ball's bladder. I would find myself, dentures fractured or hopelessly mislaid, in horrible *chambres garnies* where I would be entertained at tedious vivisecting parties that generally ended with Charlotte or Valeria weeping in my bleeding arms and being tenderly kissed by my brotherly lips in a dream disorder of auctioneered Viennese bric-a-brac, pity, impotence and the brown wigs of tragic old women who had just been gassed.

I must've read *Lolita* five times before I even noticed this hideously gorgeous paragraph, this miserable aside linking the fatally despised women with the fatally desired girl. Part of *Lolita*'s power is in its extreme oppositions: Even Humbert's fanatically one-directional desire for little Dolly is made more delicious by the sharp tonal oppositions in her "two-fold nature," the "tender dreamy childishness" and "eerie vulgarity, stemming from the snub-nosed cuteness of ads and magazine pictures," the "exquisite stainless tenderness seeping through the musk and the mud" of her female being—really, of *any* being. The tension between Humbert's near-erotic revulsion for women/his miasmic desire for girls, his human despair/his demonic joy is even more intense; the dream that tragically joins these poles suggests that one has been a palimpsest for the other all along.

So how does one, one very normal one, put this on a book jacket? How even to try? It is remarkable to me how many have succeeded in capturing even a fractional flash of Nabokov's ingeniously juggled, weirdly populated planets with their many moons. *Lolita* may be fairly described as "a threnody for the destruction of a child's life," yet a high percentage of the covers go for cute: whimsical buttons on bright red, an ejaculating pink plastic gun, a crenellated candy pink shell, a pale pink plastic necklace spelling the titular name, that name elsewhere spelled with a bobby sock *L*, still multiple elsewheres with a leopard-print mascara wand, a paper doll leg, a crushed red lollipop *o*. Some covers are bric-a-brac-ishly decorated (bleeding old-maidish mum with dripping chocolate petals, *Lolita* in crazy-quilt neon lace, a silhouette man trapped in a cubist blue teardrop, a pink bird in a rigid cage); still others are subtle to the point of opacity (the corners of two pink walls are unsurprised to meet a white ceiling); a few are deliberately ugly (horrible-looking old men, one of them openmouthed, bare-chested, and practically reaching into his pants).

They are all fun to look at, even the ugly ones. For me, cuteness (Yes, snub-nosed, even when there is no nose! Ads and magazine pictures, of course!) comes consistently closest to the book's cruel and ardent heart. For Humbert's aesthetic infatuation is based on a tyrannical ideal, and cuteness is a kind of ideal—one that is heartless, breathless, and ageless as Bambi, static and hard-edged, perfect in its way, with all excess flesh and unseemly feeling cut out—oh Humbert, there can be no "aurochs and angels" in this cartoon heaven-cum-hell!

But the best cover, I think, is not cute. It is the 1997 Vintage paperback edition of the book, featuring a simple photographic image with a complex penumbra: a bare-legged girl shown from the waist down, wearing a flared skirt and oxford shoes. The photo is bright white, granular gray, and deeply dark; it is delicate (the slender legs) and un- (the big shoes and skirt). The girl's legs are beautiful and very vulnerable, in a knock-kneed position, with a large gap between the calves, and the toes adorably, spastically touching each other. Charming, until you consider the full body posture suggested by the position: it expresses fear. Either the girl has cerebral palsy or she is cringing. (The legs could also evoke a playful flirt making a pretty pose of pretend fear combined with inviting eyes and arms. But the element of cowering is strongest in what we can actually see.) Without the full image, your first and (probably) only conscious response is appreciation of the subject's touching, awkward beauty. But a second, instinctive, and less aesthetic understanding of the image (creeping quietly up under the first) shades mild appreciation with something too dark to quite *see*, which we nonetheless *feel* intensely in our reptile spines.

The blurb on that cover is more disturbing than the image, for it sincerely states that *Lolita*, in which the heroine is seduced, kidnapped, and grossly used, her mother humiliated at length before dying violently, the seducer himself shattered, his rival murdered, the heroine finally dead along with her "still-born baby girl"—according to the blurb, this madcap orgy of Thanatos is "The only convincing love story of our century"!!! It is not shocking that *someone* said this, especially given that this *someone* was Gregor von Rezzori writing for *Vanity Fair.* But it is quietly outrageous that a mainstream publisher would choose to put it on the cover, directly over those understandably frightened legs.

I am not the only one to feel this way; if you Google the

phrase, you will find all kinds of online fussing about it: *Lolita* is not about love, because love is always mutual, *Lolita* is about obsession, which is never, ever love, and Nabokov himself was *so* disappointed that people did not understand this and take away the right message. I am in sympathy with the fussers, and am almost one myself, for how could anyone call this feeding frenzy of selfishness, devouring, and destruction "love"? And yet, consider what Nabokov said about Humbert: That while he, the author, would condemn his character to hell for his acts, he would allow Humbert, for one day a year, to leave hell and wander a "green lane in Paradise," and that this parole would occur because of the glowing particle of real love he bore for Lolita.

Although I find Rezzori's words initially repellent and even a little smug, if you rewrote the sentence without using the words *only* and *century*, I have to agree with them. *Lolita* is about obsession and narcissistic appetite, misogyny and contemptuous rejection, not only of adult women but of humanity itself. And yet. It is also about love; if it were not, the book would not be so heart-stoppingly beautiful. Here is Humbert on finding his runaway sex slave, now married and pregnant at seventeen:

> You may jeer at me and threaten to clear the court, but until I am gagged and half-throttled, I will shout out my poor truth. I insist the world know how much I loved my Lolita, pale and polluted and big with another's child, but still gray-eyed, still sooty-lashed, still auburn and almond, still Carmencita, still mine . . . even if those eyes of hers would fade to myopic fish and her nipples swell and crack, and her lovely young velvety delicate delta be tainted and torn—even then I would go mad with tenderness at the mere sight of your dear wan face, at the mere sound of your raucous young voice, my Lolita.

This is love crying with pain as it is crushed into the thorned corner of a torture garden—but it is still love. Purity of feeling must live and breathe in the impure gardens of our confused, compromised, corrupt, and broken hearts. Love itself is not selfish, devouring, or cruel, but in human beings it suffers a terrible coexistence with those qualities, as well as with a host of milder evils—say, resentment or misunderstanding or projection. These oppositions sometimes coexist so closely and complexly that the lovers cannot tell them apart. This is true not only of sexual love but of the love between parents and children, siblings, and even friends. In most people, this contradiction will never take the florid form it takes in Humbert Humbert. But such impossible, infernal combinations are there in all of us, and we know it. That *Lolita* renders this human condition at such an extreme, so truthfully, and yes, as Rezzori says, *convincingly,* is the book's most shocking quality. It is why it will never be forgotten. It is also why no one will ever succeed it describing it fully on a book jacket. But how wonderful that so many have tried.

PREFACE TO *Lolita: The Story of a Cover Girl,*
EDITED BY JOHN BERTRAM AND YURI LEVING, 2013

THE EASIEST THING TO FORGET

ON CARL WILSON'S *LET'S TALK ABOUT LOVE*

When I first picked up Carl Wilson's *Let's Talk About Love,* I didn't know what Céline Dion sounded like—and I did not live during 1996–1997 in a "Unabomber-like retreat from audible civilization," which Wilson claims is the only circumstance under which one could lack this awful (according to him) knowledge. I started reading anyway because I wondered why someone would write a whole book exploring and trying to reconcile with a singer whose music he hated. I kept reading because I liked Wilson's supple and subtle voice, and because I was increasingly fascinated to see just how much emotion and energy he and apparently hordes of others have expended in hating and despising a singer I had never even noticed.

It's not that I don't know from weird singer hate: Billy Joel, the early Boy George, and Mark McGrath of Sugar Ray all have voices that used to make me inwardly spasm with misanthropic disgust for a few seconds at least. But apparently Céline haters don't spasm in silence or for seconds; they scream and froth at the mouth *at length:* "The most wholly repellent woman ever to sing songs of love," spewed Cintra Wilson. "I think most people would rather be processed through the digestive tract of an anaconda than be Céline Dion for a day." Bitch, excuse me? We're not talking about Bernie Madoff or the Abu Ghraib torture team; this is a pop singer who annoys Your Excellency. In response to the relentless snideness described by Wilson about Dion's teeth, her Quebecois accent, her kooky arm movements, her clueless fans (whom some asshole in the UK sneeringly imagined as "overweight children" and "grannies"), by page 18, I was solidly in Dion's corner without hearing a note; I figured that anyone who got so many pricks so agitated had to be doing something right.

Then came page 23, on which Wilson informs the reader that the most "widely mocked minutes of Céline Dion's career" occurred when she had the vulgarity to get all emotional about the victims of Hurricane Katrina on *Larry King,* crying even, and doing that arm-movement thing like some kind of spaz; the next day it apparently went viral under headings like CÉLINE DION GOES CRAZY! For me anyway, that's when the book became about something more than Céline Dion, pop music, or tastes. Wilson skillfully uses the *Larry King* incident to segue at graceful length into a description of Dion's Quebecois cultural roots, which, he says, explain why she "fails most non-fans' authenticity tests" and why "her personal touchstones are off the map," this being true because Quebec's idiosyncratic pop culture and Francophone sense of oppression are "a null set in the popular imagination." Wilson can show, with his lengthy analysis, why Dion's passionate defense of poor New Orleanians who "looted" busted-up stores was as "culturally sound" as Kanye West's speech the following week, and he's very interesting while doing it; Dion's personal and cultural background makes a good read. But. While there have always been and always will be stunted creatures who make fun of people for showing emotion that said creatures are uncomfortable with, why does a plainly sophisticated, generous, and intelligent critic need to marshal lengthy cultural analysis to explain to his equally sophisticated cohort why a person might get emotional and even cry at the sight of her fellows wretchedly suffering day after day? Really, you have to explain why that is "culturally sound"?

I didn't ask these questions the first time I read the book because I got so involved in Wilson's parsing of the "signifiers," "referents," and "touchstones" that make up the horrible baroque language of modern criticism, a layering upon layering of assumptions, interpretations, and second guesses trip-wired to catch the uncool. The importance of cool in this culture is something that Wilson spends a great deal of time on, and is depressingly convincing about:

> The virtuosity that cool audiences today applaud, the sort Céline always fumbles, is not about having a multi-octave voice or flamenco-fast fingers: It's about being able to manipulate signs and symbols, to hitch them up and decouple them in a blink of an eye, to quote Homer but in the voice of Homer Simpson. It's the kind of virtuosity an advertiser deploys to hook multiple demographics, as well as the playful or caviling way of the postmodern artist.

What Wilson is describing, in this section and throughout the book, is a world of illusory shared experiences, ready-made identities, manipulation, and masks so dense and omnipresent that in this world, an actual human face is ludicrous or "crazy"; a world in which authenticity is jealously held sacrosanct and yet is often unwelcome or simply unrecognizable when it appears.

Wilson eventually seeks out and gets to know some Céline Dion fans, one of whom is Sophoan, a young Christian Cambodian-American who spent his first five years in a refugee camp on the border of Cambodia and Thailand. Wilson maintains his equilibrium as Sophoan describes his love for Céline Dion, but he loses it when Sophoan reveals that, as a toddler interned in a camp with a dirt floor, he really loved Phil Collins, especially the song "Groovy Kind of Love": "What on earth," muses Wilson, "does [Collins's] goopiest tune . . . sound like to a displaced Cambodian five-year-old? (I suppose not knowing the word 'groovy' would help.)"

I *think* the parenthetical is meant to be funny but still, on reading the question, I almost answered it out loud: "Gentle, Carl. To *any* toddler, the song would sound comforting and gentle. To a toddler surrounded by anxiety, fear, sadness, and loss, that sound would be especially nurturing, *especially* the sound 'groovy,' with its delicious 'ooo' and fun 'eee.' "(These same sounds are also nurturing to adults forced to live with chronic fear, sadness, and loss, which is probably why Dion and singers like her are (according to Wilson) popular in Iraq and Afghanistan.) At this point in the book, I had come to like and admire Wilson for his empathic and imaginative willingness to pick his way through the dark maze of signifiers and referents in order to see past his own received ideas. Still, I wanted to say, "Good grief, man, music is about *sound;* that social meaning shit is . . . basically shit. Fun, interesting shit, maybe, but . . ."

Speaking of sound, either mid-book or on finishing, I finally listened to Céline Dion on YouTube. I heard three songs, including the *Titanic* one. I thought her voice was pretty, even beautiful at moments, but her overall sound made little impression; I probably *had* heard her and forgotten it. Her appearance on *Larry King* however did make an impression; it struck me as absolutely sincere and sane. That thousands would actually spend time watching this interview so they could jeer at it, jeering especially that Dion (a singer!) had the nerve to sing a song after her speech, seemed not merely cynical but neurotically detached from reality: Dion's response wasn't only moral; it showed a sort of biologically based empathy that understands the physical vulnerability of humans in the world. News flash: Real humans are connected with one another whether they like it or not. They are awkward and dumb and wave their arms around if they get upset enough; real humans *all* have personal touchstones that are "off the map" because *there is no map*. We are so maplessly, ridiculously uncool that whole cultures and subcultures, whole personalities even, have been built to hide our ridiculousness from ourselves. These structures are sometimes very elegant and a lot of fun, and fun to talk about, too. But our ridiculous vulnerability is perhaps the most authentic thing about us, and we scorn it at our peril—yet scorn it we do.

At the end of *Let's Talk About Love*, Wilson concludes that Céline Dion will remain "securely uncool" and that this gives him "the heart to go on." I *think* this means that he's realized that someone he had despised for reasons having nothing to do with her is just a person making art that he can like or dislike, but that his likes or dislikes don't reflect on the fundamental quality of her humanity or his, a quality that independently exists and will "go on" outside of any systematized set of social/artistic judgments.

It seems the most obvious thing in the world. But in the middle of writing this reaction to Carl Wilson's reaction to Céline Dion something funny happened: I went to a reading by a writer who had been described to me as great, and I not only failed to find him great; I found him bad, obnoxiously bad, bad to the point that I was a-boil in my chair as I listened to him hold forth. When he was done, I turned to the person next to me and said, "What an idiot." That night, I called someone and expanded on that "thought," using words like "buffoon" and "conceited pig." I don't know how long I went on about it, but it was *much longer than seconds*. It wasn't until I hung up that I heard my own words in my head: *Bitch, excuse me?*

This seems to me the real substance of Wilson's book, and why it is more than an intelligent discourse on a small, specialized segment of society: The most obvious thing in the world is the easiest thing to forget, especially regarding any subject that you care about, *especially* when that subject is an art form full of costumed personalities making their most private experience into publicly projected stories, where real and unreal are fantastically or oafishly mixed. In this nonstop torrent of personae, audience and performers both, Carl Wilson has slowly and patiently come to find and respect one human soul regardless of his cherished "likes"; it's a beautiful reminder to see someone do that in any context.

Let's Talk About Love: Why Other People Have Such Bad Taste, EDITED BY CARL WILSON, 2014 (COMPOSED IN 2013)

SHE'S SUPPOSED TO MAKE YOU SICK

A REVIEW OF *GONE GIRL* BY GILLIAN FLYNN

This is not a book I would normally read; I rarely read mysteries, and the title, *Gone Girl,* is irritating on its face. I bought it anyway because two friends recommended it with enormous enthusiasm, and because I was curious about its enormous popularity— the millions of copies sold, the impending movie by David Fincher and Reese Witherspoon, the glowing reviews. I found it as irritating as I'd imagined, populated by snarky-cute, pop-culturally twisted voices coming out of characters that seemed constructed entirely of "referents" and "signifiers," and who say things like "Suck it, douchesnob!" The only reason I kept reading was that, having bought the book in hardcover, I took it with me on a long train ride and it was better than obsessively checking my messages (which *is* something). As I read, I began to find the thing genuinely frightening. By the time the train ride was over, I felt I was reading something truly sick and dark—and in case you don't know, I'm supposedly sick and dark.

The sick and dark of *Gone Girl,* by Gillian Flynn, is less in the plot (which is a masterpiece of cuckoo clockwork) than in the vision, especially the vision of Amy, the missing woman. Amy is a beautiful, rich New Yorker who is lovely and lovable, at least according to her diary entries, one of which begins, "Tra and la! I am smiling a big adopted-orphan smile as I write this. I am embarrassed at how happy I am, like some Technicolor comic of a teenage girl talking on the phone with my hair in a ponytail, the bubble above my head saying: *I met a boy!*" This boy is Nick, whom she marries, who then loses his job, who pressures her to move to his miserable Missouri hometown, where he reveals himself, according to her relentless chirping prose, as a narcissistic abuser who persuades her to use the last of her trust fund to finance his bar. On Valentine's Day, she buys a gun because "I just would feel safer with a gun."

Meanwhile, Nick (chirping in a more masculine register) is revealing Amy as an emotional terrorist who sets baroque, hurtful traps for him, especially on their anniversaries, for which she creates "treasure hunts" full of clues based on shared moments that he can't remember. She goes missing on one such anniversary, and Nick quickly becomes a suspect, partly because he's a habitual liar, but mostly because inexplicable, damning evidence keeps turning up against him, including a murder weapon. And then there's the treasure hunt, which appears to be Amy's final love letter but turns out to be one piece of her final and most malicious trap. The trap has many moving parts, including a faked pregnancy test achieved by harvesting a pregnant woman's pee from a toilet, an actual pregnancy achieved with forgotten frozen sperm, a mysteriously planted stash of porn (*Brutal Anal; Hurt the Bitch*), and a faked poisoning backed up by frozen vomit. The few acts of physical violence that occur happen off-camera and are not dwelled on. That the emotional violence is rendered in smarty-pants chirping makes it more grating than painful.

What makes *Gone Girl* scary rather than kooky is its cast of characters—what motivates them, and how they view each other. Amy and Nick do not resemble actual people so much as grotesquely smiling masks driven by forces of malevolent artifice, and it's exactly that masked, artificial quality that's frightening to the point of sickening. Most frightening of all is that the artifice is so *normal*.

What I mean by "artifice" is social language, styles, and manners—a public way of being that is by necessity coded, fixed, and hard, and which has become even more so through the emergence of the virtual world. In physical life, the hardness and (frequent) deceptiveness of such language is offset by the deep, doggishly honest presence of the body; in the virtual world, such animal presence is either absent or faked. *Gone Girl* doesn't compare to other books as well as it evokes flipping through TV shows (including the news) and glimpsing face after chirping female face, all with only slight variations on the same manner of speech, facial expressions, and the "smart," high-speed delivery common to Facebook chat, texting, and tweeting; that is to say, the book impressively evokes an artificial hive-minded way of relating combined with what has become a feminine cultural ideal of relentless charm tied to power and control.

This feminine ideal was lampooned/celebrated in the movie *Bridesmaids,* which is about adult women manically competing over things like who will pick the bridesmaids' dresses, who will have the last word in the bridal shower speech, and, of course, who has the most and best stuff. The women get food poisoning, shit in their dresses, slam one another in the tits while playing tennis; at the shower, the heroine—who is a quirky single misfit—screeches at the bride about bleaching her asshole, whereupon the bride screeches back, "I love my bleached asshole!" It's not exactly a new idea: Women are filthy, vicious idiots who must compensate with extreme self-control—dress exactly right, talk exactly right, pluck, diet, dye, and, hell yes, bleach—then claw at each other/bond over who is doing it best, and wow, is it ever cute! But *Gone Girl* takes it to a whole other level. Because Amy is rich, beautiful, sharp-witted, and thin, she has won the first part of the control game automatically. If you have observed, as I have, that people tend to treat others as they treat themselves, the next natural move in achieving such fanatic self-control would be to control others. This requires a kind of power that most women (and men) do not have—except in power fantasies such as the ones concocted in Flynn's novel.

When I called the friends who'd recommended *Gone Girl* to talk about how sick-making I found it, they both listened in baffled silence before replying, "But the character is crazy. She's supposed to make you sick." I guess that by "crazy" what is meant is that Amy lies, manipulates, switches personae, in fact sees herself and everybody else in terms of personae, and will do literally *anything* to get her way. But I don't think she's any crazier than the world we live in now. Her meanness—and the unfeeling, appraising way she types everyone she meets—just seems an extreme version of a norm or an accepted cultural language; that hyperfast hive brain that very nearly precludes seeing beyond a coded surface.

Amy—a paragon of self-possession who always has the last word—constantly typecasts others in the most rigid and nasty way. Here's how she sums up the young woman Nick turns out to be fucking: "Taking his cock in her mouth, all the way to the root so he can feel extra big as she gags. Taking it in her ass, deep. Taking cum shots to the face and tits, then licking it off, *yum*. Taking, definitely taking. Her type would." It's normal, I guess, for a woman to hate her rival. But the hatred and scorn here seem not to be about the competition for Nick's attention; they seem to be about the young woman's (imagined) receptivity or submissiveness—her lack of control.

Amy may be the nastiest, most reductive typecaster in the book, but the reductive tendencies of our cultural moment are part of *Gone Girl*'s DNA, and snap judgments emerge without question—particularly at the expense of those who, like Nick's mistress, appear to have less than total control. When Nick and Amy's families set up a Find Amy Dunne headquarters at a local Days Inn, a female detective warns Nick about the rapacious older women (forty-somethings) who will inevitably try to seduce him while pretending to help, and sure enough, one such creature instantly appears. She is, like everyone else in the book, immediately identifiable, in this case by her "giant brown pony eyes, her pink shirt ending just above crisp white shorts," her "high-heeled sandals, curled hair, gold hoops." Soon she is pawing Nick, offering him pie (!), pouting, and complaining that the female detective doesn't like her. Nick responds:

> "Why do you say that?" I already knew what she was going to say, the mantra of all attractive women.
> "Women don't like me all that much. . . . Did—does Amy have a lot of friends in town?"
> . . . "I think she may have the same problem you do," I said in a clipped voice.

Some critics have called Flynn's portrayals of women misogynist, but to me it seems like she's just amplifying an attitude that's shoved in front of us all the time—on TV, online, in countless tabloids that are constantly informing us that some woman, regardless of age, is "humiliated" because her husband "cheated" or because she gained weight or because, after being dumped by her husband, she had the nerve to get drunk and dance in public—that is, because she did not have absolute control over herself *or* the behavior of her man, and is therefore a legitimate object of derision or pity, or both. The book is a representation of everyday cruelties, along with au courant social behaviors and codes that flatten everything and everyone into instant types. Here is Nick being seduced by the supposedly disgusting young lady described above: ". . . her breasts pushed upward. She wore a pendant on a thin gold chain; the pendant slid between her breasts down under her sweater." "*Don't be that guy,* I thought. *The guy who pants over where the pendant ends.*" Who exactly is "that guy"? A guy who likes to look at women's breasts? Wouldn't that be millions of guys? There is nothing here but "that guy" or "that girl," and that means nothing, period.

There *are* elements to admire in *Gone Girl:* Some of the nasty characterizations ring true, and Flynn has a witty eye for detail; the intricacy of the plotting is insanely clever. The best and most grounding element, though, is the backdrop, the small, economically depressed town to which Nick brings Amy, where homeless people live in the abandoned mall at which Nick's mother used to work. The minor characters who populate this backdrop, including Nick's parents, are the only real humans in the book; reminiscent of the "proles" in Orwell's *1984,* their "realness" seems to consign them to poverty, illness, wan goodness, and small-time criminality—in short, powerlessness. Given this context, rage and annihilating artifice seem a reasonable response, for who would want to be like these people? Amy is just outplaying the hive mind on its own terms—and winning, on a grand-slam sweepstakes level, all the things the average woman is supposed to want. In this sense, *Gone Girl* is pure-black comedy; it is also a maniacal power fantasy that panders to (specifically) female rage and fear. I wonder if "real people" like those depicted by the book are buying it so that they, too, can enjoy the fantasy, distance themselves from it by calling its heroine "crazy," and then go back to muddling on.

What is unclear to me is how *Gone Girl* regards its nihilistic fantasy. Does Flynn represent Amy's chirping, her charm, and her control over herself and others with a sort of wild, cackling despair? Or does she promote the fantasy, or somehow cut it down the middle? (Perhaps it's unfair to note that Flynn, writing on her blog and the acknowledgments page of *Gone Girl,* sounds exactly like Amy.) Either way, it's difficult to appreciate the book without participating in the fantasy, without living, for a time, in the horrible hive brain it so successfully invokes. Unlike a TV show, which we can watch while texting, this is written fiction; we have to attentively absorb it word by word. However harsh my comments here, as a writer I can't help but appreciate Flynn's assertion of literature's superior potential to engage readers by subtly making them do more than just listen and watch. But this book seems a little too enamored with Amy's view of the world, and misuses its power in something like the way its protagonist misuses hers.

Bookforum, 2013

ICON

Icon of freedom and innocent carnality; icon of brokenness and confusion; icon of a wound turned into or disguised as pleasure source; icon of sexual victimization, sexual power, irreconcilable oppositions; icon of 1970s America; icon of Everywoman. And just another skinny white girl with average looks and a little flat voice, a type you barely notice even if some version of her is everywhere.

I saw Linda Lovelace* in *Deep Throat* because my boyfriend was the projectionist at a hippie film co-op. It was 1972 and I was seventeen; my boyfriend was twenty-five, and neither of us was interested in porn, which we thought of as a corny old person thing. But *Deep Throat*, an X-rated comedy about a woman whose clitoris is in her throat, was supposed to be something different, and we were curious, then won over by the film's dirty goof-ballery. "She just seemed to like it so much," said my boyfriend, and his voice was not salacious as much as tickled. I liked the movie, too—it was funny—but *liking* and arousal are very different. I wasn't excited by *Deep Throat,* and the only thing I could really remember about it afterward was Lovelace's sweet smile

---

*I am not using her given surname, Boreman, because it is the public persona Linda Lovelace that this essay is most concerned with.

and the strange expression in her eyes, a look that I could not
define and still can't, a look that was not happy yet which seemed
to go with her smile.

I was, however, wildly excited by the next movie I saw at the
co-op, a film that on the face of it has nothing in common with
Deep Throat but which remains, in my imagination, weirdly linked
with the porn comedy: It was Carl Dreyer's *The Passion of Joan
of Arc*, an emotionally stunning silent film made in 1928 about
the persecution, psychological torture, and death of an inexplica-
bly, helplessly powerful nineteen-year-old girl. I'm sure it sounds
ridiculously arty, but trust me, my reaction was not artistic. I was
horrified by this film, but also moved and so aroused that I was
embarrassed to be in public, even in the dark. I don't *like* images
of persecution or death or torture, but liking was irrelevant; *Passion* demanded a powerful response, and my body gave it.

Anyway, in 1980, when Linda Lovelace wrote a book (with
journalist Mike McGrady) about her experience, called *Ordeal*,
then joined Catherine MacKinnon's antiporn movement, I fleet-
ingly remembered her sweet, strange-eyed smile, and how different it seemed from the woman claiming that anyone who
watched *Deep Throat* was watching her being raped. I was
vaguely sad but not that surprised; it seemed just one more piece
of senseless effluvia flying past.

Fast-forward to 2012, when not one but two mainstream
biopics about Linda Lovelace were being made at the same time;
I learned of these films because of a brief involvement with a
guy who had some vague connection with one of the films as
well as very strong opinions on its subject. He felt nothing but
contempt for Lovelace, whom he described as a deeply stupid liar
who refused to take responsibility for any of her actions, including her participation in pre-*Throat* porn loops, particularly one
in which she enthusiastically received a dog. He told me that in

Ordeal she claimed, among other things, that she was forced by her husband/pimp, Chuck Traynor,* to "do" the dog, but that "everyone" knew it was a lie, that she was "into it"—that is, she liked it.

This was all news to me, but I shrugged and said, "I don't blame her. We've all done things that, while not embarrassing at the time, *would* be embarrassing if projected on a public movie screen. Besides, she had kids; if you had kids, would you want to talk about dog fucking with them?" "But," my friend said, "then she turned on Women Against Pornography and said *they* used her, too." I said, "They probably did; those women are bonkers." He retorted, "But *then* she posed for a magazine called *Leg Show.*" To which I said, "So what? That's not really porn, and she probably needed the money." We changed the subject and broke up that night.

But the conversation made me care about Linda Lovelace in a way I previously had not, and made me want to defend her. It also made me curious; she and her husband/pimp, Chuck Traynor, are dead (both in 2002), as is *Deep Throat* director Gerry Damiano and Lovelace's costar Harry Reems, so why was a grown man talking like a schoolyard bully about her ten years later? Why was her story suddenly of such pop-cultural interest that, forty years after *Deep Throat,* two mainstream film companies wanted to tell it?

When the biopic titled *Lovelace* came out the following year (the other, *Inferno,* floundered and was killed), I saw it and became something more than curious. *Lovelace* is a candy-colored feel-good story of a nice girl forced into porn by an abusive husband but who nonetheless blooms with the attention of celebrities like

---

*Pronounced *trainer,* a name that, in some linguistically based universe, should've been enough all by itself to get him hauled in on suspicion of *something.*

Hugh Hefner, is redeemed by feminism, accepted by her family, gets married, and starts a family of her own. Critics and viewers responded tepidly, but to me the bowdlerization was even more obnoxious than my former friend's contempt. Why, after more than forty years, were people so insistently sanitizing and simplifying this story?

I shouldn't have wondered; *Deep Throat* was an extreme phenomenon that, whimsically and unself-consciously, both confirmed and challenged the status quo of masculine privilege by creating a fantasy world of blow jobs that gave pride of place to female orgasm. This preposterous polarity was heightened by the film's combination of high and low (in terms of register or pitch), the way it put together silliness and lightness of spirit with the florid id imagery of porn, especially the image of its star, an appealing girl happily splitting her pretty face to get huge, hairy dicks impossibly far down her throat. Made in six days for $45,500, with sitcom dialogue and a kooky sound track, the film grossed fifty million dollars; *Screw*'s Al Goldstein fell in love, the Mafia made a killing (literally), President Nixon condemned it, New York mayor Lindsay banned it, and the glitterati lined up to see it, including Jack Nicholson, Truman Capote, Liz Taylor, and Jackie O. Harry Reems was arrested and eventually did time for obscenity; Linda Lovelace became an international celebrity.

She may've been average-looking, but (in addition to her famous erotic "trick" and her ardent way with it) Lovelace projected the perverse charm of innocence soiled, but blithely so, a fragile, playful persona that was uniquely, darkly radiant, dirty and ethereal both. She appeared at a time that is hard to imagine now, when porn has become normalized and commodified to the point that middle-class teenagers might sport license plates that read PORN STAR and actual porn stars are featured on mainstream news Web sites; 1972 was a transitional time, both libertine and innocent in every direction, with traditional values asserted as aggressively as they were rebelled against. It was a time when many people must've found it wonderful to see a sweet-faced young woman with a touchingly delicate figure and a girlie voice swallowing throbbin' gristle till her nose ran, yet whom you could watch without feeling nasty *because she liked it so much*. The 2005 documentary *Inside Deep Throat* includes footage of a press conference at which Lovelace appears in a long pale gown with a rose in her teeth. She looks anything but average; she is beautiful, puckishly so, and she is surrounded by absolutely gaga men who look as if they are witnessing the arrival of a woman riding in from another world astride a thunderbolt, a world in which good and evil cum together with joy, and *anything* is allowed without consequence.

It is poignant to consider this explosion of glamour and sexual exuberance emanating from an utterly unglamorous, small, abused and abusing couple, but—for a minute it seemed like anything *was* allowed, and when anything is allowed, what really *is* abuse?

Abused or not, Lovelace suddenly had offers she'd never dreamed of—from television, movies, and lecture circuits—and she gamely tried to make use of it all, trollish husband in tow. But either because she lacked the talent or because she was simply too overwhelmed by the whole thing, none of it worked for her; she dropped out of sight, divorcing Chuck and marrying childhood friend Larry Marchiano. Until, that is, she produced *Ordeal* and reemerged as an antiporn activist. Her besotted fans were disappointed; her former colleagues were *angry*, and in some cases hurt—according to porn star Annie Sprinkle, *Deep Throat*'s director was "heartbroken" by her claims.

The Other Hollywood, by Legs McNeil and Jennifer Osborne (with Peter Pavia), is an "Uncensored Oral History of the Porn Film Industry," and it is jammed with people expressing their anger and disgust at Lovelace—even people who plainly state that, yes, Chuck Traynor beat his wife. "I mean, this was a woman who never took responsibility for her own shitty choices—but instead blamed everything that happened in her life on porn. You know, 'The devil made me do it.'" In a personal exchange with me, porn diva Annie Sprinkle was gentler about it: "I do think Linda was in an abusive relationship. And she was definitely traumatized by it. . . . And I strongly believe that she had a ball doing *Deep Throat* and that she was treated like a star, and went through a horrible time simultaneously with her husband. . . . I'm sure she also associated *Deep Throat* with that horrible time in her life."

I liked that interpretation and took it further, possibly in a too-romantic direction. I thought that the relationship must've at least started as consensual, that there was probably an element of coercion from Chuck that was part fear and part willing excitement, but that at some point the excitement tipped over into real fear, and that eventually Lovelace could not tell where one ended and the other began. I wondered if Traynor, pimp that he was, knew for sure. Once out of the relationship, I imagined that Lovelace simply lacked the confidence to describe what she did and felt in a nuanced way, and the thing was very, very nuanced and contradictory. So she went with either "I liked it" or "I was raped."

This is a very rational, mild, and forgiving way to think of an experience that was none of the above. Just how "none of the above" it might've been became apparent when I read *Ordeal*. That book, which is now out of print, has been so dismissed that I almost didn't read it. I can see why it was dismissed; the experience it describes is so relentlessly, ridiculously miserable, so helpless and hapless, so utterly incongruous with how Lovelace initially presented herself. Some of it does strain credulity; as I read the beginning of it, I asked myself out loud, "Where were her instincts?" It's a good question: If her portrayal of Chuck Traynor is at all accurate, he was the kind of guy that even a very young and naïve girl could see coming from a mile off. You don't need special shrewdness or even much experience to recognize a predator; all you need is a working animal instinct. But some people's instincts have been ruined. Some people's instincts have been so ruined by such disrespectful treatment that, for them, disrespect is not merely a norm; it has a kind of hyperreality that is absolutely compelling. Such people don't necessarily identify as masochistic in a conscious way. They are sometimes just apparently weird people whose strange ways of dealing with the world can make them a pain in the ass. It's hard to want to know them—that is, to know how hurt they are, and how intractable the damage is. I'm not sure I believe everything in *Ordeal*, but even if half of it is true, expressions like "nuanced and contradictory" or "having a ball" and "being treated like a star" seem woefully off the mark.

But, while it expresses a low opinion of porn, *Ordeal* doesn't actually blame porn for anything. The book is appreciative of some people in the business (for example, the late porn star Andrea True) and depicts *Deep Throat* as a big step up from the stuff Lovelace says she was forced into previously. She describes Gerry Damiano and most of the other people involved with the film as relatively decent and considerate, including a soundman who offered to protect her from Traynor if she gave him a "signal." As grotesque as it is, I can't dismiss it; too much of it rings true. But it's also impossible to dismiss the appealing, even delightful way she looks in *Deep Throat*, or her otherworldly radiance in the subsequent press conference and interviews. In spite of her eerie, sometimes dead-looking eyes, there is nothing in her voice or body language that suggests terror or victimization, not even during a scene in which she's pretending to be menaced by a pretend rapist with a gun. Really, she *does* look like she's having a ball. A ball in hell maybe, but a ball nonetheless.

This equal-and-opposite mixed signage is what makes Lovelace into a compelling, even profound figure, a lost soul and powerful icon, defiled innocent and sexual rock star who posed for a skin mag at fifty-two. All these years later, her redemption is important for feminists (and not only those with an antiporn fixation) because, in spite of her Sadean trajectory, her experience is a fun-house version of the sometimes excruciating contradictions that many women experience in relation to sex.

Consider this mild and typical anecdote: A friend of mine, now in her fifties, told me how, in her twenties, every time she would walk into her neighborhood bar in NYC's East Village, this same guy would grab her breasts and everybody would laugh; she said thinking about it now made her furious. When I asked her what she did at the time, she said she laughed, too, because she didn't know what else to do. And I remember what she was like in her twenties; she flirted and giggled a lot, and she loved attention. So which is true, the giggly girl who just laughed when the guy grabbed her, or the angry woman in her fifties? Now consider this more extreme contradiction: A therapist once told me that some women orgasm when they are raped. I had never heard this before and found it hard to believe. I said, "So, if the rapist said, 'She liked it,' he would be telling the truth." The therapist said no, she did not like it. But for some people, the adrenal arousal of terror turns into global arousal that becomes sexual.

I thought of that when I read in *The Other Hollywood* that Linda was constantly turned on, that she was "soaking wet," and that she really seemed to be "into it" with the dog. In *Ordeal*, Lovelace writes that she was forced into the scene with the dog, that there was actually a gun on the set. But in *The Other Hollywood*, actress Sharon Mitchell says that when she briefly walked onto the set, it "didn't look like they were forcing her to do anything"; rather, that it "looked like they were forcing the dogs!" Mitchell says that she was so upset by the sight of Linda's arousal that she became terrified and ran down the stairs. The first striking thing about this anecdote is Mitchell's mean-girl brutality; did she realize how many people would talk with the same contempt about her? Was the sight of arousal really so terrifying? Or was she running from terror itself, terror blended with arousal so completely that she didn't consciously know what she was looking at or running from? The second striking thing is that although everyone else involved describes one dog on the set, Mitchell apparently saw "dogs"—kind of like Lovelace seeing a gun that everyone else says wasn't there. Chuck Traynor did hit Linda and he did own guns. If he ever pointed a gun at Linda, even once, in her mind it was probably always there.

Or not. Maybe there was no gun and she knew it. Maybe she was terrified anyway. Fear is powerful sometimes even when there is no immediate threat. Sometimes it motivates people without their knowing it except in hindsight, if at all.

When I was seventeen I was violently raped. It was horrible, but I got through it and did not believe it affected me overmuch. It did not inhibit me sexually; in the years following the experience, I was promiscuous, even aggressively so. Sometimes I had sex without really knowing why (by which I mean, I did it when I wasn't really interested), but that seemed true of many, many people at the time. Then one day when I was nineteen something happened. I was with a guy and we were fooling around on my bed, still fully clothed. Playfully, he raised himself over me, grabbed my wrists, and pinned them. I went completely blank. I don't know how else to describe it. As he put it later, my body went limp and my eyes "empty." Scared himself, he let go of me and said something like "What's wrong?" I said, "I thought you were going to start hitting me." Clearly taken aback, he replied, "I would never do that. How could you think that?" I said, "I don't know," and I meant it; I had no idea how much fear I'd been carrying and was so surprised by my own blanking out that I didn't even understand it at first. We talked some—I don't remember if I told him about being raped or not—but sex was out of the question. That incident made me realize that I was sometimes having sex because I was afraid that if I didn't, I would be raped or hit, even when the men in question did not threaten me in any way. This was not always the case; I had natural feelings. But sometimes fear motivated me without my being aware of it until that one boy's gesture brought it out of hiding. Even then it was so *physically* present in me that I couldn't stop having sex I didn't fully want for almost two years after I realized what was going on.

Because of experiences like this—not just mine but also those that other women have described to me—it's hard for me to see the Lovelace story as a simple matter of her lying or not. Even if there was no gun and Lovelace knew it, I can't see that kind of lie as coming from one simple motivation. Maybe Lovelace enjoyed what she did to the point of wallowing in it, including the abuse that came with it, and then years later, when she was ravaged, angry, and broke, rewrote it and came to believe the revision. Maybe she started out liking it and came to hate it, or liked it sometimes and hated it other times. Maybe she never *liked* it but was masochistically *aroused* by it; maybe she hated it straight up but did it anyway. Not many people could describe experiencing any of this accurately, let alone honestly, especially if it was *all* true. That is, if she felt all of the above in some hellish combination, and was so torn by the opposition that she developed a fragmented public self, one that smiled and was delightful when prompted or that assumed an antiporn stance when prompted, with nothing fully developed in support of either.

This last, terrible idea makes me remember my stunned blankness of so long ago, blankness that I acted out of for years and which, frankly, was not exclusively about rape. Blankness is a kind of dead zone, and action that comes from blankness happens in fragments. I know what it's like to be pulled in too many directions to make sense of, but to want to live and to engage so much that you act regardless. It's a hard way to be, but at least I had the space and time to try to understand my experience as best I could. Lovelace didn't have that ordinary luxury because of her fame. Becoming famous for being yourself is now an American fixation; Linda Lovelace lived the dream, and how. But what would it be like to be famous for being yourself if you didn't know what your "self" was? Imagine projecting and being projected into the world, on a massive scale, as someone who has no complex emotions, who is all persona, in this case a persona that is all about having one particular kind of sex with whomever. Because people liked the persona, it must've felt good at first; hell, it must've felt great. But some of the worst things in the world feel that way. At first.

In the documentary *The Real Linda Lovelace,* Chuck Traynor described his wife this way: "Everything she did, she had to be told how to do it and when to do it and why she was doing it . . . you always had to tell her what to do." This is self-serving; it's possibly true. After Traynor and Lovelace split, he married Marilyn Chambers, and by most accounts the relationship was good for the eleven years that it lasted. Eric Danville, a friend and fan of Lovelace (and author of *The Complete Linda Lovelace*), once asked Chambers if she'd ever met Linda; she said no but that she'd once overheard her screaming at Chuck on the phone while he winced and held the receiver away from his ear. In an interview she gave before her death in 2009*, Chambers was asked what it was like to be married to "the infamous Chuck Traynor," and she defended him all the way, characterizing Lovelace's book as "75% BS" and Chuck as "an average Joe Blow kind of guy" who knew what "turned on the average guy." According to a 2013 article by Chris-

---

* See girlsandcorpses.com.

tine Pelisek in *The Daily Beast,* Chambers acknowledged that
Traynor did hit her once but that she "hit him back really hard,"
breaking two fingernails; she said that Linda's problem was that
she was "meek." The same *Beast* article reports that when Chambers and Traynor divorced, she gave him all of her money, that
she died with nothing. That Chambers accepted the rules of the
pimp's game, and played by them till the very end, even to her
disadvantage, suggests a kind of gallantry that might, in another
time and context, be referred to as "being a lady." I admire it.
But I don't understand why she needed to disparage Lovelace
for being "meek" or (it seems to me) for not really knowing that
there was a game being played, let alone what the rules were.*

That I saw *The Passion of Joan of Arc* in such close proximity to
Deep Throat is strictly random. Still, I am haunted by it. Lovelace
was as apparently hapless as Saint Joan was fanatically determined, seemingly as ordinary as Saint Joan was extraordinary.
Yet, in the same way Joan of Arc embodied social and spiritual
forces that were most likely beyond her personality, Lovelace was
fated to embody extreme and opposing social and sexual forces
much too big for the limits of her self, for any self. Both women
were torn apart by that which they embodied, yet for a moment
glowed with enormous symbolic power. This is what seems the
most painful thing about the Lovelace story, more painful even
than domestic abuse, to live as a public vector for oppositions
that are still too much for this culture, possibly *any* culture, to
countenance, to burn with the strength of those forces without
fully being able to understand or effectively wield them.

---

*A circumstance I find poignant and slightly eerie: Lovelace died on
April 22, which was Chambers's birthday; Chuck Traynor died of a heart
attack on July 22, exactly three months later.

In the end, Lovelace divorced Marchiano, claiming that he, too, abused her. She was poor and sick with hepatitis, and, having fallen out with the antiporn movement, was appearing at porn memorabilia conventions to sign DVD copies of *Deep Throat* and copies of *Ordeal*. The recent film doesn't touch any of this, perhaps because the filmmakers felt that in omitting these aspects of the story they were casting their subject in a positive and more sympathetic light, making it easier for the audience to like her. But the bowdlerization does Lovelace a great disservice. As much as anything, her story was about enormous loneliness, and survival against odds that few people could understand; this universal condition makes her moving beyond any specifics of feminism or porn and defies a happy ending.

During *Passion,* one of the twisted inquisitors asks Joan if Saint Michael actually spoke to her; as the critic Roger Ebert described it, her face "seems to suggest that whatever happened between Michael and herself was so beyond the scope of the question that no answer is conceivable." The question of whether or not Linda Lovelace was a liar or a victim might be a joke in comparison— but still, I think that whatever happened in that place and time in her life is beyond the scope of the question.

Icon, EDITED BY AMY SCHOLDER, 2014

THAT RUNNING SHADOW OF YOUR VOICE

ON NABOKOV'S *LETTERS TO VÉRA*

We had a pleasant little party the other day, what
can I say: tra-la-la, Aldanov in tails, Bunin in the
vilest dinner-jacket, Khmara with a guitar and
Kedrova, Ilyusha in such narrow trousers that his
legs were like two black sausages, old sweet Teffi—
and all in this revoltingly luxurious mansion . . .
as we listened to the blind-drunk Khmara's rather
boorish ballads she kept saying: but my life is over!
While Kedrova (a very sharp-eyed little actress
whom Aldanov thinks a new Komissarzhevskaya)
shamelessly begged me for a part. Why, of course,
the most banal singing of "charochka," a lonely
vase with chocolates, the hostess's wail (about me):
"Oh, he's eating all the chocolates," a view from
the picture window onto the skeleton of the growing exhibition and the moon. *C'était à vomir.* Bunin
kept impersonating my "arrogance" and then
hissed: "you will die alone and in horrible agony."

—Vladimir Nabokov, from *Letters to Véra*

In life as in death: If there was a superhero called Most Loved
Yet Most Hated Dead White Male Writer, Vladimir Nabokov

could've been buried in the suit. Bring him up in interested company and the reaction may range from snooty, ululating adoration to irrational, pinch-mouthed hatred. For the haters, V.N. is an elitist of the worst kind, a contemptuous aristocrat, a probable pedophile, a cruel, immoral, emotionally empty, perhaps *even stupid*, yet freakishly gifted technician with nothing to say. For the ululators (not all of whom are snoots, I'm just acknowledging the royalist fusspots on the far end of the spectrum) V.N. is beyond reproach, a moral and intellectual saint who, among other flawless feats, wrote an erotic masterpiece about pedophiliac love purely in order to "exploit the aesthetic possibilities of the material" or, as the superb scholar Brian Boyd has written with a straight face, to express his "concern for children." Between these two poles there is such a stupefying gap, filled with so much brainiac noise, that when I find myself in such conversations, I become . . . stupefied. "Nabokov is cold," coldly comments an academic of my acquaintance. "He's not cold," I answer; "he's hot." "It's finally the same thing," he replies. "There's no warmth." "But he's sometimes even a bit sentimental," I say. "Exactly" is the inexorable reply. "It's false feeling."

In view of all this, I read *Letters to Véra*, a collection of V.N.'s letters to his wife, in part with the hopeless hope that *finally* the haters' angrily squeezed eyes could be made to open. That hope is, of course, irrelevant to the book, which is (to anyone but a confirmed hater) a gorgeous and heartening record of the intimate life of a genius. It is a delightful encyclopedia of pet names ("My joy," "floridithy," "owlthy," "lovethy," "my love," "my sweet and multicolored Roosterkin"), literary gossip, family stories, lists of boardinghouse meals ("fried eggs and cold cuts"), drawings of animals, insects, and toys, puzzles, opinions on everything from news stories to James Joyce ("Ultimately, wit sets behind reason, and while it is setting, the sky is marvellous, but then it's night"), and intense aesthetic appreciations of, among other things, street corners, dachshunds, and oil on a puddle (that is, *a huge dullish opal*). Miserly points for the haters: There *are* moments of very petty bitchiness, even toward his admiring friends (the "pink isthmus" between Nina Berberova's two front teeth is made much of) and unpleasant vanity (he seems pleased to scornfully describe an old girlfriend who repeatedly shows up at his readings). When he writes to his wife to indignantly deny an affair, he shows himself to be a flat-out liar. However, the overwhelming quality of his letters (which he wrote nearly every day they were apart) is generous, buoyant, sincere, and *warm,* most of all to Véra and their son, Dmitri (*he still walks all over my soul as if it was his own bed, my darling, my little bunny*), but also to friends, family, animals of all kinds (the big bad elitist was a great rescuer of mice!), children, and, yes, even colleagues.

> After tea and still there for dinner (our supper) were Aldanov, Vishnyak (he is very likeable, funny and round), and the invariable Kerensky, who also keeps cracking jokes with a remarkable Jewish intonation, and in general, has mannerisms a little like the old man Kaplan's . . . and Mother Maria—a nun, fat, pink, very likeable, the former wife of Kuzmin-Karavaev. And when I, not knowing this, told how Hitlerites had beaten him up, she said with feeling: "Serves him right!"

And then:

> After the meeting, Struve spoke, as well as Kirill Zaytsev, Kartashev (he speaks wonderfully, with tight-shut eyes, with amazing force and imagery), Florovsky and Fondaminsky (who was terribly agitated: they had gotten at *Novyi grad*), with great spirit.

This tone of warm, appreciative engagement with others suffuses the letters; even the snotty passages have an effervescent spirit—for example, the one I chose to lead with. And actually the way I quoted that passage is somewhat misleading because I omitted the lead-in to the scene:

> I'm really starting to feel oppressed, the enervating charm of Paris, the divine sunsets (on the Arc de Triomphe, a fragment of the frieze suddenly comes to life—a pigeon taking off), the charm and the idleness, the outlines of time are wobbly, I can't write, I'm desperate for solitude with you . . .

V.N.'s exasperation at the party didn't spring primarily from his dislike of the company; it seems he much preferred the intimate connection with his wife. He preferred love, which he, in a letter, whimsically described in terms of temperature:

> I have just returned from the Karpoviches', where it was agreeable as always, but also cosy in a new way—a very bright and light house, which has not yet managed (although it's starting to, in some corners) to blossom. The water in their tub was, as I told Tatyana, more like (warm) friendship than (hot) love.

The letters create the impression that V.N. temperamentally preferred the heat of love to the warmth of friendship. The need to escape the social nonsense to be with Véra comes up repeatedly and even incongruously; while V.N. was carrying on an affair with an émigré poet named Irina Guadanini, he was literally begging his wife to leave Germany and join him in Paris. This begging could've been purely for show, but it does not read that way to me. It suggests instead that V.N., far from cold and calculating, was in this instance not fully in control of himself. His pleas to his wife to come to Paris read almost as if he wanted her to save him. And she did. Someone told Véra what was going on and she confronted her husband, essentially saying "her or me." He broke off the affair but continued to exchange letters with his mistress for a couple of months. Guadanini asked to see V.N. one last time. He said no; he had by then reunited with his family in Cannes. She came to see him anyway. She approached him on the beach while he was with his three-year-old son. (She may've come to tell him she was pregnant; afterward, she gave birth to a boy she put up for adoption.) He told her that he still loved her but asked her to leave for good. He also asked that she return his letters, but she refused. She died—alone and in poverty—in possession of every letter he wrote her and a collection of articles that had been written about him, including some that featured pictures of Véra.

This affair might be seen as an example of what my academic friend was getting at when he said that very hot can be, in its effects, "the same" as very cold—that is, painful. Indeed, it seems that the very heat of the affair required a cauterized ending— otherwise, it might've been impossible to end it at all. Guadanini did not simply leave when dismissed. She sat down on the beach some distance from V.N. and Dmitri, and continued to sit there when Véra joined them; she was still there when the family left for lunch.

One's heart hurts for the devastated woman—but few would want such drama, and V.N. truly could not afford it. Like everyone else in the unmoored émigré community, he and Véra (who was Jewish, and often alone with her young child in Weimar Germany) were vulnerable and struggling mightily. The reason V.N. was apart from his wife for such long periods was that he was in Paris and London frantically hustling his work, hand-delivering copies of novels and stories (typewritten and posted by Véra from

Berlin) to whomever he thought might help him get published, angling for teaching appointments, networking like a fiend. The insecurity of such a life would be hard even in a stable world, and prewar Europe was brutally unstable. V.N.'s father had been murdered by Russian monarchists in 1922 (they were gunning for someone else when Nabokov senior interfered); in 1939, his impoverished mother would die in Czechoslovakia; later, his brother Sergey would die in a concentration camp.

Sergey's story is a particularly painful one; in his memoir, *Speak, Memory,* V.N. describes his relationship to his brother as "inordinately hard to speak about." Blatantly favored by his parents from birth, V.N. describes himself as "the coddled one" and Sergey as "the witness of the coddling." V.N. was a boisterous and dominant child, Sergey was mild and timid. (A picture of the two boys in 1909 says it all: ten-year-old V.N. is standing with his legs wide apart and his hands on his hips, as if inviting the world to adore him on its knees; Sergey, nine, has one leg turned in and his arms crossed over his chest, one finger pensively placed on his cheek.) By his own account, V.N. was something of a bully, although in general he simply wasn't very interested in his brother. He *was,* however, interested enough (at the age of sixteen) to read Sergey's journal in enough depth to discover that the boy was gay; he was also interested enough to show the journal to their tutor, who showed it to their father.

Sergey is mentioned sparingly in the *Letters;* these mentions are heartrending. In the most striking of them, V.N. quotes at length from a letter his brother wrote to their mother telling her that he had converted to Catholicism because "it is stricter and more demanding than the Orthodox," and because as a Catholic he would be able to "take communion every day" and thereby "kill the sin in [him]," to "make way for something new and not sinful." On quoting this letter, V.N. follows with a non sequitur that is unintentionally comic: "I had lunch (veal cutlet, cherry compote) then sailed off (in the chocolate Macintosh) . . ." He goes on about his pleasant day for about half a page before breez-ily commenting, "It's true, Catholicism is a feminine arrow-arched faith. . . . Probably Sergey's carried away by this, but in a good, deep way that will help him a lot."

The response is blithe to the point of—I almost wrote "brutal-ity," but I think the truer word is *incomprehension*. V.N. probably had no idea what it was to feel such anguish and self-hatred, and given that he was trying to create a safe world for his family amid one that was crumbling around his ears, it is hard to blame him for not trying to understand right then. He chose, it seems to me, the survival tactic he was constitutionally best equipped for—that is, to focus on the abiding beauty of the world, in the form of such things as a random cat ("that special silkiness of short fur, and some very tender white tints on its folds"), or the sea ("very lightly touched up with blue and throwing itself at everything"), or any- and everything about his wife ("how I love your hand-writing, that running shadow of your voice"). The focus on such small beauties in situations of crushing seriousness can be self-involved and light-minded; it can also be a kind of heroism.

There are comparatively few letters written after the family arrived in America, where V.N. brought his gifts to fantastic frui-tion. The tone of these letters is somewhat different from those written in Europe; the situational drama and romantic beauty is much subdued, I suppose because the couple was at that point more securely established, materially *and* emotionally. But the quality of lightness and buoyancy remains consistent, suggest-ing that V.N.'s character seems to have been remarkably indepen-dent of external circumstances. The reader of these American letters also hears a refrain of that perhaps *overly* light breeziness when V.N. was faced with the concerns of people suffering from problems outside his immediate comprehension. On a visit to Spelman College in Atlanta ("a black Wellesley") he notes that

"My lecture about Pushkin (Negro blood!) was greeted with almost comical enthusiasm," and expresses good-humored condescension toward a professor who was, in V.N.'s opinion, ridiculously preoccupied by whether or not Pushkin's African descent was "openly discussed" in the Soviet Union. Given the time and place, worse attitudes were possible, and it is true that V.N. had the same condescension toward white people who wished to see their political concerns reflected in literature. But lack of comprehension in this case was not due to any kind of survival reflex or lack of time to stop and think.

It is a questionable project to analyze a writer's personality based on the fiction he has written, or to cross-examine his fiction based on information about his life. Letters, however, are much more naturally revealing. *Letters to Véra* presents neither an elitist prick nor a sainted artist; written with easy grace and sometimes ardent haste, the letters display, rather, an artistically spectacular but morally ordinary human being whose gifts and flaws were both thrown into high relief by his transcendentally expressive genius. They also show a man of *unstoppable* energy and joy.

Letters winds to its end with anecdotes about reading tours at small colleges, slapstick mishaps at train stations, oddball characters, and the grotesque customs of the segregated South. My favorite, though, is about V.N.'s hospitalization for appendicitis in 1944:

> The nurses constantly tried to pull open the curtains of my coop and got angry saying that since all the other curtains were pulled, my poor tabernacle was spoiling the general look of the ward. By the end of my stay I was in such a state of exasperation, that when on Saturday morning I saw from the gallery (where I had gone out for a

smoke) T.N., who'd come for me, I jumped out through the *fire-escape* as I was, in pyjamas and a dressing-gown, rushed to the car—and we were already moving off, when the absolutely enraged nurses ran out—but they couldn't stop me.

They still can't.

Bookforum, 2016

Several pieces originally appeared, in slightly different form, in the following publications:

Artforum: "Toes 'n Hose," "Crackpot Mystic Spirit" • *Asymptote Journal:* "Form over Feeling" • *Bookforum:* "Dye Hard," "Mechanical Rabbit," "Lives of the Hags," "Master's Mind," "She's Supposed to Make You Sick," "The Running Shadow of Your Voice" • *Elle:* "Leave the Woman Alone!" • *Granta:* "Lost Cat" • *Harper's:* "The Trouble with Following the Rules" • *Libération:* "Worshipping the Overcoat" • *The New York Times Book Review:* "I See Their Hollowness" • *Post Road:* "Peter Pan" • *San Francisco Focus:* "A Lovely Chaotic Stillness" • SF360.org: "Beg for Your Life: On the Films of Laurel Nakadate" • *Stone Canoe:* "Somebody with a Little Hammer" • *The Village Voice:* "Bitch," "I've Seen It All" • *Zoetrope:* "Victims and Losers, a Love Story," "The Bridge"

The following pieces were previously published or collected in various works:

"A Lot of Exploding Heads," originally published in *Communion: Contemporary Writers Reveal the Bible in Their Lives,* edited by David Rosenberg (Doubleday, 1994) • "And It Would Not Be Wonderful to Meet a Megalosaurus," originally published as the introduction to *Bleak House* by Charles Dickens (Modern Library, 2002) • "Remain in Light," originally published as liner notes in the three-CD album box set of *Once in a Lifetime* by Talking Heads (Rhine/Warner Bros., 2003) • "This Doughty Nose," originally published in *A New Literary History of America*, edited by Werner Sollors and Greil Marcus (Harvard University Press, 2009) • "The Cunning of Women," originally published as the foreword in *One Thousand and One Nights: A Retelling* by Hanan al-Shaykh (Pantheon, 2011) • "Pictures of Lo," originally published as the preface in *Lolita: The Story of a Cover Girl*, edited by John Bertram and Yuri Leving (Print Books, 2013) • "The Easiest Thing to Forget," originally published in *Let's Talk About Love: Why Other People Have Such Bad Taste*, edited by Carl Wilson (Bloomsbury Academic, 2014) • "Icon," originally published as "Mary Gaitskill on Linda Lovelace" in *Icon*, edited by Amy Scholder (The Feminist Press at CUNY, 2014) • "Imaginary Light," originally published in *How to Write About Music: Excerpts from the 33 ⅓ Series, Magazines, Books and Blogs with Advice from Industry-Leading Writers*, edited by Marc Woodworth and Ally-Jane Grossan (Bloomsbury Academic, an imprint of Bloomsbury Publishing Plc., 2015)

I would like to thank everyone who was a part of this in any way, particularly Jeffery Renard Allen, Jeff Parker, Mikhail Iossel, and the unfailingly generous Beatrice Monti von Rezzori. I would especially like to thank those people who asked me to write about things it would never have occurred to me to write about on my own: Knight Landesman, Michael Miller, Greil Marcus, John Bertram, David Byrne, Lexy Bloom, Michael Ray, Dwight Garner, Marc Woodworth, Amy Scholder, Lee Yew Leong, Laurel Nakadate, Carl Wilson, John Freeman, and David Rosenberg; also my editor Deborah Garrison and my agent Jin Auh for their professional and personal kindness. Most deeply I would like to thank Peter Trachtenberg and Jennifer Sears for their unfailing intimate support.

Impersonal but sincere and respectful thanks are due to David Sim for allowing the public to use his wonderful Cerebus the Aardvark imagery."

ABOUT THE AUTHOR

Mary Gaitskill is the author of the story collections *Bad Behavior, Because They Wanted To* (nominated for the PEN/ Faulkner Award), and *Don't Cry,* and the novels *The Mare, Veronica* (nominated for the National Book Award), and *Two Girls, Fat and Thin.* She has received a Guggenheim Fellowship, and her stories and essays have appeared in *The New Yorker, Harper's, Artforum,* and *Esquire,* among many other journals, as well as *The Best American Short Stories* (1993) and *The O. Henry Prize Stories* (1998).

A NOTE ON THE TYPE

This book was set in Monotype Dante, a typeface designed by Giovanni Mardersteig (1892–1977). Dante was originally cut for hand composition by Charles Malin between 1946 and 1952. Its first use was in an edition of Boccaccio's *Trattatello in laude di Dante* that appeared in 1954. The Monotype Corporation's version of Dante followed in 1957. Although modeled on the Aldine type used for Pietro Cardinal Bembo's treatise *De Aetna* in 1495, Dante is a thoroughly modern interpretation of the venerable face.

TYPESET BY SCRIBE, PHILADELPHIA, PENNSYLVANIA

PRINTED AND BOUND BY BERRYVILLE GRAPHICS,
BERRYVILLE, VIRGINIA

DESIGNED BY BETTY LEW